Anatomy of a Schism

Anatomy of a Schism

How Clergywomen's Narratives
Reinterpret the Fracturing
of the Southern Baptist Convention

Eileen R. Campbell-Reed

University of Tennessee Press / Knoxville

Copyright © 2016 by The University of Tennessee Press / Knoxville.
All Rights Reserved.
First Edition.

Library of Congress Cataloging-in-Publication Data

Campbell-Reed, Eileen R., author.
Anatomy of a Schism : how clergywomen's narratives reinterpret the fracturing of the Southern Baptist Convention / Eileen R. Campbell-Reed. — First edition.
pages cm
Includes bibliographical references and index.
ISBN 978-1-62190-178-5 (paperback)
ISBN 978-1-62190-255-3 (pdf ebook)
ISBN 978-1-62190-558-5 (Kindle ebook)

1. Southern Baptist Convention—History—20th century.
2. Baptists—United States—History—20th century.
3. Baptist women—United States—Interviews.
4. Women clergy—United States—Interviews.
5. Church controversies—Baptists—History—20th century.
6. Christian sociology—Baptists.
I. Title.
BX6462.3.C35 2016
286'.132082—dc23
2015028628

For Joanna, Chloe, Anna, Martha, and Rebecca

Contents

Acknowledgments	ix
Introduction	1
1. (Sub)ordination: How Clergywomen Embody Schism in the Southern Baptist Convention	25
2. (Sub)mission: How Clergywomen Reimagine Baptist Identity	47
3. (Sub)text: How Clergywomen Reframe and Renew Baptist Relationships	71
4. Redeeming Humanity: How Clergywomen Embody Struggle and Sacred Presence in the SBC	93
5. Reimagining Ministry: How Clergywomen Reinterpret Schism and Remake Baptist Identity	117
Conclusion	139
Epilogue	143
Appendix A: Resolution on Ordination and the Role of Women in Ministry, June 1984	147
Appendix B: Hymns, Songs, and Poems	149
Appendix C: Alliance of Baptists Covenant	153
Notes	155
Index	205

Acknowledgments

> When the blackbird flew out of sight,
> It marked the edge
> Of one of many circles.
>
> —Wallace Stevens, "Thirteen Ways
> of Looking at a Blackbird"

Writing a book over several years is like many other practices learned over time. The effort requires trying, risking, improvising, and reassessing after missteps. The text becomes layered with meanings that a single draft could never produce. Moments arise when all confidence feels lost in wondering if anything worth publishing will finally take shape. This book, like most every large project I've ever undertaken, faltered at some moments and seemed to fly out of sight. Yet at just those moments, the practice of writing itself emerged as sustaining and consoling. When I felt lost or off kilter, I could return to the writing, attend to the stories, and sit quietly with the substance of the book. I could redraw the circle of writing. In those moments I could see: just what I needed was right there all along. Both research and writing took on the shape of spiritual practices that have sustained me and co-created with the clergywomen, a community of scholars, and the communion of saints, a new interpretation, another circle added to the many interpretations that came before.

Anatomy of a Schism is dedicated to the five women who entrusted their stories to me. Each woman's stories emerged as a narrative around which a reinterpretation of wider Baptist events and culture could be constructed. The book could just as easily have drawn on other women's stories to open up space for a new interpretation of the Baptist schism. In fact, many of the public and well-known stories of Baptist women also appear in the pages of this book. Women's stories were right there in the Baptist milieu all along, and it has simply been my task to lift them up and to articulate how they cast a new and compelling light on events at the end of the last century.

On many occasions I've searched high and low for the thing I needed—only to discover it was right there all along—in my purse, on the pages of a book I was reading at the time, or in the smile of a friend. Thus my growing up in the shadow of University of Tennessee Press seems so fitting. As a child I ran on the university track and swam in the Olympic-sized pool in summers when my dad was a graduate student. I even took a few courses at UT as an undergraduate. What a delight it was to find the welcome and partnership that was exactly what this book needed at UT Press with proficient and gracious leadership from Scot Danforth. Several important books on Baptists published by UT Press prepared the way for *Anatomy of a Schism*, a new contribution to the conversation on what it meant to be Baptist in the late twentieth century.

Many circles of friends and colleagues, fellow pilgrims, and family members cared for me, listened with me, and cheered me along the way with kindness, urgency, and joy as I completed this project. My search for partnerships and collaborations is always expanding those circles, and yet in the hands of those nearest, I found just what I needed. Lynn kept the home fires burning, and Marissa kept me laughing, curious, and always on my toes. Support came to me often from my pastors, April Baker and Amy Mears, and from many others whom I simply asked and they simply responded. I'm grateful for innumerable emails and social media messages, prayers, and gracious words of encouragement.

I'm deeply grateful for colleagues who read chapters of the book, both early drafts and later revisions. They offered feedback that sharpened the book's arguments, stories, and overall contributions. From my research partners in the Learning Pastoral Imagination Project, I've experienced the sustaining grace of ongoing dialogue over many years, a grace that was folded (almost unconsciously) into the pages of this book. Thank you, Christian Scharen and Catrina Ciccone, for your care for ministers and for doing work that matters. For pulling together a new generation of scholars on Baptists and gender, I'm grateful to Karen Seat, who brought Betsy Flowers, Susan Shaw, and me into a collaborative effort that is now growing to include Lisa Thompson and other scholars and will, I hope, continue to bear good fruit. I'm also grateful to my early and ongoing collaborations with Pamela Durso on the study and understanding of women in Baptist life. Many thanks also belong to theologians and historians who have read and commented on this book from their multiple disciplinary vantage points: Jimmy Byrd, Kathleen Cahalan, Pamela Cooper-White, Susan Dunlap, Curtis Freeman, Mary McClintock Fulkerson, Jan Holton, Bill Leonard, Molly Marshall, Bonnie Miller-McLemore, Mary Clark Moschella, Francesca Nuzzolese, Charlie Scalise, and Timothy Snyder.

Two groups of supporters have been indispensible to me in the late stages of completing this project. A weekly writing group has been sustaining me for seven years. Duane Bidwell currently anchors the group, with regular encouragement from Allan Cole, Emily Askew, Frank Thomas, Tim Robinson, Janet Schaller, and Mary Clark Moschella. My other weekly check-ins are with a women's circle, facilitated by Jennifer Derryberry Mann and Emi Canahuati and joined on the journey by Amy Nakamaru Hopeman, Lindsey Kever Magner, Dusti Ramieh, and Michelle Rivera. It is a great gift to bear witness to women giving birth to new ideas, new ventures, new children, and a new sense of self.

Over the last six years I have presented material from this book at the Society for Pastoral Theology and in the Psychology, Culture and Religion Group at the American Academy of Religion; on panels at the American Society of Church

History and the National Women's Study Association; and at the Collaborative for Women's Leadership between the Cooperative Baptist Fellowship and Baptist Women in Ministry. In each conversation, my work to articulate the research and findings in a community of scholars led to clarifications, critiques, and many improvements to the book. I am deeply grateful for each of these opportunities and conversations.

As with each piece of writing, there are so many ways of seeing, so many vantage points from which to look. Always, beyond the limits of sight, there is more to tell. Yet I trust that even with all its limits, this book may just as well take wing beyond the edges of my knowing.

Thanksgiving Day 2014
Eileen R. Campbell-Reed

Introduction

Growing up in a blended family, Rebecca was baptized in a Southern Baptist church when she was six years old. She says of those early years: "I got a really good grounding in Scripture and the stories in the Bible and that God loves me. And I got a really good grounding in women being inferior." Rebecca watched what women did and didn't do in church. The messages were never spoken aloud. She absorbed them by "osmosis."[1]

After more than a dozen years of ministry, Anna finally received ordination for her work. A few years later she wanted more pastoral responsibility, and chaplaincy looked like the best possible path. Anna wanted Southern Baptists to endorse her, but in 2002 the North American Mission Board stopped endorsing women as chaplains if they were also ordained ministers. With irony and sorrow, Anna recalls the message of a favorite Baptist hymn, one that nurtured her and taught her about God: "'Wherever He Leads I'll Go,'" she says, "is a great hymn, unless you're a woman." The Board did not endorse her, but Anna refused to be shut out. The breakaway Cooperative Baptist Fellowship (CBF) credentialed her as a hospital chaplain. She reflected on the situation with determination: "As a woman in ministry . . . I just hoped, and have hope, and I will continue to hope, that I would just get to do ministry, because that's where my heart is."[2]

When Joanna challenged a layperson about his presentation of an annual budget to the church staff, she spoke with authority. The parishioner was surprised by her questions and insights. Proud of avoiding a meltdown, and refusing to second-guess herself, Joanna still checked with another staff member to ask if she was "out of line." She received assurance that her challenge was "strong." Others were less pleased and reported her actions to the interim pastor (a woman), although no one talked to Joanna directly. Days later Joanna realized that everyone who had complained about her actions was male. That was the moment, says Joanna, "when I felt that I hit the glass ceiling." Despite years of experience as an accountant and church financial secretary, Joanna felt limited and "dismissed" by the reactions of others:

"You're a youth and children's minister. What would you know about a budget? Why aren't you staying in your place?" The interim pastor recommended that Joanna consult with a pastoral counselor. Joanna felt shamed by the referral: "I literally crawled under my desk after she left my office. I just felt lower than dirt."

When the search committee from Monroe Corner Baptist Church first phoned, Martha said to herself, "This is never going to happen. They are not going to call a woman!" Nevertheless, she took a risk and entered the search process with them. To her surprise, she and the committee "had a wonderful experience" and they "clicked." Armed with worries from her friends that only dying churches call women as pastors, Martha wondered what might be "wrong with a church" that would call her. Although she looked around and saw "many better preachers, better qualified people," somehow the "right place and timing" converged, and the church called her as their first female pastor. Despite the demise of local industries, and the church's declining membership, Martha still rejoiced: "I knew for women in ministry in 2001, this is great! I mean this is as good as it's going to get."

After three years as pastor at Cave Hill Baptist Church, Chloe pondered what it means to her to be a Baptist woman in ministry. Compared to her clergywomen friends in other denominations, who are criticized for "having problems with authority," Chloe says she has many more problems with authority than they do. This makes the "sense of freedom as a Baptist woman" very important for her. As her journey of faith and ministry unfolds, she sees the Baptist distinctives of "soul competency and priesthood of the believer" as "very crucial" to her own Baptist identity and leadership. For Chloe, pastoring means "making sure that I'm nurturing my own personal relationship with God and helping church members to do the same. And, through that relationship, encountering Scripture, worshipping and praying together ... seeking God's presence together." Ministry for Chloe is "trying as best I can to practice the presence of Christ in community."

Baptist identity takes shape by osmosis, through relational connections and family networks, through worship and Scripture, and in power struggles, long-term commitments, and serendipitous moments. Constrained by a culture of complementarity yet inspired by piety and feminism, clergywomen forged a new kind of Baptist identity in the years of struggle known collectively as the "takeover," the "resurgence," or "the Baptist holy war."[3] From 1979 to 2000, the Southern Baptist Convention (SBC) squared off and the biblicist and autonomist parties fought openly for control. The struggle polarized Baptists across the United States South and beyond, ending in a schism that produced not only major changes in the SBC but also several new Baptist groups. When the story of schism is told, clergywomen are largely ignored for the roles they played and the contributions they made to the fracturing of the largest Protestant group in the U.S. Ordained women are most often treated as an issue over which the parties fought, but only recently have scholars seriously considered the women's contributions and interpretations as active participants.

This book moves women's narratives front and center, and it shows how clergywomen's stories offer a compelling new structure for understanding the plot of Southern Baptists at the close of the twentieth century.[4] Qualitative interviews with five Baptist clergywomen offer paradigm cases showing how the Southern Baptist schism was more than a battle for the Bible or a struggle for political power.[5] The narratives of Anna, Martha, Joanna, Rebecca, and Chloe reframe the story of Southern Baptists and reinterpret the schism in broad and significant ways. Together they offer an understanding of the schism from three perspectives—gendered, psychological, and theological—not previously available together. The three perspectives don't operate side by side, but like three focal lenses, they bring a new depth of seeing that is framed by each woman's narrative yet universal in its implications for understanding changes to Baptist life in the last four decades.

First, the Southern Baptist schism grew out of a gendered psychological struggle, waged in Baptist imaginations, relationships, and social structures. Most interpretations of the schism ignore or marginalize both the internal and relational lives of Baptists, opting to investigate the political, social, or theological aspects of the fracture. The psychological struggle, however, was already present before the first Southern Baptist women were ordained in 1960s, and the novel presence of clergywomen brought the internal and relational dynamics into greater conscious awareness and visibility. The most challenging point in the psychological struggle is the effort by clergywomen and others to undo the paradigm of submission and domination, which supports a complementarity culture, reinforcing the ideal and practice of male headship and female submission. On the other side of that struggle is a sustained effort to maintain a gendered status quo of complementarity. Possibly more unsettling than the explicit polarization between autonomists and biblicists over the future of complementarity, and the host of other gendered psychological issues, is the reality that both parties also reproduced a culture of complementarity by degrees.

Second, clergywomen's narratives also reinterpret the Southern Baptist context not only as a culture of hostility and conflict but also as a nurturing space in which Baptist piety and other convictions, such as feminism, meet and reshape Baptist identity. Two forms of reimagined identity are the focus of this interpretation: the meaning of being human and the theology and practice of ministry. As clergywomen and their autonomist supporters worked to undo the culture of complementarity, they lived, worked, loved, played, served, and practiced new relational, vulnerable, and embodied ways of being human and Baptist. These shifts participated in a theological struggle among Southern Baptists against the sins of sexism, submission, and domination, and with a hope and desire for freedom and healing. Together the clergywomen's narratives reinterpret schism in the SBC as a profoundly spiritual, theological, and gendered struggle over brokenness and redemption.

And third, clergywomen's lives seek a theological renewal of ministry itself. The sustained effort to reimagine Baptist identity and assert a more authentic humanity runs through each woman's story of growing up, coming to a sense of vocation, educating herself for ministry, seeking ordination, and entering pastoral work. Each woman's life was met with a range of responses, from joy and bewilderment to reluctance and outright hostility. Thus the Baptist space was not experienced exclusively as a battleground but also as a playground where clergywomen improvised the practice of ministry and reshaped Baptist pastoral identity. In that playground clergywomen created and discovered God's presence and purpose in their lives in embodied, relational, and even mystical ways of knowing. In sum, each clergywoman's story reinterprets the Southern Baptist schism as a gendered psychological struggle over the future of complementarity, a gendered theological struggle over what it means to be human and Baptist, and a space where a new practice and theology of ministry emerges. By seeing the Baptist situation through their stories and experiences, a new set of stakes in the controversy emerges. The schism's outcomes held profound consequences for individuals and communities, and Baptists of all stripes engaged in the struggle as if their lives, identities, relationships, and ministries depended on it. In the end, they did.

Living History

The fracturing of the SBC, although addressed at length, has been inadequately understood in both academic and partisan accounts as primarily a theological battle about the Bible or a political struggle over social and institutional issues. Three related problems plague the earlier interpretations: (1) they did not take seriously enough the roles played by women or the dynamics of gender as a shaping force of the schism, (2) they did not attempt a psychological analysis of the fracture, and (3) the theological interpretations did not appreciate the gendered struggle at stake in the schism. Additionally, attention to shifts in understanding ministry was rarely, if ever, explored as a dynamic feature of the Baptist rupture.

Schism among Southern Baptists remains a living history. From 1989, written interpretations of the Baptist fighting grew steadily, and many firsthand accounts and partisan materials interpret schism out of direct participation in the events.[6] Many Baptist insiders, scholars with a Baptist background, and a handful of non-Baptists wrote academic accounts of the schism, including historical, rhetorical, and social scientific studies.[7] However, despite some careful analysis of Baptist history, politics, and theology, almost all of the academic and partisan literature interpreting the schism lacks an adequate analysis of the roles, identities, or contributions of actual women. Recently, newer analyses are taking the category of gender, and the contributions of women, more seriously.[8] Although the schism literature includes sociological and political analyses, it also lacks phenomenological readings of the situation, which psychology and theological anthropology offer. Because the "history" of the SBC schism is still unfolding, many of the actors are still living, and the institutions continue taking new shape, the existing literature does not account for later developments and much of it lacks a critical distance regarding underlying reasons and causes for the split.[9] Finally, the concern with "biblical inerrancy" functioned to distract attention from other major theological and psychological tensions at work in the lives of Baptists.

The following discussion situates this book in relation to the schism literature by presenting the major contributions and unexplored areas of the previous interpretations. A new interpretation of the meaning and significance of the Baptist struggles emerges herein by attending to the features of lived religion for Baptists and by looking through three main lenses: gender, psychological dynamics, and theological anthropology. To advance the scholarly conversation, this book takes a novel approach to the sources, methods, context, and focus of partisan materials.[10]

The most comprehensive arguments about schism in the SBC describe multiple causes and effects of the fracture and present a variety of investigative and interpretive methods, offering complex and multilayered analyses of the controversy. Several interpretations address the role of women's leadership and ordination in the Baptist controversy in a single chapter or section, but they say little about the possible contributions of women themselves as a source for interpreting the schism.[11] None of the books published before 2000 address the category "gender" in their analyses of the schism. Women and gender are often synonymous "issues" (if gender is even named) in the Baptist battles, and they can be subsumed under larger causes and outcomes. In other words, the narratives and arguments are portrayed as the activity of men, in an extended debate about the theology and politics of men, and mostly written by men.[12] Women remain a doctrinal and political issue throughout much of the literature about the schism.[13] When the issues of women's ordination and leadership were tied to financial decisions in SBC agencies, they became early signs of real fragmentation of the SBC.[14] Despite the wide range of sources for understanding the changes unfolding in the denomination, the early analysis never looked to women's lives or experiences as sources for a more comprehensive understanding.[15] A decade after the schism began, time and critical distance grew sufficiently for interpreters to begin considering the questions of women's ordination and pastoral leadership more intentionally, sometimes as one of several significant issues.[16]

Much of the partisan literature continues to quote secondary sources and repeat the canon of stories and observations about the SBC schism without introducing any new perspectives or analysis.[17] Scholars outside Baptist life have tended to take social science approaches more comprehensively than either history or theology as they interpret Baptist schism. The social science studies make substantial use of qualitative and ethnographic methods for gathering data.[18] While they utilize a variety of research methods and offer a range of perspectives on the SBC schism, none of the social science studies considered the events using a psychological framework for understanding.[19] Eventually some analyses offered a closer look at relationships or genealogies of influence in the two parties embattled in the schism; however, the analyses are hardly psychological in any formal sense.[20]

In the life world of Baptists, a potent mix of cultural ideals and practices as well as psychological dynamics in family and society shape women like Anna, Martha, Joanna, Rebecca, and Chloe. Too often psychological and cultural shaping forces are considered in isolation, but to grasp their combined power, the forces need to be considered together, particularly if a better or more complex understanding is needed.[21] For example, personal psychological experiences of the conflict, and the accompanying intense emotions, are analogous to the public and very visceral conflict that played itself out among Southern Baptists negotiating a split.[22] In addition to the intensity of emotion, the presence of particular psychological dynamics, which can be observed in individual experiences, relational exchanges, and larger social groups, is a basis for analogy. For example, the dynamic of splitting (psychological divisions of self and other, good and bad, or as a defense against harm) can be noticed in individual self-understandings, shared relational interactions, and social organizations. Additionally, certain theological ideas are themselves psychological conceptions, and they are observable in three overlapping realms of human being: the subjective, the relational, and the social.[23] This book reinterprets a variety of psychological concepts and perspectives in order to illuminate the psychological character of the schism. Often the women in this book and other primary texts name and engage psychological concepts, which can be teased out to show broader dynamics at work in the Baptist culture.[24]

A canon of stories became central to the retelling of the larger story of schism in the last three decades, and many of the interpretations depended heavily on the prior theological and historical convictions of the narrators.[25] Because it remains a living history for now, the events of the schism are not yet exhausted and new, thicker descriptions and analyses of the times, lives, and changes among late-

Introduction

twentieth-century Baptists are still forthcoming. This book adds new material from a very close reading of the lives of everyday clergywomen who until recently have been largely ignored.[26]

Even when women are perceived as more than symbols or issues in Baptist life, they still often end up as instrumental props, or at best flat characters, in a story that tries to explain the actions of men from a historical or theological perspective.[27] These histories and theologies need the lens of gender to show more fully the angles of vision about Baptist events and what was at stake in those events. Analyses of class, race, and sexuality are also implicated in Southern Baptist negotiations of schism, although they are less central in this book's descriptions of white, Southern, middle-class women and the denomination they mirror.[28]

Early on, the academic analyses made connections to trends and changes in the larger American religious landscape by focusing on one of two issues. Some writing zeros in on the apparent connection of biblicists to the New Religious Right (also called the New Christian Right).[29] Other writing focused to some degree on the academic "drift" toward theological liberalism, especially by seminary professors and some of their students.[30] Too often in the partisan literature, these connections appear in the form of accusations rather than analysis. The effect is to distract from rather than connect to religious trends in late-twentieth-century American Christianity. This book relocates the lives of clergywomen to the center of the story, allowing several previously unexplored connections to trends in lived religion in America, particularly regarding changes to the character of ministry since women began to occupy pastoral leadership positions in greater numbers.[31]

Naming Baptists

Winners write the history books, or so the saying goes. However, all the Baptists in the fracturing of the SBC have reframed the story to cast themselves as winners and inheritors of the authentic Baptist identity.[32] Language in this living Baptist history for naming the experience remains contested, suspect, and even embittered. Thus the following definitions and identifications will invite clarity for reading this book and acknowledge the disputed language, terms, and concepts. The richer meaning of many terms is among the purposes of the book and will unfold in the chapters, not through greater precision of definition but in a richer complexity of description and meaning. However, to help the reader get started, four groups of terms are introduced below: clergywomen and ordination; autonomist and biblicist parties; gender and complementarity; and vulnerability, splitting, and redemption.

The term "clergywoman" indicates training and ordination for professional ministry.[33] In Baptist life neither education nor ordination are required for the work of ministry, but they are informally expected. The two tracks of preparation—seminary and ordination—are normative for most Protestants, and by the mid-twentieth century, Southern Baptists had increasingly adopted a standard that expected an educated ministry, opening six seminaries to do the work. There is a distinction among some Baptists between minister and pastor: all pastors are ministers, but not all ministers are pastors.[34] This exact point is part of the contest between parties over who can be ordained, to what purpose, and by whom. Local churches and associations of Baptists typically ordain ministers. Baptists do not universally accept any particular set of guidelines for ordination, and given the ambivalence of the Bible on the practice, even appeals to Scripture are not uniform. As women increasingly presented themselves as called to ministry, with the hope of receiving ordination, the beliefs, guidelines, and practice of ordination became explicitly part of the disagreements between Baptist groups. The stories of ordination told by Anna, Martha, and Chloe are especially helpful in further defining the issues at stake in this debate and in reframing new understandings of the practice.

In an effort not to embrace too closely the rhetoric of either of the main parties in the schism, and to signal an academic rather than partisan engagement, this book takes the strategy of coining new terms for the two groups: *autonomists* and *biblicists*.[35] Both groups, as well as some scholars, refer to the events of Baptist life between 1979 and 1990 as "the controversy." Thus even the term "schism" is a relatively novel metaphor for describing the events of the Southern Baptist divide.[36] During the most intense conflict between 1979 and 1990, there was little doubt about who was on which side. The choice to assign new names for the two parties is not an effort to obscure their internal differences but to highlight the differences between them.[37]

Those included in the "biblicist party" are leaders who referred to themselves as conservatives, inerrantists, or traditionalists. Their Baptist detractors referred to them most often as fundamentalists and sometimes as ultra-conservatives or literalists. Scholars who have studied and written about these groups sometimes refer to those in the biblicist party as evangelicals, neo-evangelicals, or primitivists. Members of the biblicist party most often referred to the events and outcome of the SBC schism as a "conservative resurgence" or a "course correction." Biblicists coalesced around the strategy of gaining control of the SBC presidency in order to bring change to the convention. Leaders included layperson and judge Paul Pressler, Bible scholar Paige Patterson, Tennessee pastor Adrian Rogers (elected convention president in 1979), Texas pastor W. A. Criswell, and dozens of pastors of large Baptist churches. In this book, biblicist voices include Patterson and his spouse Dorothy Patterson (theology professor and outspoken advocate for biblical manhood and womanhood) and pastors Rogers, Fred Wolfe, James Draper, and Jerry Vines.

Those included in the "autonomist party" referred to themselves alternately as moderates, denominational loyalists, or conservative-moderates. Their Baptist critics often called them liberals or secular humanists. Scholars have at times called them modernists or progressives. Members of the autonomist party most often referred to events of the schism as "the (hostile) takeover." Leaders included North Carolina pastor Cecil Sherman, Texas pastor Daniel Vestal, and a group assembled in 1980 known as the Gatlinburg Gang. They made greater and lesser attempts in the next twelve years to win the SBC presidency or find a means of compromise with the biblicists. However, the autonomists never caught up in organization, support, funding, or strategy and were never successful at winning the SBC presidency.[38] During those dozen years, the convention shifted from uneasy synthesis to open schism.[39] The SBC became the domain of biblicists. The voices that shaped the autonomist party, and are given voice in the analysis of this book, include CBF founder Daniel Vestal, pastor and theologian Molly T. Marshall, pastor Nancy Sehested, seminary president Randall Lolley, professors Daniel Bagby and Andrew Lester, and pastors Lynda Weaver-Williams, Cindy Harp Johnson, Kathy Manis Findley, Jann Aldredge-Clanton, and Betty Winstead McGary.[40]

Of course the autonomists were "biblicists" in the broadest sense, seeing the Bible as a central source of authority. However, they explicitly included other sources of authority in their discernment, theologizing, practice, and ethics. Autonomists deserve this name—not because they believed singularly in the autonomy of local churches or the autonomy of individuals—but because many in the party came to prize those values highly and use them rhetorically in the years of struggle. Conversely, biblicists also valued autonomy in the sense of individual responsibility before God, and they assumed an ongoing accountability to a faith community in spite of the rhetoric of "Bible only."

The work of "gender" tends to remain hidden and/or appear natural or biological, coming into view when women move from the margins to be central actors. Male normativity renders the otherness of gender invisible most of the time, but when females are introduced as complex, three-dimensional characters into the narratives of history, both the questions and the interpretations change, destabilizing previously unquestioned narratives.

The ways in which late-twentieth-century Baptists perceived and performed gender presumed a straightforward and unambiguous difference between male and female.[41] The relationship between male and female was idealized as complementary—each supposedly needed to "complete" the other. However, both inside and outside of Baptist life, a large-scale cultural shift was underway from complementary marriages (two different types make a single whole) to mutual marriages (two different people relate in partnership and mutual exchange).[42] For Baptists, complementarity not only indicated a relational dynamic but also, being surrounded by a culture of complementarity reinforced a common state of mind. In the theological rhetoric of the day, God's delegated authority meant men are men and women are women, and by virtue of Bible and biology, never shall the two be confused. Power flowed predictably and normatively between the two genders, although in practice there was much more fluidity, and a multiplicity of identities existed and circulated.[43] Much Baptist debate about "gender" remains within the confines of this gender binary, yet it is the challenging and undoing of the binaries that fosters a crisis over gender itself among Baptists.

The culture of complementarity in which Southern Baptists were and are immersed upholds an explicit ideal for how family life and the entire order of society's relationships should operate. It is captured in writings and doctrinal statements but can't be reduced entirely into a single definition. However, because the subtlety of gender and its centrality to human identity are so difficult to see, the following definition, taken from the 2000 Baptist Faith and Message, can be a point of departure for the larger explorations of this book. After biblicists gained leadership of the SBC, they revised the confessional document, and that revision is often taken as an end marker for the schism, which began in 1979.[44] Complementarity holds that marriage unites one man and one woman for the purposes of companionship, sexual expression, and procreation. Both men and women are considered "of equal worth before God" and "created in God's image." However, at that point equality is qualified by the notion that marriage follows the "order of creation." Man is compared to God and woman to creation. As Christ leads the church, a man should love and lead his wife and family. Woman is like the church and should thus "graciously submit" to her husband. The statement calls on woman—created "in the image of God" and thus "equal to" her husband—to follow her "God-given responsibility to respect her husband and to serve as his helper in managing the household and nurturing the next generation."[45]

One aim of this reinterpretation is to show a number of aspects of a complementarity culture and how it works. The definition adopted by Southern Baptists doesn't capture the pervasive and adaptive quality of complementarity.[46] Neither does it fully capture the contradiction and double-binding features of this relational ideal. By looking at the period of schism from within the clergywomen's narratives, the persistence and recalcitrance of complementarity comes into sharper focus.

When men and women embrace a desire for work, and to own their vulnerability as well as their power, they present a threat to cultures of complementarity and produce anxiety within others in their immediate social circles and the wider system. Anxiety over the undoing of complementarity shows itself in the rhetoric of leaders who act and react to keep complementarity in place. Complementarity is a subtle and deceptive "good" that keeps domination and subordination at work by declaring both to be necessary. When complementarity is understood as "God's delegated order" for all of life, no amount of "equality" will be acceptable because it will undermine the entire system of "order" in home, church, and society.

Baptist clergywomen typified the challenges to complementarity by authoring and owning their own desire, not just for equality in some generic sense but also for doing ministry, the work of the church. They sought to do it with the authority of ordination rather than continuing on with only the power of subordination (a place Baptist women had long occupied and used to their advantage). By owning and authoring desire, these women symbolized new powers of agency, which threatened the entire system of Baptist complementarity. Particular women, such as Anna, Chloe, Rebecca, Martha, and Joanna, claimed for themselves the subjective powers of agency and authority and experienced the confirmation of communities who ordained and called them. At the same time, those communities, and the clergywomen themselves, reproduced the dynamics of complementarity relationally and socially, despite the new sense of equality that was afoot.

Life begins and ends in profound dependence for human beings who are fragile creatures. Although endowed with amazing capacities for creation, beauty, freedom, and achievements of all kinds, human lives are also finite and vulnerable, susceptible to giving and receiving harm at every turn. The most basic passions animate human lives: to be oneself, to be with others, and to grasp sense or meaning in one's existence. These drives or passions are unavoidably at odds with one another. The irreconcilability of human passions, and the finitude of human life take form in a tragic structure that is the human condition.[47] The "tragic" in this sense is not unnecessary harm giving rise to terrible sadness but the irreconcilability of the basic human drives and the inability to experience a total understanding of self or other. Thus the tragic structure of existence itself further amplifies human vulnerability; however, without vulnerability there would be no intimacy, no need, no creative or beautiful engagement, no being founded by another, and no experience of the sacred.[48]

As understood by psychoanalytic theorists and attachment theorists, psychic splitting—between self and other, good and bad, and harmful and caring—works as one of the most basic of human defenses against the potential harms to one's vulnerability.[49] Splitting is required for identity such that each infant begins to understand that she or he is a separate self and not merged with the caregiver. In fact there is likely never a time of complete euphoric merger with the mother/other from which an infant later splits away. Rather, from birth a relational self is present as well as an experience of merger with the original caregiver.[50] Splitting remains essential to both identity (this is me, and this is *not me*) and self-defense (that is bad/harmful, and this is good/caring) against inescapable vulnerability. The split between good and bad for an infant is based in the responsiveness of his or her environment and caregivers to the needs and desires for survival and connection.[51] The tragic structure of human existence is present from the opening moments of life, when the infant cries out to breathe, live, eat, and be held, all essential for survival. Vulnerability, connection, and the potential for harm are all present.

As infants mature and grow, more complex psychic defenses come into play, although splitting remains at the heart of many attempts to protect oneself from unpleasant physical sensations or affective states. Soon after an infant knows self and other, one of the next differences she or he learns is the split in "she" and "he." For millennia the split of gender has been so culturally important, power-laden, and seemingly natural and unquestioned that the achievement is not easily untangled.[52] Whenever changes to that psychic and cultural split of gender appear, a social and personal crisis of identity ensues.[53]

Even to suggest changing the meaning or significance of gender strikes at the core of identity. For many Southern Baptists the widespread defense against the vulnerability produced at the very thought of destabilizing gender was to valorize biblical manhood and womanhood and double down on "God's delegated order" in church, home, and society. The complementarian culture built on male headship and female submission was falling out of favor with many Americans, but biblicist leaders redoubled their efforts to keep it alive and make it a point of cultural critique of a godless America.[54]

Thus when Baptist women like Anna, Martha, Rebecca, Joanna, and Chloe moved into the work of ministry, they faced many complex dilemmas and double-binding messages that orbited around the human psychology of the splitting of gender and the growing influence of complementarity culture. Anna upset the assumptions of her seminary and the neighborhood "pastors' wives," bringing her face-to-face with the struggle of the "servanthood dilemma" felt by many Christian women. Chloe navigated the troublesome pathway for clergywomen between the authoritative male pastor and the servant-leader pastor. Martha struggled not to believe that only dying and unhealthy churches called women. Rebecca faced the brokenness of a church sweeping the sexual indiscretions of its staff under the carpet for years. Joanna hit the stained-glass ceiling of male criticism.

The clergywomen's presence in communities, in anecdotes, and even in the news, functioned symbolically as a major shift in thinking, and the threat was felt at both a profoundly visceral level as well as a broad political one. As symbols, clergywomen evoked fear and anxiety about changes to sexual identity, understandings of gender, and the shape of a social and ecclesial order that had long been in place. The resulting fear, anxiety, and guilt led to (or returned Baptists to) the private and public defense of splitting. The psychic and social splitting worked to keep complementarity in place. The rhetoric of pointing out differences became louder and more insistent as the years unfolded. One form the split took was for biblicists to project their anxiety and fear about the changes onto clergywomen (and their autonomist supporters) as the personification of all that was disordered and ungodly. In the other direction, the projections and fears of autonomists appeared in the form of blaming the other party—fundamentalist pastors—for being domineering, heavy-handed, and even violent predators and patriarchs who wielded power unfairly in home and church.

Introduction

Thus the projections on both sides reproduced complementarity in the two parties and kept the cultural forms of domination and subordination in place *between* the parties: autonomists were weak, ineffectual, vulnerable, and unsure of their desires; biblicists were powerful, effective, strong, and clear about their goals and desires. But it also had the effect of keeping complementarity in place *within* each party in overt and subtler ways. Although women made advances in the ownership and authorship of their desire for work in ministry among autonomists, they continued to find work mainly in associate positions where they supported men who were the more powerful leaders.

The events that Southern Baptists endured and fashioned at the end of the last century are portrayed as a split, schism, divorce, hostile takeover, controversy, battle, and/or resurgence. The militaristic imagery connotes sides that are hostile and polarized. Psychological splitting and breakdown on the largest social scale characterized the entire period. Yet clergywomen and other Baptists found ways to live creatively and sustainably even within the difficult times and personal circumstances. Redemption and reimagination become the occasions for healing the longstanding splits of gender, desire and vocation. Precisely within the defensive splits of Baptist life, clergywomen creatively renegotiated self-identity, relationality, and their social roles. This was not a glib reunification of sides but a clarification and new formation of identity out of differences. To be sure, seeds of division were also replanted and splitting was reproduced. Yet the most creative work of clergywomen came at the point of reframing, reimagination, and redemption. Healing was not simply something the women conjured. Healing emerged in spaces in which a sense of God's sacred presence made the difference for Martha, evoked the power and voice for change for Rebecca, animated the creativity for Joanna, inspired relational connection for Chloe, and offered the sense of hope for a way through the times for Anna.

Reading Sources

Each chapter in this book presents a narrative of one clergywoman, relying on her words and images whenever possible yet telling her story with an eye to what that story says and shows about the times in which she lived, learned, became a pastor, and, in several cases, lost a place of ministry. Each clergywoman's story both frames and is framed by the larger events and prevailing culture of the times. The second part of each chapter moves back and forth between the clergywoman's narrative and the larger Southern Baptist context of the schism. The analysis sections are dialogues between a woman's story and other primary sources, ranging from news releases to sermons, from conference proceedings to longstanding Baptist tensions of belief and practice, and from hymns and songs to other published stories about clergywomen. Each woman's story could stand alone for interpretation. However, the engagement with other primary sources strengthens and magnifies the arguments, resonating with each new interpretation.

To follow along with the arguments of this book, which are both shown and told, and which unfold by means of an accumulation of evidence across the stories and other primary resources, requires a particular way of seeing. By the time all of the conversations develop between clergywomen and the other instances of Baptist struggle, a portrait of the deeper issues at stake in the schism of Southern Baptists emerges. Only using a psychological lens, or only using a theological one, would produce rather flat results. Seeing both psychologically and theologically how the schism unfolded through the lives of clergywomen, and allowing their stories to frame that seeing, offers a new richer and more textured interpretation of the gendered struggle.

To see the schism psychologically this book focuses on the internal worlds of the clergywomen and on the relational and social worlds of Baptists. Psychological aspects of the clergywomen's stories are available but often need the insight or clarity of concepts cultivated by those trained in psychology to appreciate their connection to the wider struggles for Baptists. Once the psychological dynamics of the schism come into view, insights from the women's stories can be read in tension with the social world and history of ideas that have typically driven the other analyses of twentieth-century Baptists. Social conditions and human psychology are mutually reinforcing human dynamics. To see psychologically thus allows a nuanced insight into larger struggles and social changes that are often treated as *only* social or political.[55]

To see the schism theologically was a more common task over the last quarter of a century; however, theological seeing in the partisan literature is often accompanied by blame and preoccupation with moral judgments of the *others* under critique. In partisan (and some academic) accounts of the schism, autonomists generally focused more intently on the history of events and biblicists focused more on theological arguments between the parties.[56] The reinterpretation in this book sees those differences as endemic to the struggle itself and a perennial feature of the human condition.[57] This new reading tries instead to focus on the everyday lived theology of Baptists, centering on the clergywomen's narratives in order to open up the struggles that were at stake for many Baptists. Questions over the character and gender of human existence, brokenness, vulnerability, and redemption, as well as the work of meaning making, animate the reimagination of Baptist identity.[58]

To see "in depth" is not what others have critiqued as an overconfident claim to seeing some "true" or "real" interpretation. The claim about depth is based in a metaphor of perspective taking. Rather than take a singular and potentially reductive perspective from psychology or taking a similarly reductive approach from theological anthropology, the set of arguments made in this book are crafted from two kinds of vision, each two-dimensional alone, brought together to offer a third dimension—one of depth. In human sight (among other predators), two eyes, two angles of vision, create depth perception, which produce a third dimension of greater complexity and more possibilities for seeing.[59] What emerges is a critical and constructive interpretation of Baptist schism as a psychological and theological struggle over what it means to be human, shown in fine-grain detail.

Narrating the Schism

For readers unfamiliar with Southern Baptists, the following brief narrative presents some key moments from the years of schism in the SBC, framed by the lives of the five women who are featured in this book. Presenting major public events in parallel with the everyday stories and lives of Baptist women serves three purposes. First, it expands and complexifies the commonly accepted story of the schism, showing implications that are both more personal and more widespread. Second, seeing more of the micro- and macro-connections opens the way for new interpretations to emerge. And third, this chronological account helps orient the reader to each woman's story in the chapters that follow.

The summer of 1979, when biblicists first gained the presidency of the SBC, usually marks the beginning of the Southern Baptist schism. The period of conflict is typically described as ending in the summer of 1990, with a June victory celebration by biblicists in New Orleans and an August gathering of autonomists in Atlanta to launch the Cooperative Baptist Fellowship (CBF). The CBF and a constellation of moderate and progressive organizations became an alternative set of denominational structures, continuing to fracture the SBC through the 1990s and beyond.[60] To understand the intense twelve-year period of fighting in a larger context, one can set the bookends a bit wider on this shelf of Baptist history. The period between the 1963 adoption of the Baptist Faith and Message and its revision in 2000 provide the wider setting. In those decades, Anna, Martha, Joanna, Rebecca, and Chloe entered the Baptist world, experienced nurture and conflict, announced vocational callings for ministry, attended seminary, and began pastoral careers. Their stories frame the events of the schism, and they guide a new reading of what was at stake in those years.

Although she grew up to be a pastor, Martha was born into a Southern Baptist world in 1958 that included virtually no reference point for women's ordained ministry. Mainline Protestant denominations were just waking up to the idea of ordaining women as pastors. Various Methodist and Presbyterian groups passed collective denominational statements endorsing the practice of women's ordination in the 1950s, but Baptists made no such pronouncements.[61] In the early 1960s, when Martha was just learning to read, Southern Baptist leaders were arguing over how to read the Bible. The "Elliott controversy" erupted in 1961, when the

SBC's Broadman Press published *The Message of Genesis,* written by Baptist seminary professor Ralph Elliott.[62] Conservative pastors (who would eventually play key roles in the biblicist party) galvanized their arguments about the literal truth of the Bible over against new scientific methods for studying the Scriptures, demanding the withdrawal of Elliott's book. They worried that new study methods might undermine the Bible's authority. Concerns over the inspiration and authority of the Bible motivated a new revision of the SBC's Baptist Faith and Message in 1963. Although there were several small changes to the confession's statement on Scripture, the main addition read, "The criterion by which the Bible is to be interpreted is Jesus Christ."[63]

Born into a Roman Catholic family in 1960, Joanna knew virtually nothing about Southern Baptists until junior high, and even then she was notably unimpressed by their proselytizing tactics. Joanna attended Catholic school for a time, where she was nurtured and influenced by her teacher, Sister Mary Charles. Women's religious leadership still took traditional forms in Roman Catholic and Baptist life, and yet changes were also afoot. The sea change for Southern Baptist women began rather quietly in North Carolina with the ordination of Addie Davis in August 1964. It mustered a local controversy and found coverage in some state Baptist newspapers, but on the whole it was quickly forgotten when Davis departed to serve an American Baptist church in Readsboro, Vermont.[64]

Events like Davis's ordination and the Elliott controversy were slowly shifting the foundations of Baptist life, shaking the structures of the SBC, and contributing to the eventual schism. Social upheaval in the 1960s, with its open challenges to authority, prompted SBC employees, professors, and loyal Southern Baptist pastors to pay new attention to women's rights, racial equality, antiwar protests, and so on. The shifts in attention, mingled with modernism, rankled conservative Baptist pastors and some laity. Those most distressed by Baptist engagements with social issues tended to be conservatives who were also critical of SBC bureaucracy for its emphasis on efficiency and organizational growth in the name of missions and evangelism. The mounting disgruntlement fed the emergence of new factions in the convention.

By the mid-1960s more than ten million Baptists filled pews and pulpits in SBC churches, and they were paying little attention to the cracks and fissures opening up in the foundation of the seemingly invincible SBC.[65] Instead, they were carrying out their everyday lives of faith and enjoying unprecedented numerical growth, with little thought about theological controversies large or small among denominational leaders. One Sunday morning in 1967, Anna, age seven, came to faith in what she calls a "very positive way." Anna's Southern Baptist parents adopted her when she was two years old, preparing her to hear from her Sunday school teacher that God wanted "to adopt her into his family." The profession of faith set Anna firmly on a path to discipleship and ministry. That same year in New Orleans, a young seminarian named Paige Patterson and a Houston judge named Paul Pressler met for the first time to discuss concerns over leadership, authority, and theology in the SBC. Over coffee and beignets at the Café Du Monde, they started mapping a strategy for taking control of the appointive powers and decision-making apparatus of the convention, a plan that took ten years to formulate and another dozen years for biblicists to execute.[66]

In 1973 Chloe was born to parents actively involved in their Baptist church. Many years earlier, Chloe's mother had chosen marriage over a career as a missionary nurse. Also in 1973, six-year-old Rebecca was baptized in a Baptist church that taught her about both God's love and her inferiority as a female. Rebecca and her family soon left the congregation when her parents felt the critical judgment of pronouncements against divorce. For Baptist women, the social landscape of the early 1970s was less than hospitable. Nevertheless, the Baptist world was also slowly changing. An increasing number of churches, such as University Baptist where Martha and her family belonged, were ordaining women as deacons and electing them deacon chairs. By the end of the 1970s, the number of Baptist women attending seminary had grown substantially and those ordained in Baptist churches had reached nearly sixty.[67] During SBC meetings in the 1970s, resolutions about the role of women in society, home, and/or church rose and fell like barometers of the atmospheric pressure over the "woman question."[68] Through the decade a movement to maintain the status quo on the woman question, biblical authority, and other social and political issues, coalesced into a more formalized group led by Patterson and Pressler.[69] Setting their sights on change for the denomination, the biblicists were ready by 1979 to vote in a new strategy.

By the late 1970s, Rebecca and Anna were experiencing their first epiphanies about ministry. Rebecca attended Sunshine Baptist Camp with a friend, and the camp's missionary speakers led her to wonder if she was also called to be a missionary. Anna was fully involved in her church as a teenager, filling the role of "music minister" at the annual youth Sunday, and she regularly "led friends to Christ." Meanwhile, many hundreds, perhaps thousands, of Baptist women were beginning to explore calls to ministry.

In 1978 a group of SBC agency heads, seminary students, pastors, church members, journalists, and historians gathered in Nashville, Tennessee, for the first and only Consultation on Women in Church-Related Vocations. No one was elected and no committees were appointed, but the three hundred or so in attendance heard reports, survey results, historical accounts, and psychological analysis about women in Southern Baptist churches and agencies.[70] Those gathered also heard impassioned pleas and insistent questions from women who felt called by God to be ministers. Some of those women were already ordained and serving. Others were still trying to discern the meaning of a call. Southern Baptists seemed poised to hear these concerns and lend support, or at least not to hinder the women in their newfound vocations.

In the summer of 1979, the SBC met in Houston, Texas—an ordinary yet momentous meeting forever marking the official end of Baptist synthesis and the beginning of a schism. The 12,500 Baptist pastors and laypeople in attendance, gathered in the Astrodome, and they elected Adrian Rogers, pastor of Bellevue Baptist Church in Memphis, Tennessee, the new president of their convention. In the years that followed, biblicists carried out Patterson and Pressler's plan, electing a dozen SBC presidents, who in turn appointed scores of committees and hundreds of committee members, who in turn reshaped every SBC agency, school, and board with biblicist values and direction. The net effect was an increasingly conservative bearing and purpose for the nation's largest Protestant denomination, a direction that has continued with little interruption for more than three decades.

Neither the magnitude nor the significance of Rogers's election was immediately evident to all Baptists, either those at the centers or those at the margins. In the fall of 1979, Anna headed to college, taking a part-time job as a youth minister. In that work she came to clarity about her sense of "calling to ministry." She followed her pastor's advice to share her calling and to seek prayerful support. She also began thinking about seminary. However, like many Baptists, Anna was not aware of the Baptist troubles or even that being a woman could be problematic.

Even autonomists near the centers of Baptist power did not immediately perceive the urgency or durability of the changes to the SBC begun in 1979. No sincere organizing to mount an opposition began until the fall of 1980, after autonomists lost a second SBC presidential election.[71] By the time they got organized, autonomists were too far behind to regain power. They made greater and lesser attempts over the next decade to win the SBC presidency or find a means of compromise with the biblicists, but they never caught up in organization, support, funding, or political strategy.[72] Nor were they ever successful in their attempts to win the presidency. Over the next decade schism in the convention widened day by day.

In the 1980s, as the SBC increasingly became the domain of biblicists, a number of autonomist groups began splintering away from the convention in protest. The first among them was the Southern Baptist Women in Ministry (SBWIM) organization, founded by thirty-three women in ministry in 1983. It was followed by the Southern Baptist Alliance in 1987, and churches began to fracture as well.[73] Events such as the 1984 Resolution on Ordination and the Role of Women in Ministry, passed at the Southern Baptist Convention annual meeting in Kansas City, further solidified the parties and galvanized the splinter groups. The so-called Kansas City Resolution blamed Eve for the "Edenic fall," and it warned against recognizing women's ministry if it included "pastoral functions and leadership roles entailing ordination."[74]

In 1985, twelve-year-old Chloe was baptized at Milton Heights Baptist Church. Within a year, Milton Heights called a new pastor who was openly opposed to women's leadership in the congregation, and Chloe's family, led by her mother, departed the church so quickly their "heads were spinning." They joined a church aligned with the growing autonomist party. The schism not only fostered the formation of new Baptist organizations both local and national but also split churches and families over concrete issues such as abortion, interpreting Scripture, and women's ordination.

As the 1980s came to a close, Rebecca approached her graduation from a Baptist college, sensing a strong call to seminary. Friends and peers a few years ahead of her urged her not to matriculate at any of the SBC-affiliated schools, where they were students. The tide had turned, they insisted, and the "fight was over." Major changes in philosophy and direction of the Baptist seminaries were assured. Rebecca should go to one of the new autonomist-supported seminaries or find a suitable non-Baptist school. She chose a school with a Baptist house of study, and she mourned the loss of connection with the tradition of her professors, yet she clearly still planned to remain Baptist.

The summer of 1990 was a hinge point for SBC institutions and politics. In June the biblicists organized yet another presidential victory at the SBC meeting in New Orleans. They elected Morris Chapman, pastor of First Baptist Church in Wichita Falls, Texas, president with over 57 percent of the vote. Autonomists were growing weary after twelve straight defeats, and their candidate, Daniel Vestal, garnered just over 42 percent of the vote. At the close of the meeting a group of biblicists gathered around tables at the Café du Monde to commemorate Patterson and Pressler's meeting years earlier. They toasted victory and presented certificates of appreciation to Pressler and Patterson.[75] The boards of every SBC agency and school were secured with biblicist majorities, and a large-scale house cleaning was underway for the staff of seminaries and missionary boards. New sympathetic leaders would take the convention in the direction biblicists wanted it go. To their thinking, the "resurgence" of fundamentalist doctrine and practice was unique in American history and complete at the first stage (control of the boards). Further stages were yet to come and preoccupied the SBC politics of the 1990s: replacing all heads of schools and agencies and "incorporating renewal into teaching, publications, and programs" as well as extending the "renewal into state conventions, associations and local churches."[76]

While the biblicists celebrated at the Café du Monde, a hotel room near the convention center became a gathering place for Vestal and other autonomist party leaders to consider their losses and subsequent strategies. The next morning at breakfast, Vestal addressed the autonomist party faithful, who were exhausted by the decade of investing heavy amounts of time, money and energy to stop the directional change in the SBC. Vestal acknowledged the disappointing loss, and he assured those gathered that their work was not in vain. Then he called for a convocation in August, a gathering of the dispossessed to search for renewal and "to find ways to cooperate without sacrificing our Baptist distinctives."[77] Thus began the Cooperative Baptist Fellowship.

Moving from an American Baptist church in the Midwest to attend seminary in the South in 1991, Joanna found herself in a confusing Southern Baptist world. On one hand, nearly everyone at her school assumed that if she was Baptist, she must be Southern Baptist. On the other hand, the churches where she worshiped and served were cutting their ties to the SBC. The fracturing of Southern Baptist life was messy and unclear in every quarter. The CBF grew and established itself yet continued to skirmish with the SBC. The constellation of new autonomist organizations siphoned energy, money, and effort away from the SBC. Nearly a dozen new seminaries or Baptist houses of study opened in the 1990s, assembling faculty members who had lost their jobs in SBC schools, yet the new schools often continued cooperating with state SBC organizations. Countless churches spent the decade determining where their loyalties would go, often splitting funds, loyalties, and even families. Many in the constellation of moderate and progressively oriented organizations devoted themselves to redeeming some features of Southern Baptist character and identity.[78] However, as time wore on and biblicists consolidated power within the SBC, the breakaway groups increasingly identified themselves with new purposes and directions of their own, struggling to reshape Baptist identity in a crucible of conflict.

Where women's ordination gained acceptance in Baptist life, it was through the long, patient work of relational connection and trust building. Martha, who attended seminary as a second career in the late 1990s, found that four years in her seminary church yielded a deep sense of acceptance and belonging. The particular congregational relationships brought Martha to a sincere moment of pastoral calling. She and other women stopped being merely an issue over which Southern Baptists fought. They were Baptist daughters, sisters, mothers, wives, and ministers claiming gifts and calling for ministry. Increasingly, Baptists happily ordained the women they personally knew and in whom they witnessed a clear vocation for ministry. Baptist churches that ordained and employed women in pastoral roles participated in a widespread shift in American religion to embody a new theology and practice of ministry, one striving for gender equality and resisting the model of "delegated order" in relationships and authority between men and women. Nevertheless, for biblicists the delegated order approach grew in importance as a way to organize church, home, and society.[79] And biblicist leaders elected to enshrine their commitments in a 1998 addendum on the family to the Baptist Faith and Message. The statement declared the equal worth of women and men yet built an analogy that associates the male with God and Christ and the female with God's people and the church. Thus a wife is to "submit herself graciously" to her husband, and she holds "the God-given responsibility to respect her husband and to serve as his helper in managing the household and nurturing the next generation." In 2000 a full revision of the Baptist Faith and Message picked up the new article on the family, adding that the role of pastor should be limited to men. The new confessional document convinced a few more churches to depart the SBC. However, the revised confessional statement, coming on the heels of so many organizational changes, mainly signaled that the schism was complete. The interpretations for what happened and why, were however, just getting started.

Overview of the Chapters

In chapter 1, Anna's story reinterprets the Southern Baptist schism as a gendered psychological struggle. The analysis of her narratives shows in detail how her story embodies the Southern Baptist schism in three ways: (1) as a cultural symbol of schism; (2) as someone acting with agency to change her self-understanding, relationships, and situation by contesting the status quo and by making a move from subordination to ordination; and (3) by navigating the psychological and theological tension between personal agency and obedience to one's calling. The analysis portion of the chapter engages official Baptist statements, SBC resolutions and confessions, hymns, and agency policies, which present a variety of official, normative, and pragmatically written Baptist theologies. Anna's story, however, captures how everyday belief and practice both embodies and challenges the official interpretations through personal agency, relational change, and iconic struggles.

Chapter 2 shows how Martha's story of growing up in a complementarity culture reinterprets the schism in the SBC as a gendered identity crisis. At every turn, Martha's story reveals the Baptist struggle between "mission" and "submission" and another related struggle between sacrifice and ambition. Martha's relationships with her mother and father provide openings to see how gender is passed on to each new generation and the psychological work required for men as well as women. The anatomy of Southern Baptist complementarity is contested, undone, and reasserted, shaping numerous aspects of Baptist life during the years of schism and pressing the question of what will become of complementarity itself. The analysis of Martha's story engages the organizational life and programmatic piety of Baptists, delivered weekly in the teaching and programs of Baptist churches. Sunday school, the Woman's Missionary Union (WMU), deacon ministry, and pastoral ministry mutually reinforce the relational and internalized Baptist worlds.

In chapter 3, Joanna's story makes connections to a wider angle of vision on Baptist life. Also taking a winding road to the pastorate, Joanna did not grow up Baptist and never considered herself Southern Baptist, although she served in three churches that departed the SBC as the schism unfolded. Joanna's stories of relational support and struggle frame a rich way of understanding how Baptist polity is an ongoing set of relational negotiations bound up in historic and perennial tensions of Baptist belief and practice. Each of five tensions appears readily in Joanna's story: salvation and calling, soul competency, the priesthood of all believers, voluntary association, and separation of church and state. The analysis puts into dialogue Joanna's relational life and the ways Baptists continuously navigate the psychological tensions of their identity. Joanna and her friends openly challenge the sexism and dangers of abuse that relationships of domination and submission can foster. Most interpretations of the Baptist schism leave aside both the relational and gendered character of the story. However, by stepping into leadership, Joanna and other clergywomen move relationality and gender into the foreground as key concepts for understanding how the story of schism unfolded.

The analysis growing out of stories told by Anna, Martha, and Joanna shows primarily psychological perspectives on Baptist life. Chapters 4 and 5 assume those psychological dynamics and shift attention to a theological perspective on the stories told by Rebecca and Chloe. In chapter 4, Rebecca's story shows how Southern Baptists traversed the years of schism while living in the tension between life struggle and life sustenance. The tension between struggle and sustenance may give rise to despair and grief, yet it can also be a space of redemption and grace. The analysis of the chapter engages sermons from leading voices in Baptist life during the latter years of the twentieth century. Preaching for Baptists is a central task for meaning making and identity shaping in the culture. Rebecca's stories, and ten biblicist- and autonomist-inspired sermons and essays, illuminate the spiritual and theological struggles over what it means to be human. Her stories reinterpret schism as a profoundly spiritual, theological and gendered struggle over human brokenness, redemption, and meaning.

In chapter 5, Chloe's stories about her practice of ministry reinterpret the time and space of schism as both a battleground and playground for Baptists, where a new theology and practice of ministry and a new kind of Baptist identity could emerge. The changes in Chloe's practice of ministry reflect a larger movement among Baptist and Christian churches in the United States. Chloe's story shows how women's entry into ministry brought to light existing cracks and fissures to the coherence of the nearly all-male profession. Biblicists supported an "authoritative model" of pastoral leadership, while autonomists claimed the "servant leader model" as the right one. Yet both models are troublesome for women. The analysis of Chloe's story dialogues with other published narratives of clergywomen. In clergywomen's stories, one sees how the years of schism became an occasion for practicing a new embodied, relational, and vulnerable way of doing ministry, transforming the practice of ministry itself.

Until recently, Baptist clergywomen never had a chance *not* to be controversial. Since Addie Davis was ordained fifty years ago, clergywomen have been portrayed as anomalies, issues, tokens, symbols, and even jokes.[80] By refocusing attention on them as actors, ministers, and fully vulnerable yet powerful human beings, the stories of their lives show the situated possibilities of being Baptist, and a new narrative for understanding the culture and times in which the Baptist schism emerges. Reading the stories of these particular clergywomen, and many others in the late twentieth century, invites one to see how they were living a new way of being human that touched on every sense of who they were as women, as ministers, and as Baptists. They were inventing what they had never seen before. It was new to them as it emerged, yet it was shaped by the context and the liturgy of the everyday in Baptist life. They made dramatic changes internally and relationally, participating in the undoing of complementarity, but they also reproduced it at the same time. Most significantly, their lives offer a new framework for seeing an anatomy of the fracturing of the Southern Baptist Convention.

I

(Sub)ordination

How Clergywomen Embody Schism in the Southern Baptist Convention

> I didn't realize there was a huge problem about being a woman. With my upbringing we didn't have women on church staff. We didn't have women deacons. But there wasn't any "you can't do this." And at that point there wasn't any "you can do this" either.
>
> —Anna

In 1979 Southern Baptists began separating into factions, forming political parties, and taking votes that changed the denomination. That year Anna finished her first year of college, majoring in music and working as a youth minister. She grew up in a loving Southern Baptist home, adopted by her parents when she was two years old. As a young woman Anna had no idea a religious controversy was underway with Southern Baptists. She didn't know how close to her own life the Baptist schism would come. In the end the split was not simply "out there," as she put it, or "not with me." Rather, the Southern Baptist Convention schism cut a line right through her internal life and her relationships. Southern Baptist culture shaped Anna's desire and call to ministry, and in turn Anna and other clergywomen reshaped Baptist culture. Anna's story embodies the public struggle between the autonomist argument for women's ordination and ministry and the biblicist argument for women's subordination in family, church, and society.

Although Baptists treated women mainly as cultural symbols and did not see them as major players in the events of Southern Baptist life in the final four decades of the twentieth century, Anna's story shows how clergywomen embodied the schism as desiring subjects and active agents as well as cultural icons. Like other clergywomen, Anna embodies the fracture of the SBC in these three distinct and overlapping ways.[1] Her story gives shape to a reinterpretation of the Southern Baptist schism as a gendered psychological struggle, and the analysis of her narratives shows in detail how her story embodies the Southern Baptist schism:

(1) clergywomen are cultural symbols of the schism, (2) clergywomen act with agency to change their situation by contesting the status quo and by making a move from subordination to ordination,[2] and (3) clergywomen face an internal struggle between the powers of agency and obedience, played out in the "servanthood dilemma." Late-twentieth-century Baptist culture (and U.S. society) assumed and prioritized empowerment, even dominion, for men. Meanwhile, Baptist clergywomen living in the same culture coped with cultural and psychic expectations of subordination that often remained unconscious and yet pernicious. Within each embodiment of schism—cultural, relational, and intrapsychic—clergywomen seek change intentionally, yet they also participate unwittingly in the reproduction of the split, perpetuating the dynamics of domination and subordination.

The stories of Anna's calling, seminary, ministry, ordination, and endorsement vividly portray the embodiments of Baptist schism. The analysis that follows her stories invites a reading of her narrative alongside several key denominational events and texts, which together shape a different reading of the roles played by actual women. Although each party held them up as symbols of the schism, women were more than symbols. They participated in larger changes to ministry in U.S. churches, and they changed the Baptist context by virtue of their presence, personal relationships, and work. Anna's stories, interwoven with denominational arguments about women's ordination in the 1980s and 1990s, construct a new interpretation that goes beyond a mere battle by men over the roles of women. Clergywomen acting on their desires to engage ministry reshaped the Baptist world, contributing to new understandings of women and of ministry. Internally, clergywomen embodied the dynamics of the Baptist split in the "servanthood dilemma." A psychological interpretation of Anna's experience shows how the dilemma is also a paradox, both empowering and disempowering women as ministers and disciples of Jesus. Clergywomen's lives indeed reflected the splits and fissures of the denominational fracturing, yet clergywomen experienced the schism not merely as a hostile space but also a place of mutuality, creativity, and recognition of their gifts for ministry.

Anna's Story

Anna is a forty-two-year-old hospital chaplain who lives in Birmingham, Alabama, with her husband and two children. She worked mainly with youth and college students through her twenty years of professional ministry, recently becoming a chaplain. Anna grew up in a traditional Southern Baptist family, and her "very active parents" took her to church regularly. Her parents adopted Anna at the age of two, and her adoption continues to influence the way she thinks about herself. Anna says she felt love and support from her parents and siblings. Because of being given up for adoption by her birth parents, Anna notes, "I was born (I would say) wounded. Not wounded as such, but that was a pretty major thing. I think a lot of people with mothers also have wounds." Referencing Henri Nouwen's book *Wounded Healer*, she says, "I know that is at least a part of what shaped me."[3]

Anna says she became a Christian "as kind of a spinoff from being adopted." When she was seven years old, Anna's Sunday school teacher discussed with the class how to become a Christian, saying it was like "being adopted into God's family." The teacher knew Anna was adopted, so she asked her, "What does that mean to you to be adopted?" Anna told her teacher, "It means you are special and chosen." Soon after this teaching moment, Anna says she realized, "Oh! God wants to adopt me into his family!" Coming to faith in this way "felt very positive" to Anna, and she "accepted Christ."

Anna says it was common not to talk about adoption when she was growing up. Yet she insists it would have been "very helpful" if her parents might have recognized that her questions about adoption were part of a desire to know more about herself and not about her feelings for them. She regularly confronts the dynamics of adoption with parishioners and hospital patients. Overall Anna says her parents did a "good job" and handled things in "a very positive way," giving her the clear message and feeling of being "special and chosen."

Anna thought of the church where she grew up as a "very important place in that they pushed me and told me I had gifts and talents." She liked the youth programs there and learned "how to witness."[4] The church told every young person "you are important." During Youth Week, an annual Baptist program inviting teens to lead Sunday school and worship, Anna took the role of minister of music. As a teen she "led several friends to Christ." By the time she reached college, Anna says she felt God leading her to another church. She joined Willow Baptist Church, a smaller congregation, and began working as a part-time minister of youth. She recalls that Willow's pastor saw gifts for ministry in her.

Her time at Willow, Anna recalls, "was really when I felt God calling me to ministry. And I went to the pastor. He is a very wise man. And I said, 'What do I need to do?'" They talked, and he told Anna, "Just be obedient. You don't have to make a lot of promises or commitments. . . . You say, 'Okay, God, I will obey you.' And the reason that you make it public is so that people pray for you and support you." Anna made her decision public and began exploring the possibility of seminary.

Anna describes many ways she felt "very supported" by other ministers (all men), by the congregation at Willow Baptist Church, and by her future spouse, Mark. Throughout the process of articulating her call, Mark stood by her. The year before college graduation, Anna and Mark married and found a home near the church. The pastor of Willow, who had mentored and led Anna in discipleship, moved away, but the new interim pastor also offered support to her. He made ways for Anna to preach and lead, but they never talked about ordination.

In these early years of ministry, Anna recalls, "I didn't realize there was a huge problem about being a woman. With my upbringing we didn't have women on church staff. We didn't have women deacons. But there wasn't any 'you can't do this.' And at that point there wasn't any 'you can do this' either." Anna moved from Willow Baptist Church to a small town to work part-time in youth ministry. She realized she needed and wanted more education. She was ready for seminary, and "in that process," she says, "I began to realize there was a controversy." The situation clarified further when Anna arrived at Southwestern Baptist Theological Seminary and had to be "specially interviewed because I was starting school and my husband wasn't." Anna remembers: "It really hacked me off."

Seminary administrators created a pre-entrance interview especially for married women whose husbands would *not* be attending seminary. Anna estimates there were approximately ten women in seminary with her at that time in the same situation. She says even the interviewer thought the interview "stupid," yet the school required it for entrance. The main question at the interview was not directed at Anna but at her husband. The seminary official asked him, "Do you understand that your wife is preparing for ministry, and do you support her?" This extra seminary entrance interview sounded a wakeup call for Anna. She says, "Only when I got down there did I really begin to realize that there was a problem ... a huge divide ... and I really didn't care; *I just wanted to minister.* So I thought, I'll do the best I can. There will be someplace I can minister."

While attending seminary, Anna felt shunned by some of the "seminary wives" who lived in student housing and came to invite her to a meeting for "pastors' wives." Anna said, "That's interesting. Do you have one for men?" And they said, "We don't need one for men." Anna replied, "Well, my husband is the one. I'm in school, not my husband." Anna says they turned away as if to say, "We'll talk to you later ... wrong number!" Anna taught school while she took seminary classes and completed her studies in two years. She recalls about Southern Baptists at the time, "They were really shooting at each other. You know that was about the same time the [space shuttle] *Challenger* went up, and I felt like that was exactly what was happening in seminary. People were shooting at the professors. And if you were a woman, people naturally assumed where you stood theologically—without ever opening your mouth or anything. I just wanted to get my stuff and get out of there." She sums up her seminary experience this way: "You all can shoot at each other if you want. I am going to go through underneath here, grab what I need, and get out of here and just do ministry!"

The extra entrance interview and a job interview two years later functioned like sexist bookends to Anna's formal theological education. Nearing graduation and searching for a ministry position, Anna recalls that her male peers received three and four times more interviews than she did. She describes a conversation in which she felt "mocked and degraded" by one particular job interviewer:

A guy from Georgia was interviewing me. And he said, "You're married?! You want to do ministry and you're married?!"

I said, "Yeah."

And he said, "What do you think you can do married?"

"Anything I can do single." I didn't understand what he was talking about. I think he got the name, and started interviewing and assumed that I was single. And then when he saw I was married he became very degrading.

"Well, God can't use you."

And I said, "Well chances are you aren't going to hire me, so maybe we should just end this interview." And I walked out.

Anna walked out of the interview, but she didn't walk away from Baptists. Following graduation from seminary, she found church ministry jobs. She spent more than fifteen years working in churches as a minister with youth and college students. She also worked in a private high school as a counselor and coach, and now that she is a chaplain, she continues to teach youth as a volunteer at the church where she and her family worship.

Despite nearly continuous ministry in five churches before and after seminary, it took more than twelve years, after publicly declaring a call to ministry, for Anna to receive ordination. Although she "hated conflict" and hoped not to create any, Anna felt that God "put on her heart" a desire to be ordained. She remembers earlier in her ministry, when she preached at Grove Baptist Church, a member of the congregation said, "Oh! You did a great job! But it's just a shame they will never ordain you." She knew the man well and so replied to him, "You know what? You don't have to. God already has!" She laughingly teased him about *not* putting his hands on her. Later he came back and said, "You know what? You got the best ordination." Anna concluded, "I guess that's always the way that I looked at it: I really felt like God called and ordained me."

The epilogue to this story came several years later, when Grove became the church to ordain Anna at the request of Calvary, the church she served at that time. She contacted all the young women from her various youth groups, and those who served as ministry interns with her, and she invited them to the ordination service. After her ordination, Anna felt confirmed: "There is always hope. The denomination was certainly digressing, and the affirmation is limited, yet there is hope to do ministry."

Several years after ordination, Anna decided to make a change. She wanted more pastoral responsibility, and chaplaincy looked like the best possible path. But Anna found herself frustrated by the lack of support from Southern Baptists, who decided in 2002 to stop endorsing women as chaplains if they were also ordained ministers. With irony, Anna recalls, "Coming to the hospital and wanting endorsement, it's saddened me that now I had to turn—not that CBF is bad at all—but that I can't ask for the denomination that raised me and told me 'Wherever He Leads I'll Go' is a great hymn, except if you're a woman. And now they won't endorse me. And that does sadden me about the denomination. But as a woman in ministry . . . I just hoped, and have hope, and I will continue to hope, that I would get to do ministry, because that's where my heart is."[5]

Anna says that "strong women," role models in her childhood church, inspired her. Her mother, for example, was "a very good Sunday school teacher" and "pretty influential" in the congregation. Although her parents didn't fully understand her call and "weren't real sure" what to think of her career choice, Anna still felt their acceptance. She recalls, "I think they saw the big controversy picture." But Anna remained clear about the distance between the "controversy" and her calling. "I understood God called me," she says. "That was it."

Reflecting further, she notes, "From time to time, I just have to laugh." She remembers working with another ordained woman and together leading an annual SBC workshop on ministry, attended almost exclusively by male ministers. Anna and her friend didn't share the facts of their ordinations with anyone in the workshop. She says, "They would pack out [the workshop] year after year because of our experience and what we knew, and how we tried to help them . . . it was the ministry we were doing."

In the hospital when she is making rounds, Anna says people still ask her incredulously, "You're the chaplain? And you're Baptist?!" She "struggled big time" when the SBC changed the Baptist Faith and Message. She says. "I don't know how to withdraw . . . but I know I'm not Southern Baptist, or at least I'm not . . . what they're doing." When she thinks of the changes to Southern Baptist life, she wants "to get further and further away."

Embodying the Schism: Culturally, Relationally, and Internally

Anna was adopted into a family and a church that loved her and helped her feel special and chosen, yet when those feelings expanded to include a sense of God's call to ministry, she experienced the more complex and ambivalent struggles at work in Baptist life. Her life and calling were not merely her own; they embodied the dynamics of the cultural and theological shifts of the Southern Baptist context. Anna's experiences in seminary, ministry, ordination, and endorsement were shaped by those shifts, yet she also participated in bringing forth changes, despite her insistence that the Baptist controversy was not connected to her.

In part because of their novelty and isolation from each other, clergywomen like Anna functioned as cultural symbols or icons of the Baptist schism, but Anna was not a victim or passively unaware of her situation. She and other clergywomen acted as agents to change their situations, primarily in the relational realm, where they could protest the status quo for gender roles and move from subordination to ordination. Yet the struggle clergywomen faced was not only embodied symbolically or relationally. Rather, the dynamics of the schism presented themselves in very personal and internal struggles that can be portrayed in clergywomen's navigation of the "servanthood dilemma." The dilemma is a psychological bind created by domination and subordination. For men in ministry to give up their power to serve is quite different from the task faced by women, who are already expected to be obedient and subordinate. Nevertheless, women turn the dilemma into a paradox and find ways, like Anna, "to just do ministry."

Anna's life and work as an ordained Baptist minister in a place where Southern Baptists are ubiquitous demonstrates the power of the symbolic function of ordained clergywomen. In the SBC ministry workshop, other ministers admired and followed Anna and her colleague, yet the two women felt compelled to hide their ordinations lest they lose their opportunity. In the halls and patient rooms of the hospital, Anna still faces shock and disbelief that she could be a Baptist chaplain. She tries to distance herself from conflicts in the Baptist controversy, even with her own family. Baptist clergywomen lived through the years of schism in many interesting and creative ways, yet for all their efforts, most of them could not escape entirely the symbolic role they played.[6]

In their struggle for theological and political ascendancy between 1979 and 2000, Southern Baptists treated clergywomen like political footballs.[7] Both sides claimed victory, but to celebrate, biblicists spiked the ball as a sign demonstrating all things wrong in the convention and the wider American culture. On the other side, autonomists, who also claimed the winning position, held women high as a symbol of true Southern Baptist piety and vocation.[8] Clergywomen interviewed for this book were among those sometimes held high as ideal symbols and other times dashed to the ground in a different kind of victory celebration. In both cases they were treated as objects of a larger contest between men, and this location illustrates the symbolic role women embodied in the fight between parties. The very objective (and objectionable) image of a football in the hands of male players denies women a subjective place in the story and highlights the ways they were used to make an argument or tell a story rather than included among the storytellers.

The women in this book no longer see themselves as "Southern Baptist," and on one hand they might be regarded as casualties of the schism. Anna says that after the passage of the 2000 Baptist Faith and Message, she only wanted to get "further and further away" from Southern Baptists. On the other hand, the schism resulted in several new organizations of Baptists, and each clergywoman in this book is now affiliated with one or more of those new groups.[9] For Anna the change meant a closer affiliation with the Cooperative Baptist Fellowship (CBF), the group that endorsed her work as a chaplain. As did the other women in this study, Anna very clearly continued to identify herself as Baptist.

In 1984 Anna stepped into the heat of the Baptist controversy when she and her husband moved to Fort Worth to attend Southwestern Baptist Theological Seminary. She says she had no idea about the "huge divide" over women's ordination among Southern Baptists.[10] She came mainly in obedience to her call and in the hope she could "just do ministry."

That same year a pivotal event brought into focus ways that clergywomen would function as cultural symbols for biblicists and autonomists. Just five years into the controversy, a crystallizing moment—passage by a slim margin of the now-infamous Kansas City Resolution—helped the two sides coalesce in opposition, each treating women as cultural objects. For many years before, during, and after Baptists negotiated the schism, the topic of woman's role in church, home, and society came up at the annual SBC meeting as an issue to be voted on by the gathered body.[11] Between 1972 and 1984, the convention considered nine resolutions about the role of women. Some died in the Committee on Resolutions. Others were voted up or down. The polarization of positions grew over time. Resolutions proclaiming freedom, equality, and the pursuit of vocation for women were less and less favored. Statements supporting women but opposing the Equal Rights Amendment to the U.S. Constitution were more frequently adopted.[12] In 1984 the Kansas City Resolution focused on women's ordination and leadership in the church. Longtime *Christianity Today* editor Carl F. H. Henry, who had recently become a Southern Baptist, introduced the resolution.[13] It stated that Paul's letters commend "women and men alike in other roles of ministry and service," and yet Paul "excludes women from pastoral leadership." The "delegated order of authority" provided one part of the logic for women's exclusion. That order exists "to preserve a submission God requires because the man was first in creation and the woman was first in the Edenic fall." The resolution concludes by encouraging "the service of women in all aspects of church life and work other than pastoral functions and leadership roles entailing ordination."[14]

Biblicists who sponsored and supported the 1984 Kansas City Resolution viewed any ordained woman as an example, a symbol of all that was wrong with the denomination. Women's ordination was a practice considered "anathema to most conservatives."[15] Ordained Baptist women were not living according to "God's delegated order of authority (God the head of Christ, Christ the head of man, man the head of woman, man and woman dependent one upon the other to the glory of God)."[16] For biblicists, women functioned as symbols of sin personified, thus the association with "Eve's sin." They were secondary to men in arrangements of complementarity, "divinely gifted for distinctive areas of evangelical engagement."[17] Women always hold less powerful roles in such arrangements. They are assumed unsuited for pastoral calling or ordination, which are roles and rituals reserved for men. In biblicists' line of thinking, clergywomen were cultural symbols of all that was wrong not only with Baptist life but also with all humanity. By seeking ordination, women became symbols of the *violation* of God's "delegated order" and of God's relationship to creation, families, and ministry.[18] They were footballs dashed to the ground in a declaration of victory for the Bible and in condemnation of all that was wrong with a culture that rejects God's ways.

On the other side of the fast-polarizing tensions, autonomists, who lost the vote on the Kansas City Resolution by only a few percentage points, took up the symbol of ordained clergywomen in shock and outrage. They lifted up clergywomen as figures to rally their own team for the sake of Baptist "freedom and autonomy." The previous year, in 1983, a group of clergywomen and their supporters organized a support network, Southern Baptist Women in Ministry, and began publishing a newsletter for an emerging constituency of supporters of women in ministry. In the 1984 autumn issue of *Folio: A Newsletter for Southern Baptist Women in Ministry*, numerous responses to the Kansas City Resolution appeared. All six SBC seminary presidents wrote against the resolution. Their reasons for not supporting it were not uniform, and several presidents carefully couched their words. Generally, seminary presidents could not frame the debate over women's ordination because the biblicist party had already set the terms. The seminary leaders sounded on the whole defensive and reactionary. Southeastern Baptist Theological Seminary president Randall Lolley offered succinct and direct opposition: "The resolution is bad exegesis, bad hermeneutics, bad theology, bad Christology, ... bad soteriology, bad ecclesiology, bad missiology, bad anthropology, bad sociology, bad psychology, bad manners and worst of all, 'bad Baptist.'"[19]

Autonomists attempted to take the moral high ground by supporting women's ordination.[20] Years earlier, Martha Gilmore, ordained in Texas in 1977, made the "issue of women's ordination personal" to Texans by giving the issue a face. Like some other clergywomen and "progressive dissenters," Gilmore and her supporters believed her actions and ordination functioned in Southern Baptist life as an "embodied principle." She was "doing in a particular instance what Christians believe Jesus did on the universal level, making God's presence visible to people." Gilmore and others understood that ordination "embodied, or 'incarnated,' the love of God on earth in smaller versions of the grand way Jesus did."[21]

The "Calendar" of the same 1984 edition of *Folio*, which reported the news and opinions about the Kansas City Resolution, announced six conferences and Baptist meetings about women's leadership. Southern Baptist Women in Ministry leaders publicized the "woman question" as the topic of the year. And leaders of the biblicist and autonomist parties used language like "anathema" and "bad, bad, bad" to stretch a growing divide among Southern Baptists. As they continued to wage a conflict for control of the SBC, leaders of the two parties took up the cultural symbol of clergywomen to argue their cases and make their points. Indeed, the women functioned as icons for each party, upheld as objects that embodied the split symbolically.

Taking a stand on one side or the other of the issue of women's ordination clearly marked male leaders as belonging to one party or the other in the growing schism. For women, however, the matter did not unfold quite so simply. They could not merely function symbolically. Martha Gilmore observed that her ordination became a problematic issue for her pastor, but for her the possibility arose mainly because she was a beloved child of the church and not "an issue."[22] On the ground and in churches, the 1984 resolution became an opportunity for many women to speak of their own convictions and desires for work in ministry. It galvanized some women to action. It pushed others to articulate their reasons for rejecting women's ordination. The resolution provided an occasion for expanding women's leadership. At the same time it deepened the crucible of conflict in which Anna and others prepared for ministry in the 1980s.

Clergywomen also became symbols in the debates over the meaning of ordination itself. In April 1988, the Baptist History and Heritage Society met and heard papers, published later that year, articulating detailed arguments for and against women's ordination. Bill Stancil, later hired as a professor of theology at Midwestern Baptist Theological Seminary and then dismissed for his overly progressive views, framed the larger arguments over ordination in his essay.[23] In it, he articulated important late-twentieth-century questions for Baptists regarding who can or should be ordained, for which roles, and for what practical purposes. His assessment was that the Bible does not justify ordination and may undercut it. Neither apostolic succession nor a view of "ministry constituting the church" provides adequate reasons for ordination. Rather, he argued, the "need for functional leadership" in Baptist churches drives the impetus for ordination.

Changes to the profession of ministry, a growing number of paid and ordained leaders in congregations, and the extension of ministry beyond local churches (i.e., missions, chaplaincy, etc.) expanded the number and types of ministries suited for ordination. In addressing the question of women's ordination, Stancil noted how it became "one of the issues by which political and theological loyalty is to be gauged."[24] From the first ordination of a Baptist woman in the early 1960s to the present, clergywomen and the churches that call and ordain them continue to make news headlines in local papers and national syndicates. Clergywomen became emblematic of the schism itself when local Southern Baptist associations and state conventions ousted churches for calling women as their pastors. Prescott Memorial Baptist Church in Memphis, Tennessee, became a prominent example when the Shelby County Baptist Association dismissed them in 1987 for calling Nancy Hastings Sehested as pastor. In 2009 the Georgia Baptist Convention severed ties with its historic flagship, First Baptist Church in Decatur, when they called Julie Pennington-Russell as pastor. In 2011, the Surry Baptist Association in Mount Airy, North Carolina, voted "overwhelmingly" to cast out Flat Rock Baptist Church for calling Bailey Edwards Nelson as their pastor.[25] Stancil argued for considering two additional questions: the relationship between the SBC and local churches and an ethical concern for women if they must serve without "formal recognition and authorization for exercising gifts on behalf of the congregation."[26]

Two other presentations at the 1988 Baptist History and Heritage Society meeting addressed *women's* ordination more directly. Jann Aldredge-Clanton, an ordained Baptist minister, pastoral counselor, and minister to family life at a Methodist church, spoke in support of women's ordination. Dorothy Patterson, wife of biblicist party leader Paige Patterson and "homemaker and teacher of seminars in womanhood and family living," spoke against it.[27] The choice of these two women (one an ordained minister and one a pastor's wife) and the arguments they put forward contributed to the growing polarization between autonomists and biblicists and solidified the symbolic function of clergywomen in the schism.

Patterson presented a clear-cut thesis: if women should not be pastors or "hold ecclesiastical office," then discussions of their ordination are "moot" or "academic." Scripture, argued Patterson, settled the "real issue." However, she took time to point out several problems with "historical" and "emotional" arguments for women's ordination. She wondered if "Jesuitical casuistry or historical hanky-panky" were done "in order to create a female Mt. Everest out of an anthill to prove a point" that women could or should be ordained.[28] Women who left the SBC to become pastors, she argued, "bear eloquent testimony that their commitment to Baptist doctrine was superseded by their desires to attain a particular ecclesiastical office." She equated "call" to an "emotional and intuitive impulse" and saw it as a violation of "the immutable written Word." She concluded that even if Baptist history offered greater evidence of women's ordination, it remained a "tradition, without scriptural authority," and as such "not binding."[29]

In making a biblical case against women holding "teaching/ruling positions in their churches," Patterson articulated a shared logic of biblicists. The theological point she offered is that "God of the Old Testament and His covenant people" and "Christ the bridegroom and His bride the church" are central images: "By placing woman in the teaching/ruling office, the church negates this truth taught by subjection of wives to husbands, i.e., that the church is subject to Christ, thereby destroying the image." She argued that the passages in 1 Timothy 2:8–15 and 1 Corinthians 14:33–35 capture "timeless principles." Biblical writers Peter and Paul each forbade women to "teach or exert authority over men," although they may teach, prophesy, and serve in some instances (i.e., with other women). By connecting to both the order of creation and Israelite law, these passages show the "timelessness" of the principle of divine order of "male headship and female submission." The "real issue," concluded Patterson, "is not ordination itself but the authority of the Bible." And to accept the Bible is to accept "home and church order."[30]

Aldredge-Clanton's thesis, reflecting the logic of autonomists, was also clear: "Southern Baptists cannot overthrow the ordination of women because it is of God." She built her argument chronologically, giving example after example of women's equality, leadership, and service from the Old Testament, New Testament, and Baptist history. She began with stories of Genesis, arguing that God created men and women to "equally reflect the image of God and equally share responsibility for the rest of creation." Pain in childbirth, the difficulties of physical labor, and the domination of husbands over wives were the results of sin, not God's original intention for creation, she stated. Aldredge-Clanton also made a case that patriarchy is a product of the culture and times in which the Scriptures were written and thus distorts the image of God in women. Appealing to the 1963 Baptist Faith and Message, she argued that all Scripture should be interpreted through the story and message of Jesus Christ, whose life offered many examples of his equal regard for women as witnesses (Samaritan woman), disciples (Mary of Bethany), teachers (Mary Magdalene), and ministers (Joanna and Susanna).

In her theological reflection, Aldredge-Clanton argued: "The question is not whether ordination is necessary for ministry, but whether ordination is used to exclude women from certain ministry and leadership roles in the church." The logic and tradition for Baptists is to ordain for ministry. To deny women's ordination is to deny women opportunity and to deny "the call of God" and "gifts of the Spirit." Additionally, Aldredge-Clanton said, to deny women's ordination is "to limit the priesthood of all believers" and to fail "to take a prophetic stand on the equality of men and women."[31]

Both partisan and academic analyses cast schism in the SBC as a "battle for the Bible."[32] In that framework clergywomen symbolically represent two sides of the debate. However, even if clergywomen remained only cultural symbols (clearly not the case), the arguments by Patterson and Aldredge-Clanton still show how more is at stake than some "truth" of the Bible. Clergywomen were and continue to be cultural symbols of the split in the SBC. Because they are complex symbols, they carry with their presence the real relationships, actions, thoughts, beliefs, and history of Baptists. Anna resisted becoming a symbol of schism to her family. She hid her ordained status when leading workshops for Southern Baptists. In the hospital where she works, she still brings people up short when they encounter her. But this is only the starting point for understanding the work and meaning of her ministry and its embodiment of schism. Anna is also a subjective actor and interpreter of the Southern Baptist story.

To be a woman and a Baptist and to name aloud one's call to ministry during the 1970s, 1980s, and 1990s was to step into controversy. The cultural context was inescapable, but decisions for how to act remained, at least in part, in the hands of clergywomen like Anna. As they pursued their callings, clergywomen changed their situations in small relational ways, and at the same time changes underway in the convention and ethos of Baptist life reshaped their relationships. Early on in my research for this book, the Baptist controversy appeared to be an important background for understanding clergywomen's lives and work. With sustained analysis, however, the schism emerged as more than just background. The schism also animated the very stories women lived in various ways through those decades. Yet to the clergywomen, the relationship between the growing schism and their personal lives and ministries was not immediately evident. Some women, like Anna, began their journey to pastoral calling with almost no knowledge of the growing controversy.[33]

Anna didn't set out to become an agent of change in or for Baptist life. No one told her growing up "You can't do this" with regard to ministry. Nor did anyone tell her explicitly "You can do this." Only after accepting a call to ministry and arriving at seminary did Anna "begin to realize that there was a problem . . . a huge divide." She also admits that she "really didn't care" about the Baptist fight but felt convicted "just to do ministry." "I'll do the best I can," she told herself. "There [will be] someplace I can minister."[34]

Anna's pre-entrance interview for seminary, the lack of understanding or acceptance from the "seminary wives" in her neighborhood, and the job interview in which she felt "mocked and degraded" represent moments of relational engagement that drew her into the schism and made it personal. No matter her efforts in seminary to "get her stuff and get out of there," she could not avoid the "shooting," the assumptions about her theology, or the divide. Anna could not escape the implicit understandings of power and gender, being disregarded by one interviewer and disrespected by another. Anna's stories from her seminary experience reflect the context and feeling of the school more than her classroom learning.[35] Her relational exchanges with seminary wives, administrators, and job interviewers held the formative power in her memory.

In each interview and from the seminary neighbors, Anna experienced explicit "failures of recognition." If "assertion" and "recognition" are two tensions of human relationships, then at their best they are resolved in a paradox of shared mutuality. Mature relational exchanges allow individuals to assert themselves and to find recognition from the other. Recognition is an experience of the other such that feelings, thoughts, desires, and experiences are seen and acknowledged rather than denied, repudiated, disavowed, or destroyed. When two people offer each other mutual recognition, they find and create a relational space between themselves that is irreducible to either person.[36]

Anna's stories recount a number of moments of "assertion without recognition." When assertion of one's desire for love or work goes without recognition, the balance between subjective selves falls out of balance and mutuality disappears. Anna expresses her desire to be a person working in ministry. She prepares by going to seminary, and at many steps along the way she meets not merely with a failure of recognition but also with a negation. She grew up hearing neither messages of recognition ("You can do this") nor negation ("You can't do this"), leaving an ambivalent gap of silence.[37] Anna found recognition from a mentoring pastor while working in her first youth ministry job, yet overall, the loud absence of recognition of her call was more often the response to her desire to do ministry. The job interviewer's statement—"God can't use you"—was an outright rejection or disavowal. In that exchange there is a microcosm of the relational dynamics at work in the experience of many Baptist clergywomen. Whether these were his actual words or her remembrance of them, the message stands clear in Anna's mind: *You are not recognizable as someone capable, competent, or appropriate for ministry. You have a basic defect as a minister: you are a woman.*

When she left the interview, Anna might have kept walking, until she walked away from Baptists altogether.[38] However, she chose to remain and continue to assert her desire for work and calling for ministry. Like hundreds of Baptist clergywomen, she chose to act with agency and to be the author of her own desire by pursuing her education and searching for a place to "just do ministry." Clearly, the widening Baptist schism functioned as more than just background noise for women like Anna. She needed to defend herself against it, even duck under the crossfire, yet she chose to stay with both her calling and her denominational home.

During the twentieth century, biological determinism largely shaped psychological understandings of the differences between men and women. In the popular view, male sexuality and anatomy were normative and female sexuality was derived from a wish to be male (penis envy) and eventually replaced by a desire for a baby.[39] At midcentury, ideas emerged about pure "male" and "female" elements in every human personality. In this perspective, males gravitated toward doing (active and impulsive in their relations) and females gravitated toward being (passivity and sameness in their relations).[40] This dualistic thinking produces and reproduces modern notions of difference and complementarity between males and females. Stages of human development assigned "female" and "male" aspects to growing personalities: "a passive female stage" came first and a "more mature" male stage followed.[41]

Reading Anna's story through this popularized understanding of gender leads to an interpretation of her situation as one of suffering from envy of male family members and colleagues. It views her troubles as rooted in efforts to be active rather than passive. Trying to reach mature autonomy, that is, personal agency and integrity of the embodied self, which are associated with "maleness," made Anna's task impossible. This viewpoint does move the perennial problem of domination (and subordination) one step beyond "nature" or "biological determinism" and rests it in the tangled web of human relationships.[42] However, the relational dilemma remains situated within a conflict between men. The power struggles between fathers and sons demonstrate the "Oedipal conflict," and women's subordination remains an assumption.[43] This widespread twentieth-century view leaves females sidelined while the males battle to win them or other desired objects. Anna and other Baptist clergywomen, however, did not sit passively or quietly on the sidelines, nor accept passively the role of "football" tossed about between battling fathers and sons. Instead, they took their places of leadership as players at midfield.

With persistence, Anna found service in ministry, ordination, and endorsement. At each step her (sometimes unwitting) push against tacit gender inequities, rooted in Baptist belief and practice, brought change to communities of Baptist youth and adults and families. By acting as a desiring subject, a player on the field, and not merely an object to be desired or football to be tossed about, Anna participated in the unfolding dynamics of the schism. The simple fact of her existence and persistence challenged the status quo of inequality, but the reactions of others remained mixed.

The path to ordination illustrates another significant way that Anna's relationships with her family and faith community embody the schism. Despite continuous ministry in several churches following seminary, twelve years passed between announcing her call and receiving ordination. Although Anna "hated conflict" and hoped to avoid it, she says she felt God "putting on her heart" a desire to be ordained. During the long season of waiting, Anna preached at Grove Baptist Church, where she received affirmation and one man said it's a "shame they will never ordain you." The story highlights Anna's simultaneous desire for recognition through ordination and resistance to asserting her desire directly. The resistance takes both an inner and outer form. In her reluctance to create conflict, there is an internal resistance to assert desire or act to bring about change. Anna compensates for the lack of recognition by others outside herself and the lack of recognition of desire within herself by embracing "God's call and ordination" as her best—and at the time *only*—external source of recognition for her work.

Anna's relationships with her family and congregations embody the pull in two directions experienced by the SBC itself. In one direction, she gradually changed her situation and relationships, moving along a path toward ordination, which recognized her full humanity, work as a desiring subject, and leadership as a minister. In the other direction, forces of subordination and domination, residing implicitly in the thinking and social structures of her Baptist world, worked at holding Anna in place. Those forces were reproduced and reinforced by many social arrangements, popular psychological ideas about gender, and biblicist arguments, which collectively cast Anna in the object position.

Gradually the pull toward ordination won over Anna's reluctance to engage in conflict and change. Upon receiving a request from Calvary Baptist Church, where Anna served, Grove ordained her. No universal process exists for Baptist ordination, but for men the process typically follows an identifiable pattern. Some ministers are first licensed so they can begin preaching and practicing ministry. Later, upon completion of seminary or some trial period of ministry, and usually with an outward call to a place of service, a minister will be ordained and blessed for ministry by a local congregation. That process often includes (1) convening a council or presbytery, including ministers from neighboring churches or the local Baptist association; (2) examining the candidate for authenticity of call and doctrinal soundness; (3) taking a vote in the council and/or the local church; and (4) holding a ceremony (often on the same day as the examination) to bless the candidate and lay on hands. For women the process has tended to follow the same sequence, but it often takes years longer or fails to reach ordination.[44] Anna's ordination followed this pattern. When the time arrived, she contacted girls and young women, interns and youth group members from the past, inviting them to her ordination service. The denomination did not recognize her, but Anna extended the possibilities for mutual recognition to young women in many churches, magnifying her own sense of a "confirmation" and hope for doing ministry.

Anna embodied the story of schism relationally as her life and work unfolded. Together she, along with her family, friends, supporters, and *detractors,* embodied the very struggles going on across the fracturing Baptist landscape. She felt reluctant to become an agent of change, but eventually she became one of hundreds of women who in their living and working contributed to the shift in Baptist culture that shaped the schism itself. Clergywomen were not only cultural symbols but also subjects or agents who played a role in the polarization and opening up of schism. Personal relationships with family, church members, male ministers, and Sunday school teachers gave shape to Anna's call. In turn, she created changes relationally and socially in the congregations where she served. Anna and other clergywomen lived out their desires for work in ministry despite the resistance and lack of recognition or mutuality they found in their relationships, challenging the status quo for women. In situations where Baptists denied them full expression or recognition of their desire, they sometimes muted it or dislocated it onto God. Clergywomen embodied the power of relational change, and they participated in reproducing the status quo of popular psychology, biblicist arguments, and common social arrangements between genders. In other words, they changed and were changed by personal relationships, living communities, and institutions of Baptist life.

The controversy of being a Baptist clergywoman does not end at seminary graduation, upon finding congregational or relational support, or even with ordination and endorsement. The dilemma of struggling between domination and submission runs deeper still. Anna's story shows how her internal dilemmas embody the same psychological dynamics that are part of her relational world and the cultural world of Southern Baptists. Her story holds clues to the experience of living within the "servanthood dilemma," offering a glimpse into how she internalized and reproduced tensions from her relationships and from the social world of Baptists.[45]

(Sub)ordination

When Anna took the path of hospital chaplaincy she found herself bumping into yet another conundrum, saying: "it's saddened me that now I had to turn—not that CBF is bad at all—but that I can't ask for the denomination that raised me and told me 'Wherever He Leads I'll Go' is a great hymn—except if you're a woman. And now they won't endorse me." Although in Baptist life ordination comes from a local congregation, endorsement comes from denominational bodies, and it is required for most hospital and military chaplains. In 2002 the SBC's North American Mission Board stopped, after approximately three decades, the practice of endorsing women for the role of chaplain. The decision came as a direct response to changes in the 2000 Baptist Faith and Message, including the statement that the role of pastor is limited to men.[46]

Many clues about Anna's internal world are in this brief bit of narrative. Her self-assertion of desire (*wanting endorsement*) and lack of recognition (*now they won't endorse me*) are both present, just as in earlier moments along her path into ministry. Also notable are her grief (*it's saddened me*) and her way of coping (*the turn to CBF*). Some feelings of defensiveness are also present (*not that CBF is bad at all* and *except if you're a woman*).[47] Possibly the most striking feature is the voice she gives to the gendered character of the bonds of love, tying Anna to her mother denomination (*the denomination that raised me*).[48] These bonds formed and held Anna in a relationship characterized by domination and subordination, even as she separated herself from that relationship.[49]

The popular twentieth-century view that women are universally, naturally, and indisputably passive and envious of male success splits autonomy and desire by gender. The genesis of the asymmetrical split, during Anna's lifetime, granted mothers power over their children but refused them full agency in their own lives. In an effort to escape the powerful and sometimes intrusive influence of mothers, daughters turned to their fathers for identification.[50] Western society ubiquitously reinforces patterns of domination and subordination. The persistent pairing of active, autonomous, mature males and passive, dependent, objectified females shows up in heterosexual marriages—based on complimentarity. Women are responsible for home and child-rearing, while men are (defacto) left with public leadership. The cycle of reproducing the split continues as inequality keeps infecting each next generation.[51] However, these widespread views misconceive the humanity and desires of women (and men). They also hide other dynamics at work in most situations. In Anna's story it is not female envy of men alone but a total relationship with parental figures that is important for understanding how she internalized the split between autonomy and desire.[52]

Anna does not disclose a great deal about her relationships with her adoptive mother and father. She describes her mother as a good teacher and "pretty influential" but as not having much political leverage in the church where Anna grew up. And Anna rarely mentions her adoptive father. However, she describes numerous male pastors to whom she turned for advice, support, ordination, and employment in her early years of ministry. These autonomous father figures were the gatekeepers in Baptist life, and a number of them supported, mentored, and "discipled" Anna. Yet most of her descriptions of relationships with men, excepting her husband and one pastoral care colleague, do not sound like relationships between equals. Anna often sought advice and submitted herself unquestioningly to male authority when it came to work. Internal psychological dynamics surely shaped those relationships, mostly beyond conscious awareness, keeping the social status quo in place and reproducing subordination and domination internally and relationally for women like Anna who pushed the relational role boundaries.

Institutions also function as parental figures in Anna's story. She related to her "mother denomination" as one with power but no agency.[53] The SBC holds no official ecclesiastical power, yet it is perceived and experienced by members and outside observers as having enormous cultural and political power. Many Baptists reference the Baptist milieu in a maternal way.[54] It is possible to see in Anna's story how CBF functions as symbolic of powerful fathers who lost in the denominational schism and exercised autonomy by departing. Anna thus turned away from her passive SBC mother to her active CBF father, the one willing to recognize her gifts for ministry. Yet she lacked a more authentic bond of love with CBF and longed for maintaining the bond of love with her SBC mother. However, another analysis is also compelling. Rather than CBF standing in the position of the father, Anna's language suggests that she turned not just to CBF but to a particular version of Christ (master, lord, and king) when she could not find satisfaction with her mother denomination. "God the father" stands just behind the language of the hymn she recalls.

On the surface Anna is saying that the hymn "Wherever He Leads I'll Go" is great. It captures a shorthand reference to her own sense of calling and following Christ and becoming a minister. Christ has led her to a vocation of ministry that is great, unless "you are a woman," she says, because the SBC does not recognize you and your calling. However, the hymn itself is filled by images and relational dynamics signaling why this might not be a great hymn "if you're a woman."

Wherever He Leads I'll Go

"Take up thy cross and follow Me," I heard my Master say;
"I gave My life to ransom thee, Surrender your all today."

Refrain:
Wherever He leads I'll go, Wherever He leads I'll go,
I'll follow my Christ who loves me so, Wherever He leads I'll go.

He drew me closer to His side, I sought His will to know,
And in that will I now abide, Wherever He leads I'll go.

(Sub)ordination

> It may be through the shadows dim, Or o'er the stormy sea,
> I take my cross and follow Him, Wherever He leadeth me.
>
> My heart, my life, my all I bring To Christ who loves me so;
> he is my Master, Lord, and King, Wherever He leads I'll go.⁵⁵

Thousands of Southern Baptists sang this hymn, including Anna while growing up. The hymn invites singers to become completely beholden to an image of Christ as master, lover, lord, and king. The language of *surrender . . . follow . . . my heart, my life, my all I bring . . . through shadows and stormy seas . . . drawing close to His side . . . wherever He leads I'll go,* has the character of infantile dependency, erotic adult bonding, and servitude of a slave to master all rolled into one.⁵⁶ One direction a woman's desire for love or work can take is in submitting to that which she desires rather than maintaining her role as a desiring subject seeking recognition. The all-powerful presence of Christ (or God the master-lord-king) makes a container for woman's desire, a space in which she may direct desire without acting out her own agency or risking rejection. The result, however, is not a relationship of mutuality or reciprocity. Instead, the relationship reproduces the "servanthood dilemma" that Christian women routinely face.⁵⁷

The servanthood dilemma goes like this: to be a Christian and follow Christ, one must give up self and serve God by serving the other. The basis of this model is a particular interpretation of New Testament stories about Jesus. The formula asks men to give up the power and privilege of their social and familial roles for the sake of being good followers of Jesus. To be a good leader, a man must proceed as a servant. For women, the stakes of this demand are quite different. They start from a place that lacks recognition, power, or privilege with regard to gender. So to give up what they already do not own is an impossible request. Yet in Western society white women also experience (often obliviously) the powers and privileges of being in racial, cultural, and socioeconomic positions of power. Thus there is always something to consider "giving up" in order to be a better servant-follower of Jesus. For white women seeking to lead in a religious culture that values servanthood, there is a profound dilemma: give up—for the sake of one's desire to be a minister—the small amount of power one does own. As a mode of leadership, servanthood works for men (at least conceptually) because they start with something that can be heroically given up. For white Southern Baptist women this is a double bind, an impossible effort to do two oppositional things at once.⁵⁸ Although many women co-opted the servanthood rhetoric and pathway for leading, it can be psychologically daunting, even paralyzing, for those who try.

For Anna the servanthood dilemma captures the double bind of her pastoral vocation. She not only lacks recognition from her denominational "mother," the SBC who nurtured her, but also feels reluctant to turn to the "other," the CBF. At a more fundamental level she has been shaped by a sweeping religious tradition that recognizes neither Anna as a person nor her desire for the work of ministry. As a woman she is associated with "Eve's sin," and when she hears a call to ministry, biblicists see her as making a "female Mt. Everest out of an anthill."[59] The omnipotent "God the father" demands her obedience and gives her little latitude for her self-assertion other than to follow him. The only way to get love or support in this equation is through subordination.

When Anna first voiced her call, one mentoring pastor advised her to "be obedient to God's calling" and "make it public" so the congregation would give prayer and support. Anna insists she felt support from other ministers (all men), churches, and her spouse. The internal demand for obedience is supported in practice by the Christian-Baptist rhetoric of servanthood and by a multitude of practices in communities of faith such as "mentoring" and "discipleship." Yet the support offered to her insists on obedience and submission to authority rather than any sort of mutual relationship or shared recognition. Supporting women who are trying to be obedient is fairly easy work, so long as their obedience doesn't upset the status quo. So it is little surprise that just when Anna awakened to her call, she also saw for the first time how her gender was a "huge problem." Like the hymn "Wherever He Leads I'll Go" suggests, only Anna's complete servitude provided the love and recognition needed to support her desire for doing ministry. Or as she puts it, "the affirmation is limited."

Anna's bonds of love to God the father and to the SBC, her denominational mother, initially shaped her desire to do ministry. Ironically, when she asserted her desire to do ministry, it was first not recognized by the mother (denomination) and then she was advised only to be obedient to the father (God). Even as she articulated personal authorship or ownership of her desire to "just do ministry," she was handed over to the ways of obedience and servanthood. Clergywomen like Anna find themselves in a psychological and theological dilemma of stunning proportions. This situation raises questions about why Anna didn't walk away from the SBC as she did from the job interviewer and what has kept her for more than two decades pursuing the call to ministry and investing herself in the lives of Baptists. Powerful bonds of love keep Anna and countless other Baptist women in place. Despite the limited affirmation and her frustrations, Anna is ordained and endorsed, and she works with hospital staff and patients offering ministry. Yet she also participates unwittingly in keeping many of the patterns of subordination and domination in place.

Somehow Anna and hundreds of Baptist clergywomen live and work with the internal dilemmas that not only fill the space with tension and conflict but also shape it as a paradox, which appears simultaneously to disempower and empower them. They are understood by themselves and their communities to be imitators of Jesus, "embodying a principle" that gives evidence to Christians of an ultimate reality. By making this move, clergywomen co-opt the "servanthood" tradition itself and use it to reassert their desire, as Anna says, "to just do ministry." Clergywomen shift from subordination to ordained ministry, making use of a long tradition of "power through servanthood." Yet as women living in a culture in which gender is a defining feature of power, these clergywomen are also bound to operate within relationships clearly marked by domination and subordination.

Baptist clergywomen functioned as symbols of the split between biblicists and autonomists as the parties moved toward schism. For autonomists, women functioned as symbols of autonomy, embodiments of a principle, and were held high as emblems of freedom for Southern Baptists. For biblicists, clergywomen represented the failure to follow scriptural demands for "God's delegated authority." They functioned as emblems of sin, cultural acquiescence, and moral decay in family and faith. Yet clergywomen remain more than cultural symbols in the unfolding schism of the SBC, embodying the split in relational ways and by internalized modes of self-understanding. Through their embodiment of the cracking synthesis of Southern Baptists, clergywomen not only reflected change in the SBC but also contributed to the unfolding changes. By challenging the status quo through ordination and work in ministry, they—intentionally and unintentionally—changed the landscape of Baptist life over the last three decades.

Anna grew up in the silent gap between "You can't do this" and "You can do this," which created dilemmas of desire and recognition. The symbolic, relational, and internal dilemmas lived by clergywomen were not, however, merely debilitating. Clergywomen both gave shape to and were shaped by the Baptist ethos. Psychologically formed to play roles that maintain the status quo, clergywomen also co-opted the language of obedience and servanthood for reasserting their desires to work in ministry. Through their lives, clergywomen embodied a larger paradox for all Southern Baptists of living through an age of deep division and polarization—over basic questions of identity, theology and relationality. The deep divisions and contests, however, were also occasions for creativity and renewal.

Like Anna, other Baptist clergywomen reimagined and reunited the gendered character of autonomy and desire, embodying something new. In the season of schism, the denomination was coming apart and women were coming into themselves. The stories of other Baptist clergywomen, who also embody schism in similar and unique ways, open up the conflict further and raise questions about the future of complementarity and the meaning of being human and Baptist. Together the clergywomen's stories of dilemma and paradox resonate in their particularity and reinterpret the Baptist schism.

2

(Sub)mission

How Clergywomen Reimagine Baptist Identity

> This is my little contribution. This is my mission. I'm not going to Haiti and suffering and not having a bathroom and not having electricity, but I really am financially sacrificing for the sake of making the point that . . . women have a voice and women have a place in the pastorate.
>
> —Martha

Martha, forty-six, a "cradle roll Baptist," grew up as an only child of Southern Baptist parents in the Carolinas. A sense of mission, and a sense of contribution and sacrifice, led to her pastoral ministry, she says, although the road was complicated and winding. Martha spent three and a half years as a pastor in Virginia and, prior to that, sixteen years doing part- and full-time church ministry. Currently she works for a small nonprofit agency and continues to see her work as pastoral ministry. The early years of Martha's life narrate the ways family and church shaped her into a dutiful daughter and gave direction to her early sense of calling and mission. Through her young adult life, she continued searching for clarity of purpose. After several moderately successful career moves and a major accident, Martha decided to take her questions to seminary. Working as an associate pastor during seminary, Martha discovered a clear sense of pastoral vocation and calling. After ordination and a year's residency as a hospital chaplain, she became pastor of Monroe Corner Baptist Church.

Martha's narrative becomes a center point for reinterpreting the Southern Baptist schism as a gendered psychological struggle, waged in Baptist imaginations, relationships, and social structures. Martha's stories of Baptist identity mirror the dynamics of a denomination in crisis. Her struggle between "mission" and "submission" opens on to a complex anatomy of Southern Baptist complementarity, the ways it was contested and reasserted, and how it shaped numerous aspects of Baptist life during the years of schism. Complementarity assumes supposed universal, biological, and biblical differences between males and females that "complement" (or complete) each other. Martha's stories about her parents' relationship show how a complementarity culture presents both an ideal and a dilemma. It is too complex to be mapped simplistically onto female submission and male domination. The deeper problem and contest for Baptists was over the future of complementarity itself.

Martha's story presents the splits and fissures, visibly reflecting her internal and relational life, not as mere deficits but as openings for reimagining Baptist identity and community as spaces of mutuality and creativity. The analysis juxtaposes Martha's narrative of identity crisis and reimagination with other primary textual sources from the years of schism that also manifest the wider Baptist crisis. Each primary source connects to Southern Baptist organizations and programs delivered weekly in SBC churches. Programs such as Sunday school, missions education, and deacon and pastoral ministries shaped Martha's self-understanding as well as the wider Baptist identity and culture. The analysis of Martha's story shows how Baptist piety, the woman's movement, and pastoral relationships motivated both resistance and reproduction of the Baptist culture of complementarity, reinterpreting Southern Baptist schism as gendered identity crisis.

Martha's Story

Martha's parents built their marriage on traditional gender roles.[1] They divided the labors of marriage and family life and kept up the status quo for Baptists in the South.[2] Martha's dad, Percy, a World War II veteran, earned the family's income, and her mom, Kathleen, stayed home to care for the family. Percy and Kathleen were married for nearly twenty years before Martha was born. After college Percy set his hopes on becoming a lawyer, but that never came to fruition. He became a salesman when Kathleen wanted to "settle down and buy a home" rather than wait on Percy to complete law school. Kathleen also insisted that Percy not work on a straight commission basis because she preferred the security of his dependable salary. Martha believes Percy wanted greater adventure and risk, but she says he understood her mother's insistence that he forgo law school. However, Percy often encouraged Martha to try careers that he longed for but never attempted. Both parents routinely displaced their needs and aspirations onto their only child.

After several moves, Percy and Kathleen settled in Asheville when Martha was in elementary school. Having grown up in rural farming and mill-town communities, Percy and Kathleen believed that good Southern Baptists should with each move immediately join the nearest neighborhood Baptist church. Thus they joined the progressive, urban University Baptist Church (UBC) a few blocks from home. This allowed Martha to attend weekday activities at the church. Kathleen was a "stay-at-home mom," neither working nor driving due to "her health and her generation." Martha says she experienced the best of two worlds: "the typical, rural Southern piety ... an all-seeing Eye watching everything you do" and a progressive church community that opened up different possibilities for imagining herself and her vocation.[3] Joining the progressive UBC was new for her parents, yet they felt "perfectly comfortable," which taught Martha "that church is about relationships" more than theology. However, recalls Martha, "their theology gradually became more open and more socially aware," as did her own.

As a child in the 1960s and teen in the early 1970s, Martha witnessed church votes at UBC to accept Christians baptized in non-Baptist churches for membership and ordain women as deacons. When Martha reflects on these pivotal church moments, framing her parents' reactions and responses, she opens a window into her relationship with each parent. She says her mother and father agreed with the progressive church votes but arrived at their decisions by different means. Her father, she notes, was "an intellectual ... extremely well read ... very bright, interesting, and open," adopting the changes at UBC almost immediately, despite his upbringing as a "farm boy from North Carolina." Martha clearly idealizes her father, admires his character, and wishes to emulate it. The father-daughter bond shaped her desire for autonomy and independence. Yet this desire turned out to be a complicated ideal and goal for Martha.

Kathleen, who died before Martha went to seminary, was by Martha's account quite different from her father: "traditional" but not "close minded," preferring "decency and order" and seeing the "right way and wrong way" to do things. This made Kathleen a "harder sell" on the church decisions over baptism and women deacons. But, says Martha, her mom "wasn't unreasonable and she wasn't rigid, and she wasn't petty and difficult." Kathleen's mind changed because "people she genuinely appreciated and respected ... convinced her." Martha also recalls her mother was changed by the "climate" of the congregation. She perceives her mother with greater ambivalence than she does her father. She says Kathleen was *not* defensive, rigid, close-minded, petty, or difficult, yet the litany sounds like she is defending her mother against some of these less-than-charitable descriptions.[4] Martha's loyalty and first bond of love with her mother detour her from more direct criticism. Martha also sees her mother as more relationally connected and influenced by others than her father.[5] The "climate" Martha mentions includes more than congregational influences on her mother's opinions. The sense of climate also acknowledges larger reinforcing social formations that shaped marriage, work, and parenting practices, which were operational in Martha's family.[6]

As Martha grew older, Kathleen offered outspoken opinions about how her daughter ought to live her life. Although Martha recalls her mom as "delightful, sweet and special," she also remembers Kathleen as "uptight, play by the rules, and totally practical." Martha says her mother focused on being a "homemaker" and her goal was "to take care of us and keep everything together" so Percy could work and Martha could attend school, do her chores, and practice music. Her mother created "space to grow and learn," yet she was also "pretty exacting," placing many "high expectations" on her. Although she respected her daughter's "desire for autonomy," Kathleen had little autonomy of her own, never working outside the home. Martha thought her mother lived with an "inferiority complex." Kathleen wouldn't take any leadership roles or even join the church choir. "She lived out her life vicariously through enabling my father and me, and she didn't really like it," Martha says. "She chose it and she thought it was a good thing to do, but she resented it at the same time." Therein lies the heart of the dilemma in which Martha's mother lived and which Martha could not entirely escape.

Kathleen urged Martha to become a church organist in a "really large and impressive and important church." A church organist could avoid downtown traffic, park conveniently, and be present for worship and church meetings. As church organist, Martha could interact with the "leaders of the community."[7] Martha's mother wished for her daughter a kind of work that is fulfilling but not too costly in time or energy. She wanted her daughter to have public influence, something she did not have. Martha defends her mother's World War II mindset, saying Kathleen believed "important leaders . . . are going to look up to you because you're going to be on staff, and you're going to be skilled. And you're going to be front and center every Sunday doing the music. Because you know: there is no church without music." Kathleen's logic concluded that Martha could "hobnob and be important in the life of these people without having to make all the sacrifices" that Percy made.

In discerning a career path, Martha rejected her mother's ideals and advice because Kathleen was "so critical." She turned instead to her father: "I always thought my dad had it right and my mother had it wrong." Martha's dad held more ambitious—if slightly less fitting—vocational expectations for her. Based on her verbal skills and a similar temperament and social outlook, Percy thought Martha should be a lawyer, mirroring his own youthful dream. Following high school and college, Martha tried law school, but she found it to be "too adversarial." After two years of struggling through the course work, Martha went to the dean of the law school, also a powerful father figure. He named others who were "burned out" and "miserable," and he advised her "to get out now." She withdrew from the program, taking several part-time jobs, including fundraiser for the American Cancer Society and director of a church choir.

In retirement, with time to worry about his daughter, her part-time jobs, and lack of insurance and benefits, Percy advised Martha to use her fundraising skills for sales, real estate, insurance, or stocks. He urged her, "You're not married . . . you don't have any obligations, go for a commission sales [job]. You've got the personality to do it." For a second time, she followed his advice in a direction shaped again by his longing for fulfillment. Martha admits maybe Percy was not always "the wise person that I gave him credit for being." She went to work for a stockbroker with a "really sweet deal." He played golf with clients while she managed the portfolio: she did all the work and earned 25 percent of the profits.[8] When the stock market took a dive in 1989, Martha felt disillusioned, realizing the business "was all built on fear and greed." She wanted out.

Martha identified three early sources for her sense of calling and mission in life. In the beginning, her early formation at UBC gave her a general sense of vocation. She recalls that as a young person she thought, "I want my life to count. I want to serve and honor God." She did not consider herself "special or unique" but says her career and personal choices grew out of a desire to "matter" and not "waste or squander my gifts and my life." Martha said another important source of purpose was the women's liberation movement of the 1970s.

A third source for imagining her mission and calling came from Martha's significant relationships with ministers at the large multistaffed UBC. Singing in the youth choir, leading worship each week, and touring in the summer allowed her to connect with the minister of music, who impressed her and took her "under his wing." She did not, however, connect with the ministers to children or youth. "The children's minister was a woman," Martha recalls, "but all the rest of them were men.... So I subliminally knew there were women who go into ministry, but I'd never seen one. I never attended a church where a woman was on staff." The irony in these comments is telling. She describes a woman whom she calls a "minister" yet she didn't "count" in Martha's mind as a real minister or pastor.[9]

The associate pastor, Gerald Smalley, was "very critically significant" to Martha's parents. Gerald and his wife, June, also called forth a sense of mission in Martha. June "picked children up from school . . . and took them to GA [Girls' Auxiliary]."[10] She made a lasting impression on Martha, bestowing on her a feeling that she was "Mrs. Smalley's favorite." Martha says she felt the minister's wife "depending on me to be there . . . to excel . . . to take everything from this experience." Martha's idealization of Gerald and sense of obligation she derived from June repeats her pattern of relating to her parents and hints at how these dynamics resonate across clusters of relationships, drawing from and contributing to a culture of complementarity.

Interestingly, neither the admiration of her music minister nor Martha's skills or love of music led to a desire for a career in music ministry. Martha fulfilled her "true amateur" love for music by spending many years as a part-time church musician. However, it was also "the women's liberation movement" that inspired Martha's career choices. She recalls thinking,

> The world does not need somebody with a more perfect piano technique. . . . These are important times. There's a war going on. We're all falling apart. The world is terrible. And women really need to step up. And if you're smart and if you're talented as a woman, you need to step up

because you can. Our mothers and our grandmothers and our aunts couldn't, but we can. And if we don't, then shame on us. So I'm not going to major in voice. I am going to major in business.... I need to get myself into a predominately male profession. I need to go for it. And if I don't, I'm letting down my mother and Mrs. Smalley and all ... these formative, important women. I don't know that they were, but I thought they were expecting me to live up.

University Baptist also influenced Martha's thinking about calling and mission: "They definitely instilled the desire in me to be everything." She translated this desire to mean that anything leading to "wealth and prestige" would allow her to "fully support kingdom causes." Her ambitions were tempered by sense of obligation in which she imagined using her "power and prestige and autonomy" to influence public policy and allow her to "give back" to the church and other causes.

Just when Martha decided to leave the stocks and securities business and consider other career paths, she was in a serious car accident. After the accident and a long recovery, Martha says she found herself "grateful to God" as well as bargaining with God. It was not exactly "a real call experience," says Martha, but it was an experience of gratitude and learning." Long-term her body recovered, and after several years and several other administrative jobs, Martha decided to study theology, "not out of a real sense of call but out of a real interest in 'What is God about?' and 'Why is the church so lame?' and 'Why do bad things happen to good people?' And ... 'Why are we so consumed with ... not drinking and not having sex before you get married and we're not concerned about the poor and we're not concerned about ... the really immoral issues?' Is God really that punitive?" Martha's growing up "with a conservative, traditional Southern piety" also raised other questions: "Is God really looking at every thought I think? Or is there something broader?" She wanted to clarify some things: "There were a lot of things I didn't like about God and my faith." Thus Martha felt motivated as a "seeker" to attend seminary.

Martha considered her options and decided on Candler School of Theology at Emory University in Atlanta, Georgia. She chose it for its Baptist House of Study program and because it put her closer to her father, who was living in a nearby Alzheimer's unit. She was also attracted to the university setting of the school. A small inheritance from distant relatives didn't quite pay a year's tuition, but it nudged her to begin her studies.

To support herself through seminary and meet the school's requirements for field education, Martha decided to look for a part-time church job. She sought release from the field education requirement, arguing that her years of part-time music ministry meant she knew "church from the inside out." She also argued that she was going to seminary for her "own fulfillment." Seminary administrators insisted that field education and church ministry, while studying theology, history, and Scripture, would be "very good for the church" as well as for Martha. The field education supervisor said it would be a "disservice" to her and the church to skip field education. Consequently, Martha worked as minister for outreach and children at First Baptist Church (FBC) in Benson throughout seminary, and the church became a place for deepening and clarifying Martha's call.

What began as a way to earn income and fulfill a seminary requirement soon became a pivotal experience in Martha's self-understanding and identity as a pastor. Martha was happy and enjoyed her work at FBC. She says they "called out the best" in her, and over time they came to see her as their minister. She took on some of the associate pastor's work when he resigned. Her ministry with children was very visible and free of controversy. She quickly became "a fixture" in the congregation and "picked up some credibility." Although the church ordained women as deacons and ministers already, electing Linda, who grew up at FBC Benson, as deacon chair was a first. This surprised Martha, who thought of the church as "way beyond women deacons."[11]

One evening Linda invited Martha to dinner to discuss changing the structure of the church's deacon ministry. Martha explained that the pastor was introverted, relatively new, and not a "warm, fuzzy kind of person." Linda recruited Martha's help "because you're a woman and you're . . . sweet and bubbly. They're used to seeing you with the children." Linda thought Martha could help create "stability and warmth in the congregation." As the evening continued, however, the conversation with Linda shifted, and she began sharing about growing up at FBC, teenage rebellion, and her eventual marriage and divorce. Linda began "pouring out this beautiful story of . . . how God has worked in her life." Martha felt "equipped" to hear the story, yet inside she was saying, "This is a moment that cries out for benediction!" As the conversation continued, Martha realized that "Linda was identifying with me as a woman in ministry. And in her ministry as the chair of deacons, she wanted to share that with me. That's the whole purpose of calling the meeting. I thought it was to lead off at the deacon's forum and set the tone. But really what she wanted to do was receive my blessing." Martha recalls thinking, "You need to talk to your minister about this because this is that kind of moment." Then it hit her, "Oh man, she thinks I'm a minister!'" Martha says that evening was her "moment of call."[12]

When she began seminary, Martha considered being a university chaplain but never a pastor. Four years at First Baptist gave Martha "opportunities to preach" and the experience of being "treated as a minister." She became "an important person in the life of that congregation" and "a person in their heart and in their history." The evening of conversation with Linda clarified Martha's sense of call and caused her to think that "maybe the local church is the heart of it, or the source." The time at FBC felt like a "miracle" for the way everything came together to prepare Martha for full-time pastoring. The experience was so "tremendously positive" that she believed the congregation "genuinely thought that I couldn't do anything wrong." She offers this reflection: "It's me, but it's not me. It's that little alchemy that happens. It's like a relationship . . . you either click and you want to marry each other . . . become best friends . . . complete each other. Or it's an okay match but . . . more like acquaintances or . . . short-term collaboration. It's really difficult to predict that. But those really mystical moments do occur, and they don't occur all the time. I guess that's what makes them so special."

In the early 1990s, while working at Francis Marion College, Martha joined the First Baptist Church in Florence (FBC Florence). When she decided to go to seminary, the congregation supported her with a scholarship and Sunday school classes pooled money to send her a check each month. The church said to her, "We want to ordain you when the time comes." Once she was in seminary, Martha said to them, "Let's start working on that." At the same time she asked herself, "Do I really want to be ordained?" and "Why should I be ordained?" She considered various aspects of the Baptist belief and practice: "Ordination is the sense of God working through us. . . . Everybody ought to get the chance to go through a ceremony where we all encourage one another. And it shouldn't be just ordained to 'the ministry,' you should be ordained to teach or whatever it is you do." However, says Martha, "in the real world . . . we don't get to live out our ideals all the time." She also thought about the role of the state with regard to officiating at weddings, worrying about what she considered the "moral ground" of letting "the state dictate—because I'm a minister—what I can do." Martha was naming the tension in the "priesthood of all believers" entailing her hope of blessing everyone's ministry on one hand and the significance of being ordained as a woman, which she considered "an important step," on the other hand. In the end, a request by friends to officiate their wedding opened the door for ordination by FBC Florence. She recalls, "It was definitely important and a wonderful moment." Members of the First Baptist Church in Benson also participated in the service.

Martha graduated from seminary in 2000 and completed a one-year residency program in clinical pastoral education at Barrington Hospital in Benson, Georgia. She says her experience at the small hospital was positive. Friends encouraged Martha to look for a call as an associate pastor. Surprisingly, Martha was called as pastor of Monroe Corner Baptist Church in Virginia in 2001. When the search committee first phoned, Martha said to herself, "This is never going to happen. They are not going to call a woman, but it will be a great experience to go through the process of talking with them." With little hope for a positive outcome, she entered the conversation and felt surprised by the "wonderful experience with the search committee." They "clicked," she recalls.

The search process with Monroe Corner filled Martha with a mix of expectations. In the background she could hear stories from her United Methodist seminary classmates about women getting "the less attractive appointments." No church was pleading for a woman pastor. More often they accepted a female pastor to avoid an alternative, like merging congregations or cutting back to a part-time pastor. Martha worried that any church willing to call a woman was likely a dying, conflicted, or manipulative church. These worries prompted Martha to ask herself, "What is this saying, that I believe there's something wrong with any church that would call me?" On the other hand she wondered about the luck she was having and asked herself, "Why me? There are so many better preachers, better-qualified people. But I was in the right place and time."

Martha's skepticism did not immediately turn up any concerns with the pastoral search committee. She describes her time with them as "warm" and "comfortable." However, when they asked her what questions she had for them, Martha said, "Tell me what you are really excited about at your church. What makes you so proud to be a part of Monroe Corner?" She says they started positively but quickly said, "You know we're declining. We're losing members. We used to be . . ." Martha sensed that they felt like the decline was their "fault" or as if "something was wrong with them as a church." She wondered to herself, "Who am I to say it is or it isn't?" But the bigger issue she suspected was the declining community: "A huge manufacturing plant closed six months earlier, which took people and jobs and money out of the county. They are in a stagnant area, so hence they are a stagnant church. And they used to be the cool church . . . the up-and-coming church."

Martha perceived that Monroe Corner was having an identity crisis. The core of the congregation consisted of "charter members" in their sixties, who began Monroe Corner four decades earlier as young, white married couples raising children. When manufacturing moved out of the area, they faced a community in decline and feared for the survival of their church. With self-blame and doubt, the congregation internalized the situation around them, a striking parallel to Martha's ambivalence and doubt, which undercut her belief in herself as a serious pastoral candidate. She internalized beliefs about female inferiority and lack of authority as well as her classmate's ideas that only sick or dying churches call women.

Martha recalls a nagging worry that Monroe Corner might hire her because they could "afford" her. "They know I will come to be their pastor for what they'll pay me, and a man wouldn't because he wouldn't have to." Martha says she received "a higher offer to be an associate pastor" at another church. In light of the financial considerations, she struggled with a number of questions: "Is it so important for me to be a pastor? What's my motivation here? Is it my ego?" Then she concluded, "This is my little contribution. This is my mission. I'm not going to Haiti and suffering and not having a bathroom and not having electricity, but I really am financially sacrificing for the sake of making the point that . . . women have a voice and women have a place in the pastorate."

Martha's CPE supervisor advised her to determine the percentage of the church vote she could live with and still be effective as the pastor. She decided on 85 percent, and the search committee reached the same conclusion. All was agreed, and in the end 85 percent of the church members voted for her. She recalls that the size and location of the church gave her some hope. Other women pastors in Virginia were mostly in small churches or church starts, and a few were co-pastors. Monroe Corner benefited from proximity to one of the new moderate Baptist seminaries and several members who were on boards of Baptist agencies. The average attendance was between ninety and one hundred. Part-time staff included a secretary, a youth minister, and a music minister. Martha sums up her assignment this way: "I knew that was—for women in ministry for 2001—it was great. I mean, this is as good as it's going to get."

Reimagining Baptist Identity in the Season of Schism

Martha's stories of growing up in her particular family and church, coming to a sense of mission, and calling, and eventually receiving ordination and welcome as a pastor are occasions for seeing not just her life but also the larger Baptist situation in which she lived. The relational dynamics, church theology and politics, parenting practices, and cultural and religious formations in Martha's story also shaped the lives and identities of Southern Baptists.[13] Martha learned to imagine herself and the worlds in which she lived as places of both ambiguity and possibility. The Baptist world reinforced her self-conceptions as a dutiful and often submissive daughter and at the same time allowed her to envision herself as an assertive woman and Baptist pastor. This seeming dichotomy captures not an anomaly in a single woman but insight into central features of the anatomy of schism, which animated Baptist life and contributed to the splitting of the denomination.

Martha's relationship with her parents shows how her internalized sense of self was split and polarized, giving a gendered character to her identity. The same kind of gendered split was so widespread and pervasive in Baptist life as to give a gendered character to the schism itself. In the way that gender played multiple roles in Martha's identity and experience, so too did the presence and dynamics of gender play multiple roles in the schism. The split appears in everything from church staff arrangements (like the male pastors and their supportive wives at UBC) to the Sunday school and missions curriculum used in SBC churches and to the ways biblicists and autonomists responded to change and to each other.

Many relationships and cultural formations shaped Martha into a dutiful daughter. Her story renders visible the widespread and largely unnoticed ways that gender ideals in the SBC shaped thinking, roles, relationships, and practices. Although some autonomists moved toward greater equanimity for women, they were also implicated by the splits and struggles over gender. Across the Baptist landscape, Baptist girls were raised to be dutiful daughters, and when they challenged the psychological and cultural formation, gender emerged as a central point of contention in the struggle between parties in the SBC.

In childhood Martha lived in a tension between the idealized autonomy evident in her admiration of her "very bright, interesting, and open" father and her ambivalent yet dutiful obligation to and loving bond with her "delightful" yet "uptight" mother. Martha's internalized split was supported by the Baptist culture of complementarity that surrounded the family and church. Her identity internalized each of her parents' asymmetrical roles and the strategies she used to negotiate them. The widespread split of gender into complementary relationships pervaded Southern Baptist life, and exerted its force on Martha through parenting practices, family relationships, work arrangements, and religious rhetoric about male and female in the weekly teaching materials at UBC.

In 1978, the year Martha graduated from high school, Southern Baptists sponsored the Consultation on Women in Church-Related Vocations gathering nearly three hundred women and men for presentations about women's leadership and vocations in Southern Baptist life. In a report delivered at the consultation, Kay Shurden assessed images of women in Southern Baptist Sunday school curriculum and leisure magazines for preschoolers, youth, college students, and adults. She evaluated the authorship, graphic portrayals, and content of the lesson books and magazines in each age group for the period between 1973 and 1978.[14]

In 1978 women made up 40 percent of the work force, yet the primary image of women in the SBC materials for every age group was that of *homemaker*. In terms of authorship, women wrote 89 percent of the lessons for preschoolers, 47 percent of the materials for youth (ages twelve to seventeen), and only 14 percent of the lessons for college students and 18 percent of the adult Sunday school lessons. The materials portrayed women in only three church roles: teacher of small children, church secretary, and organist. All ministers were portrayed as men with one exception in 1974. One ordained female editor wrote about her frustrations over her treatment as a single person. In preschool stories boys played with other boys, took trips with dad, and imagined growing up to be truck drivers, pilots, and auto mechanics. The girls helped their mothers with meals and household chores and imagined growing up to do more housework and share coffee with friends. In the youth materials marriage was a regular topic, and the magazines consistently portrayed women with subordinate roles and status.

Women only appeared as characters in the stories 36 percent of the time. Those pursuing ministry were consistently referred to as "man" and "he." In the collegiate publications, women only appeared alone or with other women 16 percent of the time, and they were illustrations or characters in the stories 29 percent of the time. Collegiate materials offered a few limited examples of the changing roles for women's work. Men were encouraged to take up more household and parenting responsibilities occasionally in the adult magazine *Home Life,* the most widely read periodical in Southern Baptist circles. Women were overwhelmingly portrayed as homemakers, working mothers (usually part time), and subordinates in marriage. The words and images packaged and sold to Southern Baptists in the weekly curriculum reflected historically situated psychological formations, and they also reinforced images that supported and reproduced the culture of complementarity.[15]

Church decisions to affirm the baptisms of non-Baptists and ordain women as deacons were weigh stations on UBC's road to identifying with the autonomist party as the schism opened up in the late 1970s and early 1980s.[16] Churches gravitating to the autonomist party tended to hold more progressive views about work and family arrangements. By ordaining women as deacons they challenged the complementarity culture. Churches gathering in the biblicist party were much less open to authorizing women for official leadership roles as laity or clergy. However, when considering the cultural critique of gender as a category, neither party nor its churches were very far from traditional understandings of complementarity, seeing and describing women as secondary and derivative. The culture of complementarity shaped imaginations and acceptable expressions of gender, which polarized gender into male and female and maintained different roles for each.[17] Yet Martha's account of her parents' decision making shows greater complexity in the way she internalized their relationship. Martha's relationship of loyalty to her mother shapes her as a dutiful daughter and mutes her critical voice. Her idealization of her father shows up in her ambition for achievement and autonomy. The result is a split visible in Martha's self-description that imagines working in independent autonomy without fully relinquishing a more submissive and dutiful role in the church.[18]

When schism in the SBC began to open up, it was partly a response to decisions like UBC's and the actions of women like Martha, both of which challenged the status quo of complementarity. However, to blame these groups or individuals for the split misses the point that the SBC was already split in numerous ways, including along the lines of gender, a division that is evident in the program material. The split also cut through individual ways of thinking about identity like Martha's as well as political parties and family relationships. Gender was so pervasive as to be missed until it became explicit in analyses like Shurden's and pathways to ministry like Martha's. Thus the splits among Baptists, which were already present yet unnoticed, became more evident and more public as schism emerged, and gender increasingly became a central point of contention.

Martha's stories about her parents' work and marriage, entangled with her vocational dilemmas, highlight how choices about work can simultaneously repeat patterns of domination and submission and seek a different path of mutuality and shared recognition. In Baptist life, vocation is most often understood as a call to work, but it is also recognized in a call to family life. In everyday Baptist life of the

1970s, 1980s, and 1990s, vocation was often gendered in its split between work and love. Work was the income-earning domain of men and love was the familial domain of women. Martha's stories about her parents complexify this split and show how the problem goes deeper than male domination and female submission: domination and submission themselves are troublesome no matter who takes which role. Martha's stories reinterpret the Baptist schism as a psychological struggle over both the gendered character of vocation and the ways some Baptists both resisted and reproduced relationships of domination and submission, which constitute a complementarity culture.

Martha's admiration of Percy stood in contrast to her ambivalence toward Kathleen. Her parents' competing career expectations for their daughter created a split that defined Martha's sense of gender and vocation.[19] The character of her parents' relationship also reveals the complexity and asymmetry of complementary marriage relationships, including the dynamics of domination and subordination.[20] Percy did not achieve the desires or personal autonomy he expressed. And according to Martha, Kathleen forced a set of decisions that diverted him from law school. The complexity of Kathleen and Percy's roles show how complementarity rarely means a straightforward male dominance and female submission. Often autonomy is more highly valued for husbands yet also easily subverted by wives in subtle ways that keep up external appearances. For example, Kathleen subverted autonomy by using her familial power to get her own wishes with Percy, by imagining a future of autonomy for Martha, and all the while maintaining a posture of submission.

Complementary relationships, formalized and idealized in heterosexual marriage, consist of a "doer" and one "done-to." In Martha's family, Percy was the doer who worked, earned income, and moved freely in and out of the home.[21] Kathleen was the one done-to, supporting her husband and daughter, caring for their well-being, and asserting little in the way of work, leadership, or desire outside the family. These stereotypes are only one perspective on the relationship: Martha's parents also lived in reversed roles. Her mother was the doer, deciding where they lived, what work her husband would do, and what sort of commission he ought to earn. She "exacted" Martha's work from childhood chores and homework to adult career decisions. And Martha's dad was the one done-to when he gave up law school and settled into a second-choice career. The story clarifies how dichotomies of female submission and male domination are not the only problem. Domination and submission are complex in lived reality, and even a reversal of roles does not mitigate the problem.

In 1983 Daniel Bagby, a pastor, professor, and son of SBC missionaries, published a discipleship study guide for Baptist young adults, *Before You Marry*. In the guide, Bagby, affiliated with autonomists, described the sexual relationship in heterosexual marriage: "We are sexual creatures, male and female. Our sexuality is our identity; it is neither an act nor an 'appetite.' . . . We were formed with two basic identities. Sexual man and sexual woman are designed differently physically and functionally." He went on: "We believe that our dual sexual identity (man and woman) is designed to emphasize our need for fellowship and communion. Our dual identity is a call to mutuality and complementarity."[22]

The biblicist party promoted complementarity marriage as "God given," natural, and biblical.[23] Autonomists typically advocated marriage based on mutuality and equality. Clergywomen raised many questions regarding marriage and family, wondering if and how women could do both.[24] Bagby's emphasis on both mutuality *and* complementarity unwittingly captured a Baptist dilemma and double bind of gender in family and work.[25] He urged heterosexual marriage partners to relate to each other in mutuality, but he also urged them to relate in complementary fashion, essentializing some differences between men and women. The effect of the injunction was to create a double bind: it asked women to be mutual, equal partners but not to work outside the family; it asked men to be mutual, equal partners but not be fully engaged caregivers in the family. Bagby asked partners to approach each other in two nearly incompatible ways. His directive also captured a major tension between Baptist parties and between paradigms of marriage.

Complementarity was also upheld as the model for work and ministry: men should take the lead and women should follow and support. Bagby wrote about vocation as if work happened on a level playing field, yet in his illustrations, only male biblical characters made vocational choices. The guiding force for Christian vocation, Bagby argued, is the "God of the Bible who comes to us as Father . . . one who is *in control,* but at the same time deeply desires a loving relationship with His children."[26] And the God of Southern Baptists, a "father in control," sets relational patterns and reinforces a complementarity culture. Southern Baptist church staffs typically embodied the stereotype: men directed the music while women played the organ or piano. Men preached and taught while women supported in the church office, kitchen, or nursery. Such arrangements were ironic in a religious society where women were considered the "backbone" of the church and led nearly all things spiritual in the home or church.[27] Autonomists were more inclined to grasp the argument that women should lead because they *were already leading* spiritual matters in churches and homes. Yet they did not go many steps beyond biblicists in undoing complementarity as an organizing principle for relationships in work, home, or church. Neither party strayed far from the logic of complementarity in all relationships.[28]

Social and family practices also combine to reproduce complementarian culture and a gendered form of domination and subordination. Martha's inability to differentiate fully from her relationally powerful yet dependent mother, or to identify adequately with her financially secure yet unfulfilled father, mirrors a split that perpetuates the identifications of male dominance and female submission for a next generation. Martha's relational identifications contributed to ambivalence and tension about her vocation. For clergywomen the schism in the SBC was one more struggle to find their way, their voice, their "desire for autonomy," as Martha puts it.[29] The stakes for women like Martha looked incredibly high in the days of Baptist schism because not only were careers and personal fulfillment on the line, but the very future of the denomination also hung in the balance. Asserting a desire for work and finding appropriate recognition, with the hope of owning and authoring that desire for themselves rather than depending on a husband or father, and seeking mutual recognition and shared autonomy—these were the clergywomen's struggles.

The same struggle animated the larger unfolding Baptist schism. The autonomist and biblicist parties strained with each other publically to gain the upper hand for the direction and resources of the SBC. At the same time, they were wrestling over the meaning of vocational roles for men and women in a culture of complementarity. While biblicists argued for keeping complementarity in place, autonomists asserted a new mutuality yet demonstrated ambivalence in both their practice and rhetoric. Meanwhile, the vocations of clergywomen confronted yet also participated in reproducing relational patterns of domination and submission.

In everyday relational interactions, Martha and her parents navigated the double binds of gender. Martha's relationship with Kathleen shows how submission is extended generationally from mother to daughter. Her relationship with Percy, in its gaps and fissures, offers a space to explore how the double-binding legacies for men and women were different yet worked together to reproduce a culture of complementarity. Where women attempt to undo the double binds of gender and men seek to maintain control, Baptist schism emerges as a cultural struggle over the future of complementarity.[30]

Martha's relationship with her mother is a study in contrasts. Kathleen was a powerful and pervasive force in her daughter's life, yet Martha disregarded her as a source of genuine authority. Kathleen lacked social clout yet exerted influence over the careers of her family. Martha remembers Kathleen as inferior, lacking initiative, and "resentful of her choices," but Kathleen fostered in Martha a strong work ethic and high expectations.[31] She "made space" for Martha's growth, autonomy, and influence yet felt disappointed when Martha did not become a wife, mother, and homemaker.[32] Martha both identifies and rejects her mother's views about her life.[33] Her narrative expresses repeatedly a dilemma between a loving first bond with Kathleen and the need to assert herself and find recognition for her unique identity.[34]

Every Wednesday, when June Smalley drove Martha and her friends to GA, the girls learned both autonomous mission and dutiful submission in the curriculum of the Woman's Missionary Union. From cradle to grave, WMU shaped

Southern Baptist girls into "labourers together with God," devoted supporters of missionary causes, and servants of God and world through missions.[35] The world imagined by WMU through its programs, weekly lessons, religious rituals, and powerful stories urged girls to embrace God's mission without disrupting their place as women in southern society, evoking a missionary calling in Martha as a child. Nevertheless, WMU also promoted women's leadership, and links between WMU and feminism were not uncommon.[36]

Women's submission clashed with feminism in Martha's belief that the women's movement needed her to "step up" with her best talents and intelligence. She wanted her generation to "live up" and excel in a "predominately male profession." So Martha did what girls seeking autonomy can do: she turned to her more autonomous and powerful father for recognition, identification, support, and advice.[37] This led to another troublesome dilemma: Martha could not fulfill Percy's dreams for his sake or her own. The internal tensions plagued her sense of purpose until she was incapacitated by a car wreck and spent weeks facing her own vulnerability and physical limits. Then she began to imagine a new possible path, eventually choosing ministry.

As women entered ministry, their presence dynamically surfaced the double binds felt implicitly by men. During the 1978 Consultation on Women in Church-Related Vocations, Andrew Lester, professor of pastoral care and counseling at the Southern Baptist Theological Seminary, presented a talk titled "The Psychological Impact of Women in Ministry."[38] Focusing first on the problem of competition felt by *men,* Lester observed that in a tight hiring market, men, shaped by a "cultural myth" of male superiority, do not tolerate "losing" to an "inferior" woman. Additionally, men are reluctant to accept as peers and equals women who are stereotyped as "inferior and subordinate." Feelings of competition, anxiety, and discomfort also erupt when women appear in previously all-male (pastor) groups. Each aspect of male competition leads to alienation and further isolation for women in ministry, argued Lester.[39]

If the struggle for women is to overcome the impossibility of being both autonomous leaders and submissive supporters, the double bind for men is to stay connected to others without feeling engulfed or wishing to destroy them. For men called to ministry, their dilemma is also shaped by the mutually reinforcing influences of parenting and cultural dynamics on their internal and relational worlds. The task and goal for men both psychologically and socially is also for autonomy, yet the asymmetry of power and particular parenting arrangements produce a slightly different struggle. In the middle and late twentieth century, white, middle-class, heterosexual mothers still filled the role of primary caregiver and the first bond of love for many or most children reared in Southern Baptist life. In this setting, one early and significant developmental task for boys (and girls) is to separate from their mothers while maintaining empathy and emotional connection.[40]

When the developmental task remains incomplete, the structure of complementarity is reproduced asymmetrically for boys and girls. If children do not have the appropriate clarity and differentiation from mothers, boys can lean toward aggression in their need to separate and girls can remain overly enmeshed with mothers. The resulting tension between assertion of self and recognition of the other is split, and boys are left with the desire to destroy or at least have the complete domination over their mothers, who come to represent all "others," everyone else who is "not me."[41] Dutiful daughters and aggressive sons come to look like the norm, as if they are "naturally" that way. As the inheritors of domination, and the need for submission on the part of others around them to support and confirm their autonomy, male leaders in the SBC entered the Baptist schism as one more struggle for ascendancy, like other battles of will to power that men face on a regular basis from home to work to church.[42]

Church for Southern Baptists was one of the few places where men still held relatively unquestioned power and freedom to make decisions from the pulpit, if not from the pew. The pastorate was a rare cultural space where male identity and authority remained unquestioned, until churches began to extend the power of the pastorate to women through ordination. The dynamics of personal identity for men in the arrangements of a complementarity culture depend on gaining power, which is hinged on the submission of others. This dynamic cut across the landscape of Baptist life and struggle for both biblicists and autonomists. The entire schism in the SBC was in this regard a gendered struggle for power, a competition between male pastors and leaders fighting to become "fathers in control" in yet another realm of their lives. For clergywomen like Martha, the schism was a struggle to end the double bind, assert their Baptist identity, and "live up" to a hope that was unfulfilled for earlier generations of women. For Southern Baptists the years of schism were a contest over the future of complementarity.

Martha's dilemma between mission and submission, in her understanding of call, reveals a double-binding tension between gendered ideals of sacrifice and ambition. When Martha accepts a pastoral call, ambitious mission and sacrificial submission remain in an uneasy alliance within her expression of identity. Since their beginnings, Southern Baptists have put the missionary enterprise at the center of their cooperative work, uniting ambition and sacrifice. Supporting "missions" was major point of contention and the last stronghold of unity before the weight of controversy split the SBC.[43] Martha's ambivalence between mission and submission, and between sacrifice and ambition, mirrors the gendered fractures in the SBC's corporate identity, contributing to schism and remaining after the split.

Martha's practical piety and sense of purpose grew weekly by studying the Bible and missionaries, singing in youth choir, and leading worship, feeling the "all-seeing eye" of God on her. In every activity and relationship, Martha absorbed messages about calling, mission, ambition, sacrifice, and submission. Her narratives vacillate between a large sense of self-importance and a nagging self-doubt.[44] She believed her life should "count for something," and yet she was "not special or unique." Her parents and her church urged her to "be everything" yet offered very few models for women's vocations beyond children's minister, organist, or missionary. She idealized her father and the ministers at UBC, imagining success in a "male profession." Martha thought of herself in a future that contained both "power and prestige" and also a way to "give back." This whiplash of grandiose ambition and heroic sacrifice continued into Martha's stories from adult life, even as she struggled to hear a clarion call for herself.[45] Finally naming her pastoral call, she used missionary terms to describe it: "This is my little contribution. This is my mission. I'm not going to Haiti and suffering and not having a bathroom and not having electricity, but I really am financially sacrificing for the sake of making the point that . . . women have a voice and women have a place in the pastorate." Martha understood her call as making a sacrifice for a greater good. Mission (becoming a pastor) and submission (financial sacrifice, accepting a call from a small church) were deeply entangled in her thinking and action. She did not question her belief that sacrifice was required in order to find voice and place.[46] She holds within her calling both ambition and sacrifice, mission and submission.

Southern Baptist youth camps, revival meetings, Sunday worship services, and even the offering envelopes urged young Baptists to consider their many duties of Christian calling as a matter of weekly and daily practice.[47] The most serious were encouraged to commit to "full-time Christian service," meaning the mission field for females and missions or the pastorate for males.[48] Expectations of financial sacrifice or answering a call to missions or ministry were the norm. Women faced a serious tension between the call to mission and the duty to submission.

A large-scale example of Southern Baptist ambivalence between sacrifice and ambition appears in the 1970s Bold Mission Thrust campaign to evangelize and bring salvation to the world's population before the year 2000. The grandiose vision of converting every living person to the Baptist faith in twenty-five years is both astounding and naïve. Despite its apparent organizational impossibility, Baptists expanded financially and employed more career missionaries. The campaign highlights the scale of public ambition and vision, which permeated Baptist life and contributed to the grandiosity of battles between autonomists and biblicists in the 1980s and 1990s.[49] Southern Baptists did not reach the world with the gospel message of Jesus by the year 2000, but nevertheless, they gained widespread notoriety for being embroiled in decades of controversy.

The ambivalence between ambition and sacrifice appears in the long history of a Christian missionary enterprise that seeks to dominate others through religious and cultural conversion.[50] In the mid-nineteenth century, Southern Baptists embarked with a crusader's enthusiasm to convert and colonize non-Christian people and places. What they lacked in political cachet and influence, SBC missionaries made up for with sacrifice, tenacity, and dogged determination. Gender inequity was rarely questioned in the nineteenth century, when the SBC was born out of an argument over the rights of missionaries to own slaves.[51] In that schism they split from Northern Baptists, never to reunite again. Ambivalence about women's missionary service— epitomized by Southern Baptist "patron saints" Lottie Moon and Annie Armstrong—remained, yet it was one of a very few ways single Baptist women could fulfill a religious vocation.[52] Often female Baptist missionaries worked among indigenous women and under the "protection" and "guidance" of male missionaries. Increasingly in the twentieth century, mission boards discouraged single women from missionary appointment and normalized complementary roles, assigning married couples: men to be pastors or missionaries and women to serve in "church and home." Thus the "missionary position" of complementarity, with males in the lead or dominant roles and females in submission, endured as the model, despite some resistance. Submission and domination remained deeply embedded in the Baptist missionary imagination through the twentieth century.[53]

As schism unraveled in the SBC, the missionary enterprise held the center and became a rallying cry for unity and reconciliation between the parties. The call to missions literally invested billions of dollars in over ten thousand career missionaries and a Baptist presence in over one hundred countries globally. The shared mission was an amalgamation of Southern Baptist ambition and sacrifice, supported through financial giving to the Cooperative Program and two annual offerings named for Moon and Armstrong. Yet the missionary enterprise also took center stage in the skirmishes between the parties, with gender often playing a central role.[54]

When the Cooperative Baptist Fellowship and the Alliance of Baptists formed out of the schism, each group tried to distinguish itself by establishing new forms of mission work. The Alliance of Baptists advocates a partnership model, which joins the work of Christians already living and working in marginalized spaces, assuming change for all parties in the Baptist partnership as well as the situation itself. The Cooperative Baptist Fellowship took a middle way between traditional and partnership models, changing terminology, avoiding competition with other Christian missionaries, and serving significantly marginalized and impoverished people (the "least and last").[55] The CBF became a "safety net" for SBC missionaries forced to resign during the schism for various reasons, including support of women in ministry. Over the course of a decade, dozens of missionaries left the SBC to join forces with CBF. The Alliance and CBF embody new models of ministry and mission, yet the long history of domination and submission, ambition and sacrifice, remain entangled for each group, long after their departure from the SBC, reproducing the same tensions and fractures in the missionary enterprise.

When Martha approached her ordination and a congregational call, she raised significant questions for herself and all Baptists regarding who can be ordained and who can lead. She reached with Baptist piety and feminist sensibility for a way to extend the possibility to everyone. Her struggles highlight how the season of schism was a time of questioning leadership on a large scale. The questions were not limited to a fight between political parties but were shaped by gendered understandings of leadership, mostly implicit until the end of the twentieth century. Through the authority conferred in ordination and earned relationally through the presence and practice of ministry, Baptist clergywomen disrupted the character and identity of leadership. Female pastors effectively "undid" or undermined the prevalent understandings of male leadership, creating a crisis that helped Baptists to imagine authority in new ways. Simultaneously, women's ordinations reproduced the split between clergy and laity, showing how the schism was a struggle over the gendered tensions of leadership.

Martha's ordination for ministry bought up a number of questions about the power and meaning of religious leadership. The questions were personal and existential: "Do I really want to be ordained?" and "Why should I be ordained?" She imagined that each person called to particular work should be blessed, expressing a feminist longing for equality, mutuality, and the freedom of every person to know the power of "God working through us." In that desire Martha joined her Baptist piety, specifically her understanding of the "priesthood of all believers," with her feminist longing for equality.[56] She noted the opposition between ideals of equality and lived experience when differences of power were unavoidable.[57] Martha explicitly named the tension between authorizing the "whole priesthood of all believers" for ministry and the significance of ordaining women, recognizing her own complicated place in the tension.

Martha's questions continue to push at a perennial tension in Baptist history and polity between clergy and laity.[58] Women's ordination threatens to undo complementarity, which was built on a gendered split between clergy and laity. For over 350 years a Baptist commitment to the "priesthood of all believers" heightened roles in the church for laity, sharing power more broadly and diminishing the authority of ordained clergy. At the same time, the role of Baptist clergy remained available only to men, while women were left the role of laity with a few notable exceptions.[59] Questioning the character of ordination ushers Martha into a novel engagement with the "priesthood of all believers." By being ordained, she and other women have entrée to social and religious authority previously out of their reach. On the other hand, women's ordination continues the split between clergy and laity, which the priesthood of all believers aims to mitigate, maintaining an unequal sharing of power between pastors and congregations. The effect of women's ordination is both to undo and to reinscribe complementarity. In response, biblicists and autonomists were faced with new questions about the meaning, practice, and authority of pastoral leadership.

Baptist pastors hold tremendous cultural and identity-forming authority and personal power. Absent a formal ecclesial structure or uniform doctrinal statements, historic perennial tensions and individual pastoral leadership do normative identity-making work for Baptists.[60] During the 1978 Consultation on Women, Andrew Lester addressed the psychological impact of women entering ministry in relationship to pastoral authority. He argued that ministers should be seen by self and others as (1) "possessing and deserving authority," (2) claiming "particular experience with God," (3) owning a "special calling or purpose," (4) taking "ethical stands," (5) filling "a leadership role," (6) speaking "with certitude," and (7) having "special knowledge and training." Ministers, including women, "must be willing to both *claim* and *accept* these characteristics of authority."[61] Lester said that claiming and accepting pastoral authority by women is challenging for clergywomen *and* for parishioners for three reasons: the effects of a patriarchal culture, experiences of male authority and female submission, and internalized stereotypes of male and female that resist change.[62]

Lester's description of pastoral authority presents yet another double bind for women. He described characteristics that are culturally associated with male behavior and leadership then called for women to emulate them in order to be recognized as pastors. Although he suggested reasons that such emulation is difficult, he does not question the list of characteristics of ministry. Two decades later in Baptist churches and in Martha's self-identifications, the struggles, which Lester articulates, remained. Although Lester described the barriers to claiming and accepting pastoral authority for women, when women actually stepped into the pastoral roles, the effect was to raise more questions than render answers. Martha took up the task of claiming pastoral authority when she initiated ordination with the First Baptist Church in Florence. And along the way she raised more questions about the practice and authority of ordination as well as her participation in it. In the end she made a pragmatic choice to be ordained for the sake of ministry (to officiate a wedding). In effect, Martha simultaneously challenged the meanings of ordination and authority, threatening the status quo, and accepted the authority of ordination for the sake of ministry. In that latter move, she participated in reproducing the split between clergy and laity—even while questioning it—with her pragmatic choice.

After ordination, Martha continued wrestling with questions of authority: how to respond to Linda; why only troubled, small, stagnant, or dying congregations seemed to call women; and why she held such low expectations that churches might control, manipulate, or undervalue her. Martha's experience in her family of origin and employment held the roots of her beliefs. Each accumulated experience through her life worked to reinforce each layer of troublesome belief. The resulting network of beliefs about women in the pastorate was common and widespread in Baptist life, so widespread that Lester could report "stereotypes" with minimal explanation, showing the persistent and recalcitrant character of social and theological inequality between men and women.

Individual beliefs about the inferiority and inadequacy of women are harmful or "pathogenic," particularly if they work as psychological defenses that prevent growth and flourishing.[63] Widely held pathogenic beliefs about women's inferiority do not change quickly or easily. In one regard, little had changed between Lester's 1978 presentation about the problem and Martha's first day at Monroe Corner in 2001. In another regard, women's ordination placed intense scrutiny on the practices of both ordination and ministry. Throughout the years of schism and the emerging growth of women's ordination, the questions and choices, studied or pragmatic, both challenged and reproduced the gendered split between clergy and laity, interpreting the schism as a gendered struggle over the meaning and practice of leadership.[64]

Martha's narrative reveals several periods of personal identity crisis, but her conversation with Linda was both the culmination of several changes and a turning point in her larger story. The moment with Linda allowed Martha to see herself in a new way and led her to vocational clarity as a Baptist pastor. Martha's struggle with self-recognition is analogous to the major identity crisis among Southern Baptists. Although Martha's identity crisis ends with some clarification, it does not undo all the tensions which created it. Neither does the split of the autonomist and biblicist parties resolve the tensions of complementarity entirely.

Martha's part-time seminary job at the First Baptist Church in Benson gave her experience in ministry and credibility with the congregation. She saw the church as progressive and "way beyond" ordaining women, yet signs of a complementarity culture remained: no woman served as pastor or chair of deacons, Martha's ministry with children "filled in" where the pastor wasn't strong, and her role was supportive to the "real" senior pastor.[65] In her story, Martha thought Linda was calling a meeting, but it turned out she was calling her to pastoral ministry. Martha thought the purpose was strategy, but Linda's story begged for a benediction and blessing. First, Martha resisted the call. Then she surprised herself: "Oh man! She thinks I'm a minister!" A new possibility emerged, and the moment became a significant turning point for reframing her story.[66]

In the 1960s and 1970s, Baptists saw growth in the number of churches electing women as deacons, often dispensing with the older office of "deaconesses" and increasing the number of women on deacon boards in local churches.[67] In the 1970s twenty-five churches in five states elected and ordained women deacons for the first time, and nearly twenty churches elected women as deacon chairs for the first time. These small shifts paralleled the new growth of women's ordinations to ministry, and they stirred up many local controversies.[68]

Martha and Linda reached toward each other for recognition as "real" ministers. Deeply held and unconscious beliefs, forged in homes and in a culture devoted to complementarity, shaped their thinking. These beliefs presumed a serving, supportive, and even submissive role for women. Martha was still imagining herself as a dutiful daughter who supported the leader in charge, the "father in control," the male pastor. Yet Linda's imagination pushed beyond dutiful daughter and ministry of support to "identify" with Martha as the pastor from whom she wanted a blessing. Mission and submission were so intertwined in Martha's internal world that she struggled to recognize the call. Upon hearing more clearly, however, she found a new inward calling, purpose, and mission, preparing her for the outward call of a congregation.[69]

Biblicists are most closely associated with complementarity culture, yet autonomists also perpetuated it under the cover of self-proclaimed progressivism or being "way beyond" the issue of women's equality in leadership. Autonomist churches increasingly hired women on their church staffs, yet the positions were often assistant or associate positions or non-ordained roles, and thus supportive or secondary to male senior pastors. Churches in both parties hired women to work with children, clean, cook, and provide clerical or programmatic support for other senior (male) ministers.[70] Like UBC and FBC Benson, some Baptist churches elected more women as deacons and deacon chairs, yet the practical functions of deacons also shifted in many churches from decision-making bodies to caring ministries.[71]

In SBC churches women experienced calling to ministry both inwardly and outwardly by congregations and individuals who experienced them as pastors.[72] Some were just as surprised as Martha by the awakening. The wider denomination was slower to recognize what they were seeing and hearing, and opposition met many of these new callings.[73] There was no place for the phenomenon of women's ordination yet to appear.[74] Mission and submission were as entangled culturally as they were in Martha's expressed thoughts and expectations. The growing presence of women in seminary classrooms, pulpits, and ministry settings changed the wider context of Southern Baptists, evoking a crisis of identity. As more women embraced a call to ministry, autonomists and biblicists responded differently to the crisis, and both groups experienced a growing clarity about their organizational and spiritual mission. Yet for all the contest and eventual severing of ties, the culture of complementarity remained a powerful force in the lives of Baptists. Martha's statement about her call to Monroe Corner captures the ambivalence: "I knew that was—like for women in ministry in 2001—this is great. I mean, this is as good as it's going to get." The church took its vote and called her, but the power of complementarity couldn't be voted out of existence.

Martha's stories from childhood, family, church, calling, and ordination offer a way into a closer reading of the psychology of a Southern Baptist culture of complementarity. Her story is not the only way to understand the schism psychologically, but it opens up space for a significant reinterpretation of the times in which she lived. When read alongside organizational and programmatic materials and primary sources from the same period, Martha's story provides a framework for seeing the double binds and dilemmas of gender at work in Southern Baptist life and contributing to the fracturing of its convention. Women do not equal gender, but they make it visible when they break out of expected performances and roles. In cases like ordination, they contribute to the polarizing of groups and formation of parties around seemingly opposing sides of an issue. Biblicists and autonomists fought over gendered ideas and relationships previously implicit and made explicit by clergywomen. The result was a crisis of identity. Martha's navigation of her own identity crisis, one between dutiful submission and autonomous mission, between ambition and sacrifice, and between complementarity and mutuality, mirrors the crisis of Southern Baptists. Both Martha's story and the story of Baptists demonstrate the complex and multiple locations where the performance of gender, the future of complementarity, and the meaning of human being were contested, undone and reproduced.

3

(Sub)text

How Clergywomen Reframe and Renew Baptist Relationships

> It was a whole new way of thinking. Like, wow! Maybe I could be a solo pastor. I hadn't considered it because I just felt like I couldn't do it, because I was too "wounded." Even though I knew I had the skills.
>
> —Joanna

Supportive and challenging relationships created a context for Joanna's calling to ministry. After growing up marginally Catholic, Joanna, now forty-three, found her spiritual home at First Baptist Church in Russetville, where the emphasis on community, justice, and faith for everyday life nurtured in her a vocation as a Baptist pastor. The relational spaces in Joanna's life offer keys to understanding her personal changes across time as well as how personal stories are interwoven in the larger stories of one's context and communities. Joanna came face to face with her relational woundedness when her father died, and she found healing and support from her American Baptist congregation. In seminary she learned to navigate the tension between her personal freedom and relational connections amid the challenges of classroom and chapel. Joanna's relationships—with friends, teachers, co-workers, and parishioners—offer a unique shared space, sometimes filled with innovative possibility, other times polarized by hostility. Each of Joanna's major life stories highlight the relational and gendered character of her wounds, healing, losses, gifts, insight, vision, and vocation.

Most accounts of Southern Baptist schism, academic and partisan, leave the relational and gendered character of the story as subtext, but for clergywomen and many other Baptists, the story of schism unfolded mainly in the relational spaces of their lives.[1] Joanna's story of navigating relational woundedness and healing, rupture and renewal, opens up a way of reinterpreting Baptist politics as a relational space shaped by enduring Baptist tensions of belief and practice. In the same way Joanna negotiates a variety of tensions between her self-understanding and her relationships with others to make life choices, so Baptists on a large scale negotiated a host of psychological tensions that are embedded in their historic principles. At times in Baptist history, these negotiations resulted in growth and greater connection. However, during some extended periods, such as the battles between biblicists and autonomists in the SBC from 1979 to 2000, growing hostility dissolved the creative negotiations, polarizing the Southern Baptist world into new splinter groups. The analysis in this chapter moves back and forth between Joanna's story and the larger story of Baptists negotiating five perennial tensions of belief and practice—salvation and calling, soul competency, the priesthood of all believers, voluntary association, and the separation of church and state—demonstrating how Baptist polity is a relational and psychological set of negotiations.

Joanna's story also highlights the gendered character of the schism. In the relational space of Baptist life, roles for men and women are produced and reproduced, and they are complicated and challenged by individual actors like Joanna. In her "constant drive to integration" and "creating a new thing," Joanna found ways to serve God creatively and meaningfully while challenging the Baptist restrictions on her as a woman. By drawing on her Baptist piety and also feminist convictions, Joanna and her friends explored new dimensions of salvation and calling, claiming the Baptist tradition of prophetic critique and the competency of each individual to question the tradition itself with God's guidance. Joanna challenged the culture of complementarity that rests within the priesthood of all believers, overcoming her woundedness and learning to manage her gifts and insights for ministry. Later she found herself pastoring a church in isolation, exposing Baptists' troublesome devotion to rugged individualism, which keeps pastoral and congregational associations tenuously connected. And when she led her church through the crisis of September 11, 2001, she came up against the challenges of separation of church and state. Joanna's negotiations of Baptist tensions open a space that allows a reinterpretation of schism in the SBC as both a relational rupture and time of renewal.

Joanna's Story

Joanna grew up in a "kind of Catholic" family and rarely attended church. Her parents lived "on the radical edge" of Roman Catholicism, working for social justice and "teaching adult education classes for the NAACP [National Association for the Advancement of Colored People]" organized by a local priest. Joanna attended a few years of Catholic grade school. Her first grade teacher, Sister Mary Charles, was "the most influential person" from that period of her life, and she gave Joanna the nickname "Joy." Joanna says she "loved singing in Mass," and her favorite song was "Spirit God in the Clear Running Water."[2]

As a child Joanna was rarely exposed to other Christian groups and held a rather poor opinion of Baptists. Her first up-close view came from the kitchen of a

Southern Baptist camp where she worked summers as a teenager fending off Baptist teens who tried to proselytize her. She recalls, "I went in a lapsed Catholic and left agnostic." Joanna was "shocked and flabbergasted" that anyone would "treat Catholics as though they weren't Christian." She was quite surprised to find herself a few years later in college attending an American Baptist church with "a real focus on community" and social justice. Although she had "sworn off" religion, the enthusiasm of her friends about First Baptist Russetville, the charisma and influence of a young pastor and his family, and food and hospitality for college students drew Joanna into the community. Having worked as a camp counselor, scouting leader, and swimming instructor, Joanna delighted in working again with children. At First Baptist she found people "who thought your faith actually mattered in your day-to-day life." The community nurtured and shaped Joanna's Baptist piety and invited her to consider a pastoral vocation.[3]

Quickly Joanna became fully involved in the life of the church, working with children, taking part in a Bible study, occasionally leading worship, and feeling a genuine part of the community. In the small congregation where everyone shared ministry, she assumed that she would continue on that path but did not see herself "being dependent on a church for an income." Following college and several job-related moves, Joanna returned again to First Baptist, working and earning her MBA in the evenings. When she graduated from business school, she opened a financial services firm in Dayton. Soon she discovered not all American Baptist churches are oriented to justice and community.

At First Baptist, Joanna worked with children, teaching them music. One day she was teaching the song "Behold What Manner of Love." The song repeats the lines, "Behold what manner of love the Father has given unto us / That we should be called the sons of God."[4] Rather than teach the song with "sons," she changed the word to "children" to make the song more inclusive. She recalls, "I don't think I even changed the word 'Father.' This was the eighties!" One of the children who had learned the song before complained, "Why did you change the words? It's supposed to be 'sons!'" Joanna recalls that before she could respond, another little girl piped up and said, "Well, we're not all boys, you know." Joanna said to herself, "Okay, thank you, I'm done."

While she was in graduate school Joanna's father died. However, she recalls the grief did not prevent her from doing well. In fact, she says, "I get better at school when I'm depressed. I make better grades . . . I can do schoolwork. I just can't do people work." His death and the death of one of her brothers from human immunodeficiency virus (HIV) put Joanna on a quest to come to terms with the fact that two family members had sexually abused her. Her experience of surviving sexual abuse and her desire to confront the issues in a larger way had an impact on her career path. It became one of several concerns to converge and prompt Joanna to attend seminary. Other influences included her love of arts, music, and drama; a concern, love, and advocacy for children, particularly those who survived abuse; and her experience and relational connections in her church and with progressive Baptists.

Joanna recalls her decision to go to seminary was a matter of personal exploration.[5] Ordination was a possibility but not a priority. She says, "I really felt called to doing further work on issues of abuse and violence against women and children, and the church's role in that. Or how churches could be pro-active [in changing it]." She saw how the church was complicit in the domination and abuse of its members, particularly those portrayed as "naturally weaker" and in need of protection. She also saw how churches might use their resources to help undo the problems of domination and abuse. Joanna recognized her need to know more, yet not simply *more* knowledge but a particular kind of theological and pastoral knowing that would help her bring change to churches.[6]

Relational connections at Crowder Seminary, and in churches nearby played a significant role in Joanna's choice of schools. Right away she wanted to put her "gifts and passion" to work for the sake of change. Joanna reached out to Safe Haven, a center committed to making religious responses to women who experienced violence, hoping it might be her placement for Crowder's field education program. The staff at Safe Haven and the field education staff at Crowder agreed Joanna could complete an internship if she could find her own source of income. "And so," says Joanna, "I sent out a letter to people and ended up raising about $1,500 for an internship."

Joanna described her choice to go to seminary as "a coalescing" of ideas, skills, and values. She wanted to bring social and ecclesial change "through creative ways, through programs with children, and through the curriculum." And Joanna thought she might need to use her MBA and training to support herself financially in ministry. "Because," she notes, "I knew if I was bringing issues of abuse into churches, it wasn't necessarily going to make me any friends. It wasn't necessarily something you could sustain from the pulpit." Joanna tried to be realistic about the cultural and relational limits of her passion for ministry with survivors of abuse.

Joanna ran into resistance in her first year of seminary, becoming frustrated by the school's assumptions about how "to mold each student into a certain kind of minister" without consideration of past personal experience. In the first week she recalls feeling angry—even furious—at the school's orientation when the seminary dean announced, "When you're buried in this we know what your experience will be." Joanna turned to the person next to her, whom she had just met, and asked, "Did you hear that? How could he possibly know what our experience is? He doesn't know who I am. He knows what they're giving us, but he doesn't know how I personally am going to respond!"

Rather than openness to her skills and experience at the intersection of art and worship, Joanna found the seminary to be among the most "liturgically conservative" places she could imagine. She also discovered that being a Baptist in a non-Baptist school held its own challenges. She says, "I was outcast because I was Baptist." As an American Baptist in the midst of "a great influx of Southern Baptists," she also endured confusion over the different kinds of Baptists.[7] Later in the semester, Joanna met Darlene, a woman in whom she confided her feelings of total lack of understanding and her personal experience of being "a Baptist, a feminist . . . and being punished for having a life before seminary." It seemed to her students could not "stand out" because the seminary wanted to "mold you to all look the same, so that there was something wrong with admitting you had gifts in certain areas." She questioned her choice of schools. Then Joanna and Darlene decided to put up a sign: "Feminist, front steps, chapel." And they found a group of other "self-identified feminists."

Also in her first year, Joanna discovered the Eleanor Witek Center (EWC) for women in ministry. A faculty researcher from the school hosted a focused conversation about women's experience in seminary. Joanna arrived feeling livid about her classes and ready to vent about her frustrations, but she met with resistance. She recalls that those gathered "got on me for being angry." Joanna remembers thinking, "Wait! I thought this was the gathering of women in ministry?" She found the researcher's response rather "bizarre." The woman told Joanna, "There are people concerned about your being able to be in a church placement." Joanna gave a quick retort: "Well, you know maybe they should come over to [my church] where they can see me in action if they're concerned." She explained that she assumed "people in seminary are here to learn" and could tolerate the criticism. Despite the researcher's stated intention to understand women in ministry, she managed to further alienate and frustrate Joanna and her peers.

The group disbanded and stopped meeting very soon after Joanna's inauspicious beginning with them. However, weeks later, students reformed the group at the EWC, and many confessed to sharing Joanna's feelings of anger and frustration. Joanna recalls that by the midterm of the semester other female students began hearing the regular dismissals of women's top grades because professors were "grading women more easily" or "being softer" on them simply because they were women. Eventually Joanna and Darlene became student co-coordinators of the EWC, and Joanna's connection with two communities of women (the EWC and Hope Haven) became part of her "saving grace," keeping her in seminary. She also won a financial scholarship to pay for her second and third years of school. She considered leaving for an American Baptist school, but her lack of relationships at any of those schools and the new found connections at Crowder prompted her to stay.

Joanna's second year of seminary proved to be more "fun." She co-chaired the EWC and exercised some "authority" using "resources to effect some change." She and her fellow seminarians began to focus their anger in a constructive direction. Joanna and Darlene determined to make their efforts count, taking on "good cop—bad cop" roles to make some change on campus. Joanna says, "I was the pushy, obnoxious one and Darlene could speak up and still look so sweet." They advocated for EWC to lead a week of chapel services during "child abuse awareness" month. They drew other students into an intentionally shared worship planning group that attended to "specific issues around abuse." The small group of volunteers, mostly women, planned a healing service for the seminary community, modeling something that students could recreate in their churches. Joanna saw the entire process as an important learning moment as she moved toward a vocation of ministry.

The planning group struggled to determine the best healing ritual around which to build a worship service. Some rituals felt too "self-identifying," potentially singling out or shaming survivors. The ritual of anointing created feelings of ambivalence in Joanna and others: "I have a problem with any sort of physical act over someone as an abuse issue." On the other hand, they liked the possibility that women might "reclaim the ritual." For Baptists the ritual carried little meaning.[8] They continued brainstorming until someone said, "I just see colors." And someone else said, "I see colors moving." And someone said, "It must be a dancer," and a creative solution emerged. The planners recruited a liturgical dancer, and Joanna enlisted a little girl from her church to take part in the service.

At the opening of the service, the planners gave permission for worshipers to leave if they felt overwhelmed, unlike churches "where you feel like you have to stay." They arranged in advance for counselors to be present. At the time of the liturgical dance, the little girl rocked a teddy bear and the dancer interpreted a Darrell Adams song, "Holy Spirit, Comforter." The dancer moved all around the child, carrying fabric and creating a weaving, while the soloist sang, "Holy Spirit, Comforter, come and comfort be / Rest our fears, dry our tears, set your children free."[9] Following the solo and interpretive dance, the music continued. A leader invited worshipers to take fabric from a basket and participate in creating the weaving. An amazing thing happened for the planners, says Joanna, "when people came up to do the weaving, the dancer didn't stop. She actually took her cloth and blew on them with the cloth as they came up. And then when they were all done, she made motions blessing the weaving." The planners experienced it as a "wonderful moment." A poem closed the service: "Now we pick up this broken thread, my weaving God and me . . . we do the work of repair. . . . Out of the torn places, I reclaim wholeness. Out of the broken places, I reclaim strength. . . . Out of the horror and the shame and the pain, I reclaim openness, innocence, courage."[10] The service was "an incredible experience" for Joanna and her friends, and the planning modeled the best of ministry for Joanna, clarifying her passion and cultivating her gifts for designing worship services. The work was part of her "constant drive to integration" and "creating a new thing." In the creation Joanna found "a way to live out serving God."

Joanna says in seminary another thing became clear: "I definitely had a prophetic bent to my goal." Her vision emerged for helping churches confront and offer words and rituals "about recovery and healing and acknowledging the violence and abuse." The prophetic impulse showed up in several notable ways: in her participation and leadership at the EWC, in the healing services, and in her biblical interpretation and preaching classes. Giving voice to violence and abuse in a setting of worship was rare and novel. Inviting stories of survivors into "sacred space" showed worshipers that despite the "horrid language," both biblical and personal stories of harm "belong in church" precisely because "some people's lived reality" needed and deserved acknowledgment.

Joanna recalls how the healing service ritualized "being prophetic within the context of worship." Several worship leaders physically formed a symbolic church building, making "church walls and a steeple" with their bodies while speaking a corporate confession. Joanna and the other planners carefully avoided a confession that said "we as a church" have failed, because, as Joanna notes, "if you say 'we' and everybody thinks it's a collective group of 'I's,' then you could be battering a person further."[11] Instead, the ritual drama enacted "pieces of the church taking ownership" for the violence and abuse. This action allowed worshipers collectively to "state the confession without people necessarily having to own it themselves." The thoughtful theological thinking allowed individuals to "own that part which they're complicit with" but avoid inflicting further harm on survivors of abuse.

From her first Bible and preaching classes Joanna "challenged the church's status quo and complicity with violence in terms of biblical interpretation." She remembers one class in which she called out her peers for using language such as "taking up your cross," "this is my burden to bear," and "women be submissive to your husbands."[12] Joanna says, "You have to apply corrective, and you have to be explicit about your corrective because you have [to know] statistically how many women are in your congregation who are in a battering relationship. And you can't believe 'it doesn't happen here' because it does!"[13]

In her final year of seminary and at the end of a unit of clinical pastoral education, a progressive Baptist church in Virginia hired Joanna as minister of youth and children. During her three years, the pastor retired, and in the months following his retirement, staff conflicts arose and finances fell. A difficult moment came when a layperson in the congregation presented a new annual budget to the staff. When no one else spoke up, Joanna challenged the thinking behind the recommended cuts. She recalls speaking forcefully and the lay leader appearing to be "taken aback." After the meeting Joanna felt relieved that she had avoided a meltdown and had not second-guessed herself. Still, she asked another staff member if she was "out of line." But the staffer said her arguments were "very strong." Others felt less pleased and called the senior interim pastor to complain about Joanna's confrontation. Although no one talked to Joanna directly, the interim pastor, a woman, called a meeting to talk to Joanna about the incident.

As Joanna sorted out the issues, she noticed right away that the layperson and each staff member who complained in the situation was male. At that moment, says Joanna, "I felt that I hit the glass ceiling." Despite her previous experience as a business person and church finance administrator, she felt limited by the expectations of her present role: "You're a youth and children's minister. What would you know about a budget? Why aren't you staying in your place?" She "felt dismissed," she says. The interim senior minister suggested that Joanna consult with a pastoral counselor, but Joanna felt shamed by the directive: "I literally crawled under my desk after she left my office, I just felt lower than dirt."

When Joanna met with the pastoral counselor to "process her anger," she felt as if she were being assigned to "remedial therapy," assuming her own therapy group inadequate. However, the outcome of her work with the counselor altered Joanna's career and life. In the second session, the counselor asked Joanna, "You get things fast, right?" Joanna replied, "Well, I don't know. I get things. I see things in their larger context. So when this guy's presenting a budget I'm seeing a whole slew of fall-out problems. . . . I see things in a bigger picture." The counselor followed up: "And you see that instantly?" Joanna answered, "Yeah, because it's right there." And then he said: "And you don't get that that's a gift?" Joanna said, "What?"

Joanna focused on the event as "another way my woundedness was coming out . . . and another way I will never be functional in a church." The pastoral counselor persisted: "It's a gift! This isn't out of your woundedness; this is out of your giftedness. . . . You have to learn to manage a gift, but it's a gift." For Joanna the new insight was "a complete narrative shift." She was delighted to see how the actions of her life were not a result of being flawed but because she was really good at something. After her final session, Joanna saw her own role in the situation over the budget more clearly. The counselor urged her to stop taking sole responsibility for a situation in which other members of the staff also played a role. Several months later the entire church staff began as a group to work with the counselor on their conflicts and power dynamics.

In the months that followed, Joanna thought more about her new discovery and what it meant for her pastoral calling. She thought about how to distinguish between "gifts to manage" and "woundedness to recover from." The recovery did not mean she had to "leave the gifts behind." She thought about using her perception and quick insight more patiently, bringing others along. She sums up her learning: "It was a whole new way of thinking. Like, wow! Maybe I could be a solo pastor. I hadn't considered it because I just felt like I couldn't do it, because I was too 'wounded.' Even though I knew I had the skills."

With a newly articulated sense of calling, Joanna attended the next American Baptist Churches USA (ABC-USA) biennial meeting with her résumé in hand. An executive minister told her about a small church that would likely be willing to call her. He said Joanna could bring a new "kind of birth" to Gentry Memorial in three to five years. The search committee at Gentry Memorial Baptist Church in Turner, Illinois, presented Joanna to the congregation. The church initially voted no. A church member, serving as interim pastor, appeared to undermine the vote. The district ABC-USA minister intervened, and the interim pastor left the congregation. Several weeks later the church voted again, calling Joanna as their pastor at thirty hours per week. She recalls, "In retrospect I shouldn't have [accepted the call], but at the time I didn't have anybody to counsel with me."

Joanna's "honeymoon period" with the church went well, and she led them in choosing a new hymnal. The same shift in self-understanding that led her to the pastorate also allowed Joanna to "consider being a single parent." She recalls parenting as another opportunity to "manage gifts" rather than "wallow in woundedness." Joanna adopted her son Lawson when he was sixteen months old and believes the adoption extended the church honeymoon.

Eighteen months into the pastorate problems began to arise, including a difference of opinion about the best way to teach and lead youth, a concern about the ineffectiveness of the financial secretary (which the church board insisted Joanna should handle), and the fallout from September 11, 2001. Joanna did not have a partner for ministry or parenting, and she became increasingly isolated in a relatively new church. As problems escalated, Joanna still lacked anyone to whom she could turn for counsel.

On the first Sunday following 9/11, Joanna preached a "comforting sermon" with guidance from materials provided by the Baptist Peace Fellowship, including letters of lament and support from around the world. In the weeks that followed, Joanna's gifts of seeing things quickly and contextually, and her "prophetic bent," led her to see clearly "the drums for war were accelerating." She felt compelled to preach against war: "This was not the way to respond to the terrorism" and "as Christians we stand in a different place than we do as citizens." She questioned the direction of the U.S. government. Her choices put distance between her and the congregation. Some responded to her with subtlety. However, she recalls, "one guy confronted me directly: 'I don't have to hear this, I shouldn't have to hear my government being critiqued in church.'" But Joanna was not wrong. "The bombs started flying two weeks later," she recalls. "I didn't misread the drumbeats."

As the relationship between Joanna and the congregation deteriorated, she says things took on an "aura of disrespectfulness." For instance, a church member who cleaned the church broke a microphone in the sanctuary, only taping it back together. Then, says Joanna, he "tried to fix it standing right in front of me while I'm trying to make announcements. . . . It was just bizarre." Joanna believed he would not have treated a man in the same way. In October, Joanna led a "Children's Sabbath" service, including stories about children's exposure to violence in their homes and after 9/11. Some thought the stories "too graphic." Joanna took the precaution of consulting with Bob, a church member and pastor search committee chair, who supported her choices. Nevertheless, complaints from the congregation grew louder. Some thought Joanna only "preached about women." Bob said, "Well she's preaching from the lectionary, so frankly that's what the stories are about."[14] Joanna also learned the church was paying her and staying afloat financially with funds borrowed prior to her arrival. The money would run out eventually. She decided to study for the certified public accountant exam to supplement her income.

Finally all the intense factors converged, making a miserable situation for Joanna and prompting her decision to resign. She waited until Lawson's adoption was complete before announcing it. "I couldn't stand getting up in the pulpit any longer," she says. "I felt . . . such absolute disrespect." She asked laypeople to lead the pastoral prayer. She recalls thinking, "I just can't do it. I can't pray in front of these people. I barely survived. I lived through the end of May and a couple of weeks into June. They paid me through the end of June. In many ways I wished I'd waited until they ran out of money because I let them off the hook for making hard decisions. I felt like I did. But I had to be self-protected. And I had to get out." Within a year following Joanna's departure, the small church folded under the weight of internal conflict, power struggles, and financial distress.

After leaving Gentry Memorial, Joanna returned to the financial services industry and searched for a place where she might also engage again in full-time ministry. A solo pastorate with its demands and isolation seemed "crazy-making" rather than appealing to her, fueling her ambivalence. Today, Joanna would like to be part of a ministry team or to serve as a co-pastor. Yet a ministry built on complementarity in which "team members" are required to be subordinate to a senior pastor is not appealing to her, and ministry outside of Baptist circles fails for her at the point of polity and practice. As for her gender, Joanna says she wishes being a woman would "just be a fact" and not a major "issue." It frustrates her that "just because you have a white man in the pulpit that's a non-issue because that's a normative, while being a woman is not the normative." She would like to minister where she is neither "dismissed because I'm a woman" nor "feared because I'm a woman."

Reflecting back on her wider journey, Joanna says that despite feeling derailed after leaving Gentry Memorial, she always felt a sense of "progression," that she learned something that led her to each next place. Her life holds "a constant drive to integrate all the facets." Her calling is "to find a place where . . . who I am as an intellectual is not in a different place than who I am as a youth and children's minister . . . not compartments for my gifts." Her life's entire journey, Joanna says, has been "a way to live out ministry, a way to live out serving God [as] God is calling me at that juncture."

Reinterpreting Schism as Relational Rupture and Renewal

Joanna's story reveals the relational and gendered character of Baptist polity and reinterprets schism as a rending and renewing of relational connections. Because

Baptists lack formal doctrinal agreement, and structures for organizing are minimal, they operate most immediately within a set of tensions of belief and practice, which usually remain tacit yet offer durable relational patterns for Baptist life. Each pair of tensions holds a creative and improvisational space, yet they can pull contentiously against one another coloring the relationships with conflict and hostility, making way for polarization and eventual schism. Within each tension, gender plays its part, and the gendered character of each tension came into sharp relief when clergywomen took leading roles in the world of Baptists and moved from margins to center stage.

Baptists in the 1980s, 1990s, and 2000s often referred to the struggles in the SBC in militaristic terms: "holy war," "hostile takeover," or "resurgence." Written analysis, both partisan and academic, used terms such as "uneasy," "crisis," "dissent," "struggle," "politics," and "battles," capturing the character of the changes. Biblical images such as Babylonian captivity, exile, and "God's last and only hope" emerged to describe the subsequent rift in Baptist life.[15] These images illustrate the sheer size of the changes for those living through three decades of it, particularly those who departed the SBC. However, none of them quite portray the relational character of the losses with their titles or their arguments. Like America's Civil War of the 1860s, the divisions in Baptist life were personal, familial, and relational (as well as geographical and political).[16] Baptist polity itself rests on kinship and other relational networks. Examining schism by starting in the firsthand stories of women in ministry reveals the relational character of the changes, conflicts, and renewals. Because Baptist polity lives and dies on relational networks and connections, the schism was an unavoidably relational struggle, deeply personal and grievous yet holding potential for healing.

Examining Joanna's story in terms of five major historical tensions in Baptist life displays the relational and gendered character of Baptist polity.[17] Focusing on relational dynamics shows how the stakes of schism were personal as well as political, and how the stage was set for a crisis to unfold.[18] Each pair of Baptist tensions is discernible where belief and practice can be observed publically, and they are internalized as psychological models for human relating.[19] Baptists carry forward these patterns of thought and action unintentionally but enduringly.[20] Baptist clergywomen decentered stories of *salvation and calling* among Baptists, exposing the subplot of God's care for the vulnerable and the harmed and God's call to those without political power to subvert the power available to them, remaking space for healing changes. Women embraced their own *soul competency* to speak prophetically and enact corrective for relational harms committed in the name of Scripture, church, and religion, thereby reinterpreting schism as a time of undoing complementarity and embracing relational mutuality. As women reframed their personal stories to embrace their gifts and calling as full members of the *priesthood of all believers,* they also changed the larger Baptist story, revealing a subtext of gender inequality and shifting the relational power to lay groundwork for renewal of the breakaway groups and retrenchment among those who stayed with the SBC.

Women serving as solo pastors experienced a pervasive and chronic isolation, felt by many men before them, a practical side effect of *voluntary association;* however, women's stories challenged the brokenness of Baptists' rugged individualism, and they highlighted the ways that schism unfolded as an extended struggle over how Baptists should or could cooperate. Although Baptist parties fought openly over the *separation of church and state* in the 1980s and 1990s, women's leadership—amid tremendous differences of opinion—highlights a subplot of relational deficit, a lack of capacity for recognizing the other and staying connected through conflict, setting the groundwork for separation, distance, and, finally, schism.

Joanna grew up "kind of Catholic," but as a teen and young adult, she encountered Baptists at two extremes: pushy proselytizing campers and welcoming hospitable church community. In college Joanna joined First Baptist Church Russetville, where "faith actually mattered in your day-to-day life." Becoming a Baptist Christian grounded Joanna relationally in the communities of First Baptist and the larger network of progressive Baptists. They shaped Joanna's piety, Christian feminism, and vocation, nurturing her faith and connecting it with her love of children and the arts. The congregation remained her primary support through college, graduate school, the death of her father, and facing her coming to terms with childhood sexual abuse. As Joanna encountered her relational woundedness, and that of others, she articulated a prophetic calling to engage communities of faith and make much needed change. The church blessed and supported her choice to attend seminary.

Two influential views of salvation and calling coexist in Baptist history and context. "Dramatic conversion" offers a psychological view of salvation that idealizes personal change, framing it as an individual experience of the divine—unmediated by anyone or anything.[21] In contrast, the "nurturing process" understands salvation and calling as human change over time that is relational, gradual, and infused with the sacred.[22] Both views offer psychological models of human change that require the interaction, support, and recognition of others. Neither model exists in isolation, although one may take public or rhetorical prominence in a given community. Both models depend on divine and human relationships as indispensable for Baptist conversion.[23]

Southern Baptist and American Baptist churches offer cradle-to-grave programming that shapes Baptist piety for faithful living. They sponsor traditional preaching revivals and circulate historical stories, which expect, even demand, singular moments of repentance and conversion as a way to salvation. Across four centuries, the creative tension between these two psychological models of human change contributed to notable growth in Baptist adherents.[24]

Although salvation holds an egalitarian impulse, vocation in Baptist history and polity has decidedly gendered overtones. Calling may be for everyone, but the call to ministry is usually reserved for boys and men. Like salvation, a calling to ministry may come dramatically, as if from outside, to a single person, who can then respond with individual agency. Or a calling may be nurtured over time, with communal support, guidance, and relational give and take. In practice, both salvation and calling unfold in immediate, dramatic ways *and* gradual, nurturing ways, defying any neat fit into either category *and* making the notion of tension useful. Salvation and vocation are not singular, autonomous, or isolated decisions. Both are relationally grounded, putting faith and vocation at stake in every aspect of life. The dynamics of gender are challenged, negotiated, and changed precisely within the tension of these relational spaces.

To work out her call to ministry, Joanna used relational connections and networking skills to choose a school, navigate her time in seminary, and raise funds for her field education placement. When she felt alienated in seminary classrooms, she found part of her "saving grace" in her connection with women's groups that offered peer support for women seminarians, ministry to survivors of abuse, and worship for the seminary community. Worship embodied Joanna's vocation to engage churches with questions about abuse, violence, and healing. The chapel services openly named the harm and expressed a healing impulse. Joanna was not defined solely by her status as a victim, or even as a survivor, of sexual abuse.[25] She acted with agency and made connections rather than waiting passively or submitting in isolation to her situation.[26]

In Baptist culture, particularly among ministers, most things happen through networking. Southern Baptists know one another through multigenerational connections of church membership, summer camps, college, seminary, kinship ties, business affiliations, and more.[27] In the absence of official hierarchies and formal doctrinal requirements, a relational network teaches the knowledge and skills for individual spiritual formation, group growth, cultivating leadership, organizing volunteers, raising funds, gaining political power, and making change. Ministers make networking an art form, and longstanding bonds of loyalty raise the relational, emotional, and material stakes when any disagreement or crisis arises. Baptist schism was not only a protracted political argument but also a deeply relational drama requiring negotiations of meaning, faith, and purpose played out in innumerable personal and communal relationships.

A significant but ignored subtext of the schism took shape in women's work to examine and transform abuse, violence, and relational woundedness. Women working for personal and communal healing from physical and relational wounds embodied an immediate and practical kind of salvation. Some women, like Joanna, embraced vocations of naming and confessing sins of domination, abuse, violence, and submission. Joanna and her seminary peers took on the task of subjectifying themselves in an environment where they felt objectified or dismissed. They subverted the power available to them to gain space for making change. And finally, they drew out the subtleties and subtexts of relational woundedness and the collusion of the church in harming its most vulnerable members, making room for lament, grief, and healing, all of which became occasions for transformative creativity.[28] As actors in one another's stories, clergywomen changed the story of the unfolding schism, enacting important subplots, exposing subtexts, and decentering the very subject of the story.[29] They lived in the tension between nurturing process and dramatic conversion, drawing on the language and imagery of the Spirit's energy and power for healing and transforming the lives of Baptists, especially the most vulnerable, who typically did not reside at the political and theological center of the schism.

At her non-Baptist seminary, Joanna felt alienated and "outcast" as an American Baptist surrounded by Southern Baptists, as a feminist, and even for "having a life before seminary." She got the message that the seminary wanted to shape students in a uniform way rather than focus on individual gifts or call. Eventually Joanna pulled together a group of "self-identified feminists," and over the next three years, they claimed the power of "corrective" or prophetic critique from the Baptist tradition to engage worship, Scripture, and tradition in classroom and chapel. Joanna felt especially concerned to make use of this critique to correct misappropriations of Scripture and practices of worship that supported violence against women and children. She and her friends both created and discovered new ways to see, understand, and relate to human frailty and vulnerability. They made use of their religious traditions to critique those traditions by enacting care, lament, and healing through embodied worship, preaching, and Scripture interpretation. In their actions they "undid" the split of complementarity and embodied a new mutuality.

Baptists' longstanding commitment to the corrective of biblical prophetic traditions places the individual believer within the religious tradition to critique, change, or improve the tradition based on her or his sense of the situation and God's leading. Baptists call this particular baptistic commitment "soul competency."[30] The commitment holds in tension an individual's internal wisdom and authority (or liberty of conscience) and the external wisdom and authority of Scripture and tradition. The two convictions create an intertwining psychological model for understanding how Baptists relate to history, tradition, the sacred, and the communal. The tension of soul competency also makes space for Baptists both to create and to discover a sense of authority for decision making.[31] On one side is the belief and practice of "individual liberty of conscience," a psychological model of personal autonomy drawing on the authority of immediate religious experience for interpreting traditions and texts of faith. On the other side is the longstanding Baptist commitment to the authority of Scriptures, a psychological model that defers to the biblical canon up as the final (or only) word on matters of faith, giving direction to one's choices and actions.

The problem of gender in soul competency is immediate and demanding. Biblical texts and traditions offer conflicting rules and roles for men and women. Ancient cultures of patriarchy called for male protection of women, children, and society's vulnerable members. The same patriarchal cultures also sanctioned violence against the vulnerable.[32] Faith communities negotiate this tension in endless variations as they move back and forth between questions of authority, biblical revelation, the experience of members, and meanings of texts and traditions in new times and places. When the creative tension between individual liberty of conscience (and personal experience of the sacred) and the authority of Scripture breaks down, understandings of gender are often split and polarized, allowing, and even condoning violence and harm.

Speaking and acting from the perspective and experiences of harm to women and children, Joanna and her friends searched for a new locus of authority. They took seriously the need for healing and the call for mutual collaboration in the community of faith. They created new rituals for worship out of a mutually shared and creative process. They honored the authority of women's experience as a source for interpretation. They made space for women to decide, act, and bring corrective to the harms that churches tolerated and perpetrated in worship and scriptural interpretation. In the schism, the autonomist party championed equality and mutuality for men and women in the name of individual liberty of conscience, while the biblicist party defended complementarity as the authoritative scriptural model for relationships between men and women. Neither party could claim freedom from responsibility in the harm of vulnerable people.[33] The season of schism was a struggle over the proper forms of authority by which Baptists would live, and clergywomen highlighted the trouble that emerges when a creative tension melts away or when the authority of biblical texts goes unchecked by the experiences of those harmed in the name of the Bible and its particular harmful texts or in the name of God. Joanna and others pointed out the failures of complementarity when it leads to violence and abuse, and they offered a corrective by exposing the problems and embodying a new form of work, worship, and mutual care.

Joanna took her first full-time ministry job working with children and families in a progressive Baptist congregation where the staff thought of their work as collaborative and mutual.[34] Nevertheless, the milieu for making decisions and navigating conflicts held a longstanding tension between ordained clergy and church laity. When Joanna challenged a lay leader over the possible impact of his proposed budget, she crossed several boundaries of power, gender, and staff role. In the follow-up meeting with the interim pastor, Joanna says she felt "lower than dirt," as if her supervisor dismissed her to "remedial therapy," and like she had hit a stained-glass ceiling.[35] However, when a pastoral counselor accompanied Joanna through understanding her intelligence and quick insight as "gifts to be managed" rather than "woundedness to be healed," Joanna experienced "a complete narrative shift" and developed a new self-understanding.³⁶ Her newfound sense of giftedness led to an improvement in the working relationships for the entire church staff. When Joanna's relational and narrative life changed, so did the wider community and system.

Joanna's freedom, as with that of every other Baptist, operates within structures of Baptist polity and participates in a form of communal discernment and leadership understood as the "priesthood of all believers." Decision-making authority and leadership in Baptist churches are bound up in a congregational polity. Discernment takes place in local churches with guidance from the Scriptures and the Spirit of God in Christ, rather than being the sole domain of pastors, bishops, or authorities beyond the local church.³⁷ The practice holds in tension understandings and expectations about how ordained clergy and others in the church function as leaders. The tension between clergy and laity in Baptist congregations can be at times creative and at other times polarizing. Through four centuries women led Baptists in a multitude of ways, even on occasion garnering official recognition as clergy.³⁸ Yet the gendered character of the tension in the priesthood of all believers is clear. Until the last fifty years, the clergy side of the equation has (almost always) been understood as the domain of men, while men and women populated the laity side and women usually constitute more than half of Baptist congregations and most of its volunteer work force.

As women entered into ministry more consistently and transgressed the implicit yet clearly marked boundaries between clergy and laity, they bumped their heads on stained-glass ceilings. The change created conflict, yet with patient relational work, clergywomen also gained greater clarity of call, and as they shifted their own narratives from "woundedness and liability" to "giftedness and call," the stories of other Baptists around them also changed. The multiple layers of subtext regarding gender are exposed in stories like Joanna's, reframing what it means to be a Baptist leader. The relational work of clergywomen creatively changed long-held understandings of Baptist polity. The years of schism in the SBC extended and expanded relational shifts already happening in situations in which women were bumping their heads on stained-glass ceilings. As women took action, leading congregations and learning to manage their gifts, they contributed to a groundswell of change that invited both renewal and retrenchment among Southern Baptists.

Joanna's new self-understanding that her insight and intelligence were gifts and skills, not wounds or liabilities, renewed her imagination for future possibilities.³⁹ Her sense of prophetic vision, love of arts and worship planning, and experiences of leading came together in a decision to seek the role of solo pastor.⁴⁰ However, relational conflict in a supportive and collaborative setting is dramatically different from the isolation and eventual crisis that Joanna faced in her ministry at Gentry Memorial. From college, Joanna relied on numerous relational connections to support her discernment and decision making. Yet in the decision to take the call and in subsequent conflicts at Gentry Memorial, Joanna worked without adequate counsel. Seclusion, loneliness, and lack of support for leaders of small churches can be troublesome. Joanna's struggles became especially acute as a single parent, as a first-time solo pastor, and at a geographical distance from her communities of support.[41]

The isolation experienced by Joanna was shaped by a commitment in Baptist polity to the belief and practice of "voluntary association," animating the Baptist ethos since the church's seventeenth-century beginnings. Baptists reject coercion and interference from external authorities on any religious body. Each local Baptist church is autonomous and does not answer to any other spiritual authority (group, individual, ecclesiastical, or governmental) outside of God and their congregation. Yet Baptists learned early to accomplish certain tasks and guard against isolation by way of mutual cooperation between churches, retaining the benefits of connectionalism without so many hindrances. Often churches assumed doctrinal agreement for such cooperation, but as Baptists grew in doctrinal diversity, they still found ways to cooperate for larger purposes, such as theological education, missionary work, publishing, and social justice, even when they did not agree on every doctrine.[42] These two psychological models of group relationships hold self-sufficiency, individualism, and containment of "local church autonomy" in tension with relational and connected networks in "associational cooperation."

In practice, the difficulty of these two different psychological models of group relationships shows up in a pervasive isolation among churches and ministers. Pastors must find whatever support they can muster on their own. The underbelly of Baptists' rugged individualism is a freedom with little or no relational support. The chronic isolation leads to a host of ecclesial and personal problems. After benefiting from years of nurturing, supportive, and challenging relationships, Joanna became a pastor and moved out on her own in a profound new way.

In the years of Baptist schism, autonomists usually took up the side of "associational cooperation" as their cause. They, after all, wanted to save the SBC, the world's largest cooperating body of Baptists.[43] Leaders in the biblicist party, however, often came from churches that lacked cooperative relationships beyond their own walls. Ironically, biblicists built "megachurches" as virtual minidenominations on multi-million-dollar campuses, complete with schools, businesses, restaurants, retirement villages, and scores of paid staff.[44] Notably, megachurch pastors organized a campaign to win control of the convention's decision-making apparatus. As the parties split, each group coalesced around particular doctrinal standards for belonging that opposed the other party. They also split the creative tension of Baptist polity and practice. Women entering ministry tested cooperation among Baptists doctrinally, and they literally became a test of fellowship in Baptist associations, the local proving ground for "associational cooperation."[45]

The skirmishes revealed a more chronic and devastating problem for Baptists: the sheer lack of connection and support necessary for pastoral effectiveness.[46]

When men burn out, give up, or become embroiled in controversy with their congregations, the story doesn't make headline news. But when isolation takes its toll on women, because female pastors remain novelties, it becomes a kind of "evidence" that it wasn't going to work anyway.[47]

Schism in the SBC was an extended negotiation over how and why Baptists could or should cooperate. The arguments about cooperation often took the public form of doctrinal and political differences. In both parties women's ordination and leadership shows up as a doctrinal and political "problem." However, the stories of women's pastoral leadership shows how a deeper struggle was at stake over the question of the need for cooperation and support. Their stories highlight the brokenness of the rugged individualism model. Relationality and personal networking are the bread and butter of Baptist life, the connective social tissue of the denomination. The story of chronic and debilitating isolation is surely present in the narratives of clergymen, but the losses and early disruptions to pastoral relationships between women and their congregations became more visible.[48] And the clergywomen's stories highlight the troubles with autonomy and the indispensible need for voluntary cooperation.

Joanna's conviction that "as Christians we stand in a different place than we do as citizens," and her commitment to speak out against violence, directed her to choices in preaching and leadership that distanced and eventually alienated her from her congregation. She and the congregation moved beyond the honeymoon period at Gentry Memorial when the tragedy of September 11, 2001, struck. She responded the first Sunday with a sermon of comfort and lament, and in the following weeks she preached a prophetic call of justice for innocents and plead for resistance to war. Differences of opinion are unavoidable, but when the differences are over something as significant as war, the challenge to maintain openness and relational connection increases. Some members of Gentry disagreed with Joanna, and they grew increasingly distant and conflicted. Joanna's attempt to maintain the relational connections while offering an unpopular opinion was complicated by the collapse of other aspects of her relationship to the congregation, including theology and finances.

Baptists have championed the "separation of church and state" from its earliest days in U.S. history. At one side stands the ideal of "religious liberty," which is a psychological construction of independence and autonomy for churches and individuals to be free from interference and coercion from state authorities in matters of faith, religion, or conscience. The other side of the tension is "loyalty to the state," which insists on the necessity of a free state to ensure (or enforce) the freedom of religion for every group and individual. The tension can be a creative space for negotiation or a foreclosed space haunted by fighting and hostile disagreement.[49]

Some Protestants born in the Reformation envisioned a renewed Christian church that continued to share power with the state. However, Baptists, Anabaptists, and other reformers imagined a more radical free church in a free state. The freedom went beyond toleration of other religious groups toward allowing liberty of conscience to every citizen to follow any religion (or no religion) of their choosing.[50] Psychologically, the separation of church and state can be understood as a social and political expression that allows mutual recognition of differences between individuals with far reaching consequences. During the years of SBC schism, biblicists questioned the historicity of this Baptist ideal and began to advocate for the ideal of a "Christian nation," which reunited church and state in both subtle and more overt ways. Autonomists continued to call for a clear separation between church and state as well as religious liberty for all citizens.[51]

A corollary of the separation of church and state is the freedom for religious leaders to criticize publically the actions taken by their government without fear of state retribution. Joanna's quick insight into what was coming after the events of 9/11 was supported by her view of the separation of church and state and her religious obligation to speak out against violence. However, some church members heard her sermon as disloyal to the country (a widespread reaction during the months following 9/11). They reacted with criticism, but also by withdrawing relationally from their pastor. The tension between the two views of separation of church and state broke down at this point, and Joanna was perceived as disloyal and unpatriotic. The congregation could not recognize Joanna's location within a Baptist tradition of dissent, nor as one free to speak with conviction about an unpopular point of view.

The story shows how gender can work subtly to undermine the relational stability of a situation even when gender does not seem to be a major factor. In the midst of the breakdown of many tensions, Joanna says she felt disrespect and heard complaints related directly to her gender. Meanwhile, Southern Baptists fought openly over disputes about religious liberty and separation of church and state. The SBC defunded the Baptist Joint Committee on Public Affairs (BJC), replacing it with the Ethics and Religious Liberty Commission. The Alliance and CBF picked up on funding the BJC. However, more widespread was the relational breakdown borne out of many kinds of polarizing differences. Parallel to Joanna's story, a widespread lack of recognition and respect for the differences of others, followed by criticism and relational withdrawal, fueled the growth of alternative Baptist groups, and fostered disparity and distance from each other. In the end Baptists split over many disputes and conflicts, including an experience of relational breakdown with little healing or repair in sight.

By the final months of her pastorate, nearly every relational space between Joanna and her congregation had collapsed. The mutual recognition between people and pastor was gone, replaced by an "aura of disrespect." Feelings of destruction or desolation became overwhelming, and Joanna felt she "barely survived" the end of her time at Gentry Memorial. The failures were not simply relational.

The historical tensions of Baptist life between clergy and laity, between religious liberty and loyalty to the state, between liberty of conscience and authority of the Scriptures, and between associational cooperation and church autonomy shaped the psychological context of Gentry Memorial, and many other Baptist churches and relationships, contributing to local and large-scale breakdowns and conflicts.

When the creative tensions failed, members of the congregation saw Joanna as inadequate as a clergyperson, disloyal as a citizen, and incompetent to handle the Scriptures. Neither Joanna nor her congregation benefited from accountability or support beyond the local church. Much of the blame and guilt that accompanied these breakdowns was cast as a problem of gender by Joanna *and* by her congregants. The breakdown of mutual recognition and respect moved those in otherwise intimate relationships from seeing each other as equal subjects toward seeing each other as problems, increasing the potential for harm and multiplying wounds.[52] In the end both Joanna and the congregation lost something vital.

The dynamics of polarization and splitting in the SBC unfolded in a parallel fashion. A decade into the schism, autonomists held turf at one pole of every tension in Baptist life and biblicists staked out positions at the other pole of tension. Autonomists contended for empowerment of the laity, women's ordained ministry, and equality and mutuality in home, church, and society. Biblicists argued for a greater authority of the male (only) pastor and complementarian marriages and families. Biblicists called for a return to school prayer and the acceptance of a Christian nation. Autonomists insisted on religious liberty for everyone and a clear separation between church and state. Autonomists rallied to a cry of liberty. Biblicists marched under the banner of a return to the Bible. Biblicists assumed local churches (especially mega churches) and dramatic, individual salvation to be hallmarks of Baptist identity. Autonomists assumed widespread cooperation (emblemized in the SBC's Cooperative Program) and community nurture of calling and salvation to be the marks of the genuine Baptist heritage. Sermons, news stories, and each party's journal traded insults and criticism. Biblicists accused autonomists of putting the SBC under the "curse of liberalism" and called them "skunks" and the "fanatic fringe." Autonomists said biblicists used "dinosaur rhetoric," "intimidation," and "hostile forces of harassment."[53]

Autonomists interpreted their own departure from the SBC as a "renewal movement" born out of conflict. Biblicists often refer the split as a "conservative resurgence," seeing a reassertion of tradition, especially in relation to roles for men and women, as an energizing victory.[54] Every struggle and victory in the years of schism was unavoidably relational in character. Competing psychologies of how to engage one another are woven into the very fabric of Baptist polity and practice, giving rise at times in Baptist history to creative, improvisational relations. The same tensions, however, when they collapse, become a source of political hostility and relational rupture.

(Sub)text

As an empowered actor in her own story and the stories of others, Joanna changed lives and communities around her. After reframing her sense of woundedness into a sense of giftedness, Joanna pursued her call to pastoral ministry with creativity. When these creative tensions fell into conflict, severing the ties of love, money, and shared history, Joanna felt the pain and "crazy-making" dynamics of church leadership. Her story articulates the relational pain of broken Baptist tensions, and it points to the parallel situation of the schism, which was a poignant relational split for many Southern Baptists. Bonds of love, kinship, and history fostered a loyalty to Baptist principles and relationships, which in the end were painful to sever. Yet the durability of the relational and creative space in Baptist life also endured beyond the schism, allowing each group to renew its vision for life together.

4

Redeeming Humanity

How Clergywomen Embody Struggle and Sacred Presence in the SBC

> I got this very clear message that I was important and worthwhile and loveable, and also this very clear message that I was inferior and that my family didn't fit in.
>
> —Rebecca

Rebecca grew up in a blended family and attended Baptist churches, camps, and schools. At thirty-six years old, she is a Habitat for Humanity employee, a married mother of one, and an ordained Baptist minister. After college and seminary, Rebecca took her first call to ministry at Winstead Baptist Church, an urban, progressive, and mostly white middle- and upper-class church, where she worked with youth. Despite its progressive stance, the church also embodied structures of sexism and racism that shaped troublesome relational patterns. Still, it was the place where Rebecca "cut her teeth" on ministry and, despite various limits, honed her craft of preaching and pastoring.

Rebecca's stories are an occasion to see the spiritual and theological struggles over what it means to be human and to witness how clergywomen's narratives interpret the protracted Baptist battles as a profoundly spiritual, theological, and gendered struggle over brokenness, redemption, and meaning. Rebecca thinks in theological terms and crafts meaning from the significant moments in her life of discipleship and vocation.[1] At many major turning points, Rebecca says she felt clearly that "this was where God meant for me to be." And when struggles came, "no matter how bad," she still knew the feeling of being in "the right place." That feeling came with going to college, going to work for Habitat for Humanity, choosing parenthood, and deciding to be "a stay-at-home mom." Her intuition was less clear with choosing seminary and ministry at Winstead Baptist Church. Rebecca says she can't control the right-place feeling or "make it happen." In some seasons, such as at college and during youth ministry, her sense of calling was simply "for right now." When situations were more challenging, however, Rebecca depended on a "sustaining presence of God," a knowing that accumulated over time into a "pattern in life." Rebecca knows "when I'm right where I'm supposed to be. . . . I feel sustained through the difficulties."

Two theological aspects of Rebecca's story insist on articulation. On one side is the challenge and struggle. The other side is God's sustaining presence and her clear feeling of right place. Thus struggle and sustenance, distress and call, and conflict and renewal portray the theological character of many clergywomen's lives and ministries. The paradox of this experience is also endemic to the character of the Southern Baptist struggle that led to schism. The SBC was more than a place of profound struggle for women pursuing a call and ordination, or a place of conflict and hostility for Baptists embattled with one another; it was also a place of redemption and being founded by grace, a place of God's sustaining presence in difficulty, accompanied by a feeling of being in the right place.

Tremendous vulnerability marked the years of schism. Clergywomen and other Baptists lived in a world structured by the irreconcilability of one's longings for meaning, the need for being authentically present in the world *as oneself,* and the need for belonging to other individuals and communities. These basic human desires can never finally be fulfilled and so carry with them struggle, doubt, woundedness, and grief.[2] And the particular form of this human condition of brokenness, sin and struggle, deserves to be honored by being disclosed rather than suffered in isolation. However, interwoven in these experiences are the simultaneous and paradoxical stories of calling, grace, empowerment, and renewal. Rebecca sometimes felt "left on her own" by God, and other times she found God waiting patiently, giving her "gifts that I didn't expect, didn't want, never anticipated." The schism of Southern Baptists is a story of struggle, harm, sin, and evil entangled with stories of gift, freedom, grace, and sacred presence.

Preaching is a significant aspect of Rebecca's call, a bright thread woven through her experience. Southern Baptist preachers brokered Baptist identity by narrating stories of schism and being Baptist, using language and rhetoric to capture the struggle over the meaning of being human.[3] For many Southern Baptists, including Rebecca, believer's baptism and communion are central, liturgical, meaning-filled, and contested practices. However, the high regard for a preached word coming from Bible and pulpit is a central means and mode of storytelling, narrating the meanings found and fashioned in one's spiritual life and shaping local and far-flung communities of faith.[4] Sermons and essays from five autonomist and five biblicist leaders interweave with Rebecca's narrative to articulate a story and theology of struggle over what it means to be human, including the gendered shape of that story.[5]

Rebecca's Story

Rebecca remembers being baptized at the age of six in a Southern Baptist church. Within the year, her family stopped attending that church because her parents felt censured by the "preaching against divorce" (both her mom and stepdad were in a second marriage). In those early years, she says, "I got a really good grounding in the stories in the Bible and that God loves me. I got this very clear message that I was important and worthwhile and loveable, and also this very clear message that I was inferior and that my family didn't fit in." She adds, "The messages about women were never spoken. . . . You saw what women did and didn't do in the church: osmosis."[6] Also by "osmosis," Rebecca says she learned "we weren't a real family" because her parents fought and didn't have a "perfect relationship." To Rebecca, her family did not look or act like "families in my Sunday school books," which left her feeling "inferior" and like "my family didn't fit in." The "very strong message" of God's love, however, sustained Rebecca throughout her life. She witnessed adults who "cared about me enough to teach Sunday school" and helped her feel "important and worthwhile and loveable."

Rebecca remembers vividly the morning she decided to be baptized and "went forward" in a children's worship service.[7] In that service she felt "this very clear sense that God loved me," and baptism was her response to that love. "That's a pretty good theology of baptism," she concludes. "I don't question it even now." About the baptism ceremony itself, she recalls a Sunday evening service "wearing this very fancy white dress with layers and layers and layers, which was very cold when it got wet." Reflecting on the experience, Rebecca says, "There are controversies about baptizing children so young in Baptist churches, but I have never regretted that because, to me the part that I understood very clearly was that God loved me and that my response in baptism was my way of responding to God's love and saying that I loved God, too."

Although she didn't attend church regularly after her family dropped out, Rebecca found ways each summer to attend Sunshine Baptist Camp for girls with a friend. Her initial "sense of call" came while "listening to the missionaries." She recalls, "Like lots of Baptist women, I thought I was being called to be a missionary because I knew I wanted to do those kinds of things, and the only place that women got to do them was on the mission field." A deeper sense of calling came for Rebecca during high school when she attended Youth Builders, a Christian camp focused on improving living conditions for low-income families. Her first summer she participated in building an outhouse, fitting a house for running water, repairing steps, and fixing a leaking roof. Rebecca said she learned "two very powerful things" that summer. First, the mission field no longer existed only in a foreign country. She witnessed "people living in those conditions *right next to me*." Additionally, she felt for the first time a "sense that God was using me to do something about it." Each evening campers participated in theological reflection about their ministry by gathering in a "fish bowl." A small group of people described the day's experiences while others listened. She found the theological reflections "powerful," and for the first time she also met Christian adults who "live it out . . . Monday through Saturday." Rebecca returned for several summers and says the camp helped propel her into "full-time Christian service."[8]

Rebecca started college at Mercer University amid high expectations from her mother that she achieve the greatest possible success in terms of grades. Her mom dropped out of college to put her father through school before they divorced, when Rebecca was a toddler. The expectations for college success rested with greater weight on Rebecca's shoulders than on those of her siblings.[9] During her freshman year, Rebecca's father and stepmother divorced. Rebecca says she was "just devastated" and recalls, "I just fell apart. I was completely, utterly hysterical." Because she was so young when her parents divorced, the second divorce opened up "grieving both divorces at once."

The news of the divorce came from Rebecca's stepmother, with whom she shared a positive relationship. As the loss unfolded, Rebecca says she experienced "an incredibly graceful thing," gaining clarity about her family. Her stepmom told Rebecca stories about her dad's life and his relationship with his first family. She learned that he remained distant in hopes of making space for her as a young child to adjust to the new blended family with her mom and stepdad. She also learned that her grandmother had tapped her dad to be a pastor: "She told him God was calling him into the ministry and that he would be miserable his whole life if he didn't do it." However, Rebecca says her dad did not in fact have that calling, yet whenever "he was struggling or miserable," he wondered. Laughing, Rebecca wonders if her grandmother was "a generation off!" Although her grandmother didn't live to see Rebecca as a pastor, her grandfather did live that long, and he was "very, very proud." The family stories clarified Rebecca's identity and made her father's life more intelligible.

In college Rebecca sampled various Christian groups and then joined the Baptist Student Union, continuing the mission work and ministry that fostered in her "a real sense of the power of God working through me and other people's lives." Engaging in ministry kept alive for Rebecca "the basic idea of letting myself be used by God." Her sophomore year she sensed a call to attend seminary, a choice Rebecca's father didn't understand. He wanted her to have a marketable job, so seminary left him "completely flabbergasted." Rebecca's mother was more supportive of seminary and ministry, but she did not want Rebecca "going off to be a missionary in a foreign country." The epiphanies lingered from Sunshine Baptist Camp and Youth Builders, and missionary work looked to Rebecca like "the only way" women might "live out . . . a calling in Baptist life." She was not certain about a career or vocation, but the call to seminary was clear.

Prior to Rebecca's graduating class at Mercer, students went almost automatically to Southern Baptist schools to study for ministry. However, in the late 1980s, Southern Baptist seminary boards of trust shifted power from autonomist to biblicist party leaders and faculties retreated.[10] Southern Baptist Theological Seminary in Louisville, Kentucky, admitted Rebecca and offered a scholarship, and then, she says, "the bottom just fell out . . . literally." She recalls, "My friends who graduated in 1988 went to Southern." But when she graduated in 1989, not one of her "compatriots" went to an SBC seminary. The reason was clear: "Students at those schools stopped saying, 'Come! Help us fight this battle.' And started saying, 'It's over. Don't bother.'" The "obvious choice" was suddenly not so obvious, and Rebecca needed to find a "new pathway" to seminary. As graduates of SBC seminaries, her professors didn't want their students to give up on the SBC schools, and Rebecca notes that "they were not one damn bit helpful" in her crisis to find the right school. She doesn't blame them, however, for "having a harder time giving it up." Rebecca's generation, including those "fully immersed in Southern Baptist life, . . . were not as invested as the older generation." The new generation said with Rebecca, "Okay, it's over. We're out of here. What's next?"

When she graduated from college, Rebecca says, "I was twenty-one years old and I just didn't have any clue." She was also "absolutely exhausted from school." Exhaustion and the need to find a new seminary prompted Rebecca to take a year away from studies. She worked and lived at home, saved money, and enjoyed friends and volunteering at her church. In that year off, Rebecca "found her new place" and enrolled at Crowder Seminary. Perceptively, she recalls the larger context: the school was unprepared when "suddenly all the Baptist seminaries go to hell and there are one hundred Baptist students all knocking at the door saying, 'We need a place to go to seminary' [chuckling]. So they didn't know what to do with us."[11]

Rebecca's choice of Crowder was one of convenience and not "blinding revelation." Soon Rebecca discovered several major challenges. Located at a research university, the school's atmosphere was nothing like Mercer. Rebecca was shocked when the school denied tenure for two of her favorite professors. She felt frustrated by the lack of personal connection with professors and the lack of intellectually demanding curriculum for ministry students like herself, who excelled at religious studies in college. The most basic shortcoming for Rebecca was the lack of "good preparation for working in the church."

Rebecca assessed that far too many of her professors taught with disdain for "working in churches." Rebecca says she received a "very clear message that congregants are the enemy and seminary was all about defending yourself against this enemy." Professors portrayed laypeople as "country bumpkins" who would reject everything taught in seminary. They taught her that church consisted primarily of "adversarial relationships," a portrayal Rebecca deeply resents. She walked away from seminary with a need "to unlearn a lot of stuff."[12]

Rebecca found the "best preparation for working in the church" in two courses: one on grief and one on preaching. A local Rabbi who "worked in a congregation with people that he loved" taught students how to "pastor people who were grieving." He showed students his faith and tradition and how to make use of them, translating what would be appropriate from the Christian tradition. Rebecca spent "years dreading and avoiding" the required preaching class.[13] But when she finally took the class, Rebecca says, "an amazing, astounding thing happened. . . . My classmates and my professor . . . said that I had a *gift* for preaching. I was shocked."

Seminary was also a time when two significant relationships unfolded for Rebecca: a college friendship with her future husband, Daniel, blossomed into a lasting relationship, and she discovered Montrose Hill Baptist Church. The church offered support for her ministry preparations and a sanctuary for her fears surrounding the crisis of her brother's Gulf War deployment. Rebecca says she learned about good preaching by listening to Pastor Clyde's sermons. She also found collegial relationships with all the church staff. Montrose Hill is where her "preparation for church work really happened." And worship became urgent and essential to her well-being. She would "literally get through every week" by anticipating how her church would pray for her "brother and other soldiers *and* for the Iraqis." Sometimes she would weep through the entire service. Worship, she asserts, helped her maintain her sanity. Never before or since, says Rebecca, has the church been "so absolutely necessary to my survival."

Rebecca's transition from seminary to work was complicated and strained by several major life changes. She says as a "hyper-responsible person" she recognized she "might have a hard time finding a job," thus she decided to start her search a year before graduation. In October she was engaged to Daniel, who supported Rebecca in her call to ministry and was "on the same wavelength" with many values. He occasionally wore a T-shirt that read "Real Men Marry Preachers." In November she interviewed for a position at Winstead Baptist Church, and in January she began part time there, commuting in her final spring semester at Crowder. Meanwhile she was planning a wedding and preparing for ordination.

About her new ministry at Winstead, a theologically liberal urban congregation in the southeastern United States, Rebecca recalls, "There were no lightning flashes about this job. I'm a Baptist woman in ministry. I'm incredibly liberal. And this was a job I could find." She knew she needed to be "realistic" and would not take a job she "actively disliked" or felt inadequate to perform. Rebecca says, "I clearly took it with the idea of this is what is possible." She spoke honestly with the committee, saying she didn't feel a specific calling to youth ministry, nor did she plan to do that work for an entire career. Rebecca and Daniel married the weekend after graduation. Montrose Hill Baptist Church ordained Rebecca a few weeks later. She stepped up her work at Winstead to full time that summer. She and Daniel bought a house and moved in October to close a year of transitions.

Winstead Baptist Church offered a great deal of space and freedom for Rebecca to test her pastoral gifts and skills. The church was without a permanent senior pastor most of her five and a half years on staff, and no interim minister was in place when Rebecca began her pastoral work. The church brought in a series of temporary preachers over an extended time. For Rebecca this meant "pretty much anything I wanted to do, ministry-wise, there was room for me to do. So I said, 'I want to help lead worship.' They said, 'Great.' I said, 'I want to preach.' They said, 'Oh good.' I said, 'I want to visit the hospitals.' They said, 'Perfect.'" In the absence of a senior pastor, Rebecca grew quickly in pastoral practice. The church's long and imposing history of strong preachers fostered confidence in Rebecca as she "cut her teeth" in Winstead's pulpit. She calls preaching at Winstead a "trial by fire," and through generous congregational affirmations, it was also a "great gift." She said to herself, "If I can preach here I can preach anywhere." Very little in the way of preaching intimidates Rebecca.

Youth ministry filled Rebecca's day-to-day responsibilities. When the search committee hired her, they asked her to remain as long as possible because the church's history included a high turnover with youth ministers. In that work she struggled with divergent parental expectations, competing and "inflated" comparisons with neighboring churches about overseas travel and mission trips, and a subtle competition over who put on the "best retreat programs." Rebecca believes "all the controversies in the church play out in every department," especially in the youth department. She saw the overall perfectionism of the church as a dominating factor in both youth ministry and worship.

Rebecca's ministry at Winstead began a few months after a longtime senior pastor retired. During the interim period, the congregation learned "all at once" about years of past sexual indiscretions by staff ministers, which had remained mostly hidden.[14] Rebecca sums up the revelations this way: "So there was an awful lot that had been swept under the rug for a long time that came to light, and it was an immensely painful time." From inside the church system Rebecca was able to see how the brokenness was perpetuated. Having a really strong senior pastor allowed the problem to stay hidden. The pastor could say to another staff person, "I understand that this [indiscretion, extra marital affair, etc.] has happened, and I think it's time for you to move on. And you can stay here until you find a new position." Rebecca notes that it was "a real systems problem and yet nobody in the church knew about it."[15]

The next senior pastor who came on board stayed less than two years. In Rebecca's estimation he was exceptionally winsome but unprepared for the expectations of a church accustomed to a powerful, assertive leader in both the pulpit and behind the scenes in all the decision-making arenas of the church. In fact, Rebecca says the "church turned on him the week he started." A consultant helped her see the dynamic of the situation. He told her the church "brought in this senior minister and immediately emasculated him, so . . . you couldn't have somebody screwing the church again." From the whole experience, Rebecca says, "I learned a lot. It was painful."

One of the lessons Rebecca learned was how to be more supportive to those in her care. When she first arrived and the revelations were just becoming public, an older colleague advised Rebecca to choose sides. Later she saw her choice to take a side as "a real mistake." Although Rebecca says she would "never defend sexual misconduct," she also saw how the congregation "mistreated and mishandled" the situation, giving another minister a "raw deal."[16] She says she acted "rebelliously in taking his side against the church." Her early mistake was not in being supportive to her colleague, she notes, but rather in "defining myself over against and taking a side." When the new senior pastor was forced out four years later, Rebecca says she didn't make it a secret that she supported him. However, she was more "balanced" in her efforts "to help people on both sides and help people through the whole process."

Rebecca says Winstead is also "a place where sexism is so entrenched that people don't even notice it." Although she doesn't think of herself as "a real flaming feminist," she detested the sexism. Once in a staff meeting about new church directories someone said, "I think we should put e-mail addresses in it." Rebecca said, "I think we should put women's phone numbers in it." When another staff member asked, "What are you talking about?" Rebecca pointed out the missing work phone numbers of female church members, something the staffer had never noticed. When the new directories arrived, Rebecca noted a hierarchy of organization. On the first page: "all white men." On the next page: the "Minister of Youth and Children and Preschool. They are all white women." Then, Rebecca continues, "flip the page and there are all the people of color who clean the church." She found the arrangement both telling and deeply frustrating.

After four years Rebecca felt her time as youth minister coming to a close. The timing coincided with the new senior minister's firing, however, making it a bad time to "jump ship." She stayed for another eighteen months until the new interim pastor sat her down to say, "We really think you ought to be doing something else." Although Rebecca found his words painful, she also knew it was "really true," and she wanted to try something new. After announcing she was leaving and agreeing to a two-month transition, Rebecca sat down one evening at a deacons' meeting. The chair of the deacons said, "You know, if we're going to get somebody good in this [youth ministry] position, we're going to have to pay a lot more money." All Rebecca could think was, "Thank you so much for that ringing endorsement!"

Salaries remained secretive, yet Rebecca could make an educated guess that the men on staff earned "at least twice" her salary. Church leaders argued it was based on the position, but Rebecca thought, "Well, isn't it a great coincidence that only women are in these positions that you underpay, so that you would have to go out and pay somebody 'a lot more money if you were going to get somebody *good'*?" The next youth minister only stayed a few months. Rebecca coped with her frustrations by staying "wryly bemused" rather than spending her life energy "being pissed off" with the church.

Rebecca says her time at Winstead was "interesting" and full of "really good experiences . . . and wonderful people." Although she was able to do "some good things in youth ministry," she found it "hard being in a position where my gifts were clearly not a great fit." Because of the turmoil and her "very high sense of responsibility," Rebecca says, "I stayed longer than I meant to and longer than I probably should have." Eventually she came to "a point of peace about it," concluding she "probably did as good a job as anybody would have done under the circumstances." Although she gave two months of notice to the congregation, Rebecca departed "without knowing what was next." Despite her usual need to have a plan in place, Rebecca said it was also "one of those times where I felt like I was totally doing the right thing." Within a few months she began working with Habitat for Humanity, allowing her to utilize her gifts in managing, planning, organizing, and speaking.

Looking back, Rebecca notes that "the times that I've been able to feel like I'm in the right place at the right time, that I'm doing what I'm supposed to be doing, that's a very sustaining belief for me." One of the most sustaining experiences has been "the knowledge that wherever I am, I'm being the role model that our generation didn't have." Rebecca says one of her "very favorite possessions in the world" is a church bulletin from a Sunday when she preached. A church member "noticed two young girls sitting behind her in church passing notes back and forth." After the service the church member scooped up the note, which read, "What I love about this church is that a girl preached today. Girl power!" Reading it reminded Rebecca: "No girls will grow up in this church believing women can't preach because they have seen it."

"I hope that I'm good at what I do," says Rebecca, "and that there's some sense in which the fact that I do it is almost more important: just to embody that feminine role." During the first interim time at Winstead, Rebecca found herself presiding at communion. "It didn't seem like any big deal to me, and yet elderly women came up to me in tears saying that they had never known how powerful it would be to sit there and watch a woman play that role," she says. "I really am sustained with the thought that I represent something that's beyond me." She adds, "It's like this message of you're okay because somebody like you is standing in the pulpit. I do find that very sustaining thing, a very graceful thing. It's not important that it's *me*, but something beyond me." She says, "One of the privileges we have as ministers is to represent things, and no one of us can represent all that needs to be represented, but it's a very powerful thing for me when I'm able to do that. I think it's sustaining to me to have some basic congruence between what I'm doing and what I think is important."

Redeeming Humanity through Struggle and Sustenance

The struggles, tensions, and graces of Rebecca's life are unique to her and yet powerfully illuminating for the struggles of every Baptist and the tensions that played out corporately in the schism. Baptist clergywomen's narratives interpret the SBC schism as a deeply spiritual, theological, and gendered struggle over what it means to be human. The stories reveal the work of God's redemption in and through their lives in multiple ways. Within the Baptist ethos, longstanding tensions regarding the questions of being human are deeply entrenched and play themselves out in each generation. Sometimes autonomists and biblicists polarized the tensions; at other times they resonated in surprising ways.

Moments in Rebecca's story show the spiritual and theological character of both the brokenness and redemption of humanity. The contradictory messages of belonging and alienation received in Rebecca's childhood illuminate the Baptist struggle over the significance and meaning of vulnerability in the human experience. From her baptism at age six, Rebecca's participation in very human struggles and losses caught her up and intertwined her with experiences of God's sustaining presence through loss and grief. Coming to clarity of calling and finding God's sustenance was accomplished amid her family crisis and the "bottom dropping out" of the Baptist world.

Rebecca's work at Winstead was an unsettling mix of profound learning in ministry and living within the harmful effects of sexism and racism, demonstrating how gender animates both personal and ecclesial efforts to nurture fully human lives of purpose and meaning. Like other clergywomen, Rebecca's presence and perception of the situation highlighted the explicitly gendered character of church brokenness. Over time she learned to confront that human brokenness and to participate knowingly and intentionally in the redemption of humanity through God's sustaining presence.

Each of Rebecca's stories is juxtaposed with sermons and essays by ten noted Southern Baptist preachers in the 1970s, 1980s, and 1990s. The words and events of both autonomists and biblicists, when read alongside Rebecca's story, reveal the abiding spiritual and theological struggles over what it means to be human. These perennial questions of the human condition took on particular forms as they appeared in the very fabric of the schism. Taking time to focus on each theme, and seeing how the struggles appear in the everyday preparations, practice, and participation in ministry, leads to a new interpretation of the Baptist struggle. At its deepest theological point, schism in the SBC was an opportunity for Baptists to face their brokenness over the meaning of human being, and to participate with vulnerability, clarity, and purpose in the sustaining and redeeming presence of God.

From their beginnings in the seventeenth century, Baptists navigated questions of power and vulnerability by imposing a hierarchy of values on human relationships. Baptists reflected wider and older cultural and religious traditions of the West: men hold greater power and significance than women, adults hold more than children, and people of European descent hold more than "people of color" or non-Europeans. Wealth and privilege trump poverty and vulnerability. Such tacit forms of supremacy and racism, patriarchy, sexism, and classism, however, are not the full story. A liberating and equalizing impulse was also born into the Baptist ethos, showing up in early readings and interpretations of Scripture that challenged the systematic oppressions of the state church in seventeenth-century England. The Baptist impulses toward liberty and equality fostered in each generation a piety of vulnerability (to God and people). Liberty and equality remained key to confronting prevailing social norms of gender, race, and class, although rarely did Baptists realize the implications. On the whole Baptists in America adopted the same enlightenment projects of equality, which gave birth to the democratization of religion, religious and political feminism, and other theologies and politics of justice. Yet Southern Baptists fell prey to the cultural oppressions of American slavocracy, becoming unwitting defenders of a piety of power.[17] The ensuing struggles carried on a centuries-old wrestling match over what it means to be human, in other words, to what end one lives in the freedom and liberation of Christ.

Rebecca learned what it means to be human in two clear but contradictory childhood messages: "I was important and worthwhile and loveable" and "I was inferior and my family didn't fit in." She saw what women did and didn't do in church, perceptions she received by "osmosis" and internalized as both "God's sustaining love" and her own "female inferiority." As a young person doing mission work, she learned more explicitly about the requirements of vulnerability for a fully human and faithful life. Yet this central theological task remains a double-edged sword for women. To trust God's sustenance and the power of "being in the right place" is to risk new vulnerabilities of change and loss when one is already vulnerable. The question of how to become fully human was not mainly existential for clergywomen like Rebecca. It was a practical, everyday confrontation with the dilemmas of vulnerability, grief, and loss in the web of life and leadership in ministry. Rebecca's quest to embrace her full humanity mirrors dynamics in the larger Baptist struggle for power and control in the SBC, a struggle at its heart about the meaning of being human.

At the height of Baptist adversity in mid-1980s, two pastoral teachers captured different understandings of vulnerability in the Christian life. In 1985 Paige Patterson was president of Criswell College in Dallas, Texas, and Molly Truman Marshall was a newly hired professor of theology at the Southern Baptist Theological Seminary in Louisville, Kentucky. Each pastoral academic played a significant role in the unfolding schism: Patterson, together with Judge Paul Pressler, was one of the chief architects of the biblicist plan to take control of the apparatus of the SBC.[18] Marshall was an organizer of Southern Baptist Women in Ministry, an advocate for women's ordination, and targeted by biblicists to be removed from the Southern faculty. In 2003 Patterson became president of Southwestern Baptist Theological Seminary, a flagship SBC school. In 2004 Marshall became president of Central Baptist Theological Seminary, which is aligned with American Baptists and the Cooperative Baptist Fellowship.

In the spring of 1985, Patterson, emerging as an outspoken leader of the biblicist party, wrote passionately about the theological struggle for meaning in the six-year-long tussle with autonomists. He believed the schism might allow space to confront the "apparent impasse" between parties. "Controversy has been an ever-present accompaniment of Christianity," he argued.[19] Although "some bad resulted" from controversial events, Patterson saw "infinitely more good" coming from them, including "greater understanding, sharper definition, increased evangelistic fervor and, most of all, fervent and humble supplication to God for His intervention in the affairs of men." He suggested that the "present controversy . . . may result in the demise of the Convention as we know it, but more likely, it will yield to an epoch of unprecedented growth and to a renewal of Baptist doctrinal commitment."[20]

Patterson named the losses and vulnerability he felt as a pastor, "sometimes threatened, sometimes ostracized by the 'establishment.'" He described his theological frustration and hurt as "one who believes in the realities of heaven and hell and in the substitutionary atonement of Jesus as the only way men can be saved from eternal condemnation." The most painful loss was "the spectacle of formerly aggressive evangelistic young ministers no longer interested in the plight of the lost." Patterson blamed the loss of zeal on historical-critical methods of study, which undercut "confidence in the accuracy of the Bible."[21] With both the meaning and accuracy of Scriptures on in the line, biblicists perceived these life-and-death matters worth the fight. Reducing the schism to a "battle for the Bible" does not capture the feelings of threat felt by biblicists regarding the familiar ways of thinking, believing, and living. They clung to a piety of power because it yielded a way of life they wanted to maintain.

Through the 1980s, Marshall emerged as a key player in the controversies, teaching, writing, and preaching in support of women's ordination. When biblicists gained control of board at Southern, they elected Albert Mohler president. He threatened Marshall with heresy charges, and she was forced from the faculty in 1994, despite having earned tenure in 1988.[22]

When Marshall preached at a pre-SBC meeting in Dallas in 1985, it was to nearly five hundred men and women at the third annual gathering of SBWIM. She posed a question at the heart of the search for theological meaning: "What are we to be about during these storm-tossed days as Baptists?"[23] She declared support for "the role of women in ministry" and called the meeting itself prophetic. Then she turned to deeper concerns: "We hunger for direction in what it means to be the people of God at this critical juncture in the life of our respective churches and in our convention as a whole. We long for our rhetoric to become enfleshed in constructive, transforming actions. Yet many of us feel powerless and voiceless even in the face of God's beckoning Spirit." Marshall lamented the struggle of "manifesting the Christian graces in the face of injustice, unrighteousness and hopelessness."[24] Her sermon reached for the paradox of living a meaningful life in the face of adversity.

Marshall named a challenge felt by many autonomists: "When we 'put on Christ,' we are committing our lives to a different form of change agency that requires our vulnerability."[25] The more progressive among the autonomists believed the SBC struggle was a place where vulnerability and change went hand in hand. Even when engaging directly and forcefully in the politics of the struggle, they pursued a piety of vulnerability that would lead to "inevitable conflict that following Jesus incurs."[26] Marshall urged listeners "to implement the gospel fully" and "not be afraid."[27] To Marshall and others, implementation meant the full inclusion of women in the church. The call also meant increased vulnerability, greater criticism, and political losses for the autonomist party, as well as greater risk to clergywomen, including Marshall.[28]

Both Patterson and Marshall voiced a central task and drive for humanity: to seek meaning and purpose for human existence.[29] Patterson emphasized vulnerability as a result of unwelcomed losses to a way of belief and life. Marshall's vulnerability lamented losses, but she also extended it into a call to authenticity and planned risk on the way to fuller inclusion for women in the church. Squarely at the middle of the Southern Baptist world, and precisely within its brokenness and schism, stood the question of what it means to be human and how the human condition should or ought to embody power and vulnerability.[30]

Previous interpretations of the schism do not appreciate the centrality or struggle over questions of vulnerability, risk, and loss. Rebecca's story is one caught up precisely in the basic human task of finding and making meaning. Like Patterson and Marshall, she laments the vulnerability of loss in her feelings of female inferiority. She also reaches for the constructive gifts of vulnerability in trusting God that she was "in the right place."[31] Rebecca's lived theology, and the articulations of Marshall and Patterson, show how the schism was a forum for profoundly personal and widespread corporate struggles over the character and meaning of being human. The role of vulnerability in that struggle was shaped by different understandings of gender. The desire to settle these questions animated the struggles on both sides. Despite the open drama, conflict, and anxiety, the schism of Southern Baptists was also a generative context for the work of becoming human. It was in Rebecca's words, "the right place," where many wrestled not only with each other but also with God to squeeze out a more blessed—and vulnerable—sense of living a fully human life. In this space Rebecca and others found "gifts they didn't expect, didn't want, and never anticipated."

Believers' baptism is the central theological practice in Southern Baptist history and polity.[32] The ritual practice brings together sin and salvation, and in Baptist history it is replete with fights over its meaning, the fitting age of believers, and its function in communal belonging and church discipline.[33] Baptism shapes public and personal Baptist identity. Theologically baptism becomes a focal point holding together dispute and love, struggle and sustenance. In the protracted controversy between biblicists and autonomists, minor disputes over baptism broke out, but in a larger sense the entire schism was yet another predicament over love and belonging—to God and to each other.

Rebecca's stories, from her earliest memories of church, embody both the struggle and sustenance of being a Baptist. As a child Rebecca experienced both the welcome of God's love, on one hand, and the lack of belonging for her family and her divorced parents on the other hand. As an adult Rebecca sees how being baptized at six was part of a "controversy about baptizing children so young." Yet she feels no regret: "I understood very clearly that God loved me and that my response in baptism was my way of responding to God's love and saying that I loved God, too." Rebecca's baptism also held hidden and reinforcing dynamics of gender.[34] Her visual and embodied memory of "layers and layers and layers" of frills and the cold waters of immersion seal together a baptismal promise of love and also reinforce the inferiority message about her gender. For Rebecca, love and belonging are sealed with inferiority and dispute. Her embodiment of struggle and sustenance mirrors the perennial Baptist disputes over love and belonging that animated schism in the SBC.

In June 1983, prior to the SBC annual gathering in Pittsburgh, Pennsylvania, at the first meeting of SBWIM, Nancy Hastings Sehested, associate pastor at Oakhurst Baptist Church in Atlanta, Georgia, preached, "Our spiritual pilgrimage as women is like the lives of our spiritual ancestors. As the Hebrews passed out of bondage and slavery in Egypt, there was great anticipation, great excitement, a vision of new lives and new possibilities. A new land. A new place." Sehested captured the sense of possibility that spread as a growing number of Southern Baptist women voiced a calling to ministry. She turned immediately, however, to the difficulties of that call: "The expectation and vision of a new place, a new way of living, came crashing into the experience of the desert."[35]

Sehested also compared clergywomen to new Gentile converts in Paul's day: "We live in the great in-between time. We are ready, but still waiting. We are called but not confirmed. We are trained, but not employed. We are willing, but not able." Her litany also captured the worries of the day over women's ordination: "Pastors tell us their congregations are not yet ready and able to accept us. Congregations tell us their pastors are not yet ready and able to accept us." She continued: "Our calling is clear, and our gifts are manifest. But the desert is a severe, unforgiving place." After recounting stories of women who gave up or moved on to other denominations, she said, "We can't fully understand why we stay, although all of us would have some partial reasons. The deepest reason is not fully fathomable. The best we can say is that this is where we're called to be. And that's enough." Sehested's account echoes Rebecca's feeling that even when she felt mired in struggle, she could know she was in the place God called her to be.

Just days after Sehested preached at SBWIM, across the city of Pittsburgh, James T. Draper Jr., delivered in the presidential address to the annual meeting of the SBC, which registered 10,603 messengers.[36] Draper, pastor of First Baptist Church in Euless, Texas, preached, "Wherever we [Southern Baptists] have gone we have been used of the Holy Spirit to change the face of the world for the better. We have been that special kind of people because we are a people of DEEP BELIEFS AND CONVICTIONS. We have made a firm commitment of Biblical principles . . . for which principles our forefathers even dared to die. We carry these beliefs in the spirit of Christ and in obedience to the Word of God. Only people with such commitment can become God's change agents in a sin-cursed world." He reviewed a list of "deep beliefs" central for Southern Baptists, including "the full humanity and full deity of Jesus Christ, the lostness of mankind, substitutionary atonement, justification by God's grace through faith, holiness of life, and the urgency of mission." Draper placed doctrinal belief and conviction on the highest plane, declaring all else "heresy."[37]

Rebecca's story of baptism and sense of God's presence and sustenance, like Sehested's and Draper's sermons, capture ways each Baptist argument and struggle to belong was interwoven with an enduring sense of sacred presence. The season of schism for Southern Baptists was no different. Dispute over right practice (Sehested's "calling and gifts" for ministry) versus right belief (Draper's "deep convictions") animated much of the controversy over women's ordination and pastoral leadership. Gender was a major point of struggle and an ever-present factor in Baptist history, yet the questions about gender became more explicit as more women asked for ordination and more churches called them to pastoral ministry. Despite the struggles and theological name-calling, an unfathomable presence, like the love Rebecca felt in her baptismal moment, sustained clergywomen through that time. Such powerful sustaining moments, captured by preachers on both sides of the controversy, held together deep conviction even through controversy and even through wilderness. These profound moments show how the entire schism participated in an enduring struggle over what it means to be human, to belong and yet to be left on one's own, to live in wilderness and yet to be sustained.

Creating and discovering who one is and what personal or communal meaning one can make of life are among the chief existential tasks of late modernism in the West.[38] Baptists, in their modified Calvinist beliefs and pragmatic worldview, are conversant in the individual and communal work of finding or prescribing vocation and responding with life-changing action. In the twentieth century, the question of calling in the SBC was a highly individualistic and moralistic one.[39] However, toward the end of the century, questions of call and the centrality of vocation rose into greater consciousness when women began to claim a Baptist piety of calling and the vocation of ministry for themselves.[40]

Entering college was one of the major life events that gave Rebecca the feeling that "this was where God meant for me to be." That sense of being in the right place also accompanied her call to work for Habitat for Humanity and the calls to marriage and parenthood. Other callings were less clear and full of challenges. Yet Rebecca says she found clarity in those situations through "knowing that this was my calling for right now." She began to recognize a pattern in her life of feeling "sustained through the difficulties," reaffirming her calling for each place and time. Even in her certainty of calling to Mercer, Rebecca found herself "devastated . . . falling apart . . . utterly hysterical" when she learned that her father was divorcing a second time. The grief was compounded by the earlier missed opportunity to grieve her parents' first divorce when she was a toddler. Rebecca learned from her stepmother about her father's lifelong struggle with his mother's hopes that he would become a minister. She found some ease in the story by thinking perhaps her grandmother's vision "missed a generation." The pastoral call was more evidently hers and not her dad's. Sorting through the family stories and working through grief became a surprising source of comfort and personal clarity.

When pastors of large congregations ran for SBC president, they became spokespersons for the autonomist or biblicist parties, often calling for renewed purpose and direction, consolidating each group, and articulating differences. Considered "theologically conservative but politically nonaligned," Daniel Vestal joined the SBC Peace Committee in 1985.[41] After a year spent hoping for reconciliation between the parties, Vestal concluded, "Only one side really wanted reconciliation. . . . The Fundamentalists only desired control, total control, absolute control, and they wanted no participation except with those who had that same desire." By 1987 Vestal had decided that "shared decision making, open communication, acceptance of diversity were gone." In his estimation, "a political machine that governed committee appointments, trustee selection, platform speeches, and even floor debate" had replaced the former ways, and he left the 1987 St. Louis convention "in a state of depression and grief."[42] For three more years Vestal worked for reconciliation on the Peace Committee, but to no avail. At the urging of autonomists, Vestal stood for election as SBC president in Las Vegas in 1989 and again in New Orleans in 1990. He was defeated both times.

Vestal ran against incumbent Jerry Vines in 1989. Vines and Homer Lindsay Jr. were co-pastors of First Baptist Church of Jacksonville, Florida, a megachurch affiliated with the SBC. The autonomists won not a single presidential election in ten years. The Peace Committee process was widely seen as a failure. Biblicists gained the upper hand in SBC agencies and schools by electing Baptists who agreed that the convention needed a "resurgence of conservative values."[43] Running up to the convention in Las Vegas, rhetoric and accusations escalated on both sides. Vines called for a new focus on "missions and evangelism," asking convention goers to canvass Las Vegas, knocking on the doors of "sin city," in the days prior to the SBC. Nearing the end of his first term, Vines said, "To my view, we have settled the debate over the nature of Scripture.... The theological renewal of our convention is underway. I am confident that our administrations and the boards of trustees of our institutions will lovingly monitor its progress until resolution."[44]

Vines said about all the newly elected biblicist trustees, "I am confident these Bible-believing Southern Baptists will carry out their assignments with the desire that God's will be done in our SBC and without any personal hostilities or private agendas."[45] Meanwhile, at a biblicist party rally prior to the 1989 SBC meeting, one young pastor was quoted as saying, "The rats and skunks are still inside the wall [of the SBC]. Are we just going to leave them there?"[46] The same week Vestal was quoted as saying, "I don't want to make a threat, but if we don't see a significant change soon, the fragmentation which we have seen is just a harbinger of what you will see."[47]

The Southern Baptist "divorce" was messy and contentious. Both sides declared their own innocence and accused the other side of divisiveness and ill will. In New Orleans in 1990, the evening after being soundly beaten, 58 to 42 percent, Vestal gathered friends to call for a new direction, saying, "I sensed this defeat was an end to the Moderate political effort." After twelve years, "people were tired of the conflict."[48]

Vestal addressed a group of autonomists the next morning at a breakfast meeting. He spoke of his deep disappointment, of his inability to provide all the answers, of his assurance they did the right thing. He recalls, "Beyond the sadness and disappointment was a genuine conviction that God was at work." He called for a convocation, which met with "resounding affirmation that the time had come to move beyond political contest and theological debate." He recalls a shared understanding "that the time had come to forge the future, to act instead of react, to find ways to cooperate without sacrificing our Baptist distinctives." He called for healing and a renewal of mission.

Spokespersons for each party spoke in terms of division and renewal. The two parties cast their language differently, yet both experienced limit, loss, and grief, despite the sometimes-triumphal accounts of right and wrong, winners and losers. The decision by autonomists to cut their losses and walk away was simultaneously a genesis of greater clarity, identity, and purpose.[49] Like Rebecca's clarity of calling, which came in the midst of separation, loss, and grief in her family, Southern Baptists also found themselves clarified and renewed, by their own accounts, through the schism.[50]

As in other Christian communities through history, Baptists are fully acquainted with sin and brokenness. And as in other traditions, women in Baptist cultures often bear a larger share of both vulnerability and fault for sins related to sexuality and marriage.[51] Churches and the bureaucratic structures of the SBC participate in a pervasively (and unconsciously) sexist culture. Rhetoric and relational practices of complementarity shaped roles for women as ideally subordinate and disempowered, on one hand, and threatening and troublesome, especially when they stepped outside those roles, on the other hand.[52] This is a double bind for women: remain subordinate to the "authority" of a husband or pastor, but when those men misuse their power, don't defend against the violations to one's personhood, security, or integrity. It is a no-win situation for women. Although less obvious, it is also a no-win situation for men. As clergywomen stepped increasingly into pastoral roles and asserted a desire for shared power, authority, and partnership, their presence challenged the status quo, highlighting problems and abuses already present in culture and churches. This dynamic is a significant feature of the ongoing theological struggle over what it means to be human. For women the question of full acceptance of their humanity and empowerment was on the line. Men felt a dramatic threat to their power and privilege, and more pervasively, yet harder to grasp, was the threat to the wider Baptist system itself.

Human brokenness was not unfamiliar to Rebecca. In her childhood she saw the differences between the work of women and men, messages that came to her by "osmosis." And in college she felt the "bottom fall out" of Baptist life while she was trying to choose a seminary. She lived through grief and loss in her family, including divorce and her brother's wartime deployment. In her first ministry assignment, she was immediately confronted by a longstanding, systemic pattern of sexual infidelity and misuse of power by ministers in the congregation. She witnessed how stories "previously swept under the carpet" came to light "all at once." Her time at Winstead also exposed the hierarchy of gender and race codified in everything from the church directory to secretive salaries and the structuring of church staff. Daily she and the congregation faced the losses and wounds of the community. Revelations of misconduct set the next pastor up for the church to "emasculate" him the first week and fire him in less than two years. When he departed, Rebecca drew on the wisdom of her earlier experience, choosing not to take sides openly. Rather, she offered support to those in pain on all sides of the brokenness and loss. Schism was for many Southern Baptists an opportunity to confront both personal and communal brokenness and loss, and in some cases to offer or receive healing. As women stepped into places previously dominated by men, they exposed troubling kinds of brokenness. Their stories are emblematic of schism as a theological and spiritual struggle over complementarity, *and* they show how women embodied responses to this brokenness, which demanded both God's mercy and communal accountability.

Two sermons by congregational leaders, one autonomist and one biblicist, confront the losses and desires of communities of faith. At the 1990 gathering of the SBC in New Orleans, Fred Wolfe, pastor of Cottage Hill Baptist Church in Mobile, Alabama, delivered the convention sermon. Although the biblicist party was on a twelve-year winning streak and a "conservative resurgence" looked certain, Wolfe still preached a sermon lamenting a decline in churches, nonresident members, low attendance, and divisions resulting from the controversy. He said, "Instead of marching united under the banner of the cross, we label each other moderates, conservatives, fundamentalists, liberals and a host of other names that would not do for publication. We question each other's integrity, character and motives. To use Paul's words, we bite and devour one another. God have mercy on us."[53] He continued, "We must repent of our apathy and luke warmness. We have been content to live without a mighty outpouring of the Spirit of God. Content to try and do it ourselves." He pleaded with his listeners, "These are desperate days in our denomination and our world. This calls for desperate prayer for the wind of God to blow, the breath of God to come."[54]

In 1988 Betty Winstead McGary, one of SBWIM's founders and assistant pastor at Calder Baptist Church in Beaumont, Texas, preached on "Becoming Community" at South Main Baptist Church in Houston, Texas: "Community requires *relationship and respect for others*. This is called intimacy . . . somewhere between closeness and distance. . . . With Christ in the space that is between us."[55] McGary lamented the barriers that prevent community, including "lack of effort," a "desire for sameness and predictability," and "the need to dominate and control." Achieving community requires people "to actively listen to others, to hear and internalize their stories, to see the world through their eyes . . . to become self-aware, to risk our illusions by facing reality and to share ourselves without giving ourselves away."[56] The process in these changes, said McGary, "can be both painful and exciting." Domination of others, she preached, is motivated by "fear that there is not enough and that we must compete and control to assure that our place will be secure and our needs met. . . . Love is snuffed out by dependency. We make alliances of weakness rather than strength. It happens in families. . . . It is happening in our denomination. Against our great heritage as champions of religious freedom, one group has decided that they know what is best for all of us and that their agenda, when accepted by all, will lead to the betterment of our whole society."[57]

Wolfe and McGary both cried out in longing for relationship and in lament over loss of community. Both saw the necessity of God's mercy and presence for healing. Biblicists and autonomists articulated these feelings in different ways. Yet the basic human desire, sometimes desperation, to be with the other underlies the grief over the separation and loss of belonging.[58] In other words, the losses Baptists experienced in the schism were not merely about being right or wrong, an argument over the Bible or doctrine or Baptist principles. Underlying those arguments was a more basic human drive to belong, to be in relationship with the other, to know love and support in a community. This need is theologically grounded in God's creation of humanity for relationship and in the human striving for survival, for meaning, for expressing personal initiative, and for belonging to others in one's daily round of life.[59] Yet so much can derail these human strivings. Everything from discouragement over the demands of knowing others genuinely to dividing up into camps and hurling epithets. McGary and Wolfe mourned the failures of human striving when they described the failures of Baptist community. They each participated in the blame of the other party for its failures of community.

Wolfe and McGary also reached for the courage to recognize beneath all the striving for the other, for shared belonging, for meaning and self-understanding, is a striving for the sacred, for God. Uniting every other desire is a desire for being fully known and beloved.[60] Because the underlying longing is so powerful, the possibility for brokenness and loss and subsequent grief are also powerful.[61] When Southern Baptists split open their institutions and churches with decades of fighting, name-calling, making "alliances of weakness rather than strength," and questioning one another's "character, integrity, and morals," they also harmed the deepest human desires and needs. Rebecca felt these losses profoundly when she could not enroll in the Baptist school she desired, when support from the wider Baptist community was no longer available, and when she found herself in a progressive church still harboring sexism, racism, and communal brokenness. Countless Baptists felt these losses even as their spiritual homes and identities disappeared from under their feet.

In one regard stories like Rebecca's, and sermons like Wolfe's and McGary's, set the schism in a wider context, recasting it as one more expression of the brokenness in the human condition. However, this aspect of the Baptist schism has rarely, if ever, been considered in the analysis of recent decades. Looking through Rebecca's stories, a particular context and character of human brokenness appears. Clergywomen working to find a place, a community in which to belong and contribute, came face to face with brokenness, long hidden in the structures and secrets of churches and denomination. A major task in the spiritual and theological work of becoming fully human requires facing brokenness, pain, and loss in communities, institutional systems, and people who are also connected by love and care. The assumed relational patterns of gender and race contributed to the brokenness and harm present throughout the unfolding drama of schism. The presence of women in places of pastoral power and authority clarified the harms and in some cases opened new opportunities for healing. Clergywomen like Rebecca participated in healing the brokenness in churches (and beyond) through challenging complementarity and offering the sustaining presence of love and reconciliation amid profound loss, grief, and brokenness.

Becoming fully human is founded in the radical hospitality of Christ's table: forgiveness, grace, and a full sense of belonging that sustains life and ministry, heals brokenness and alienation. Historically in Baptist churches, women set the table of fellowship but didn't often sit at the tables of leadership. They could prepare communion but not serve it. Women share in bearing the diversity of God and of creation, yet ritual and liturgical spaces muted or eclipsed their presence in the family of God. When Baptist women received ordination and began serving at the table, they offered a more radical hospitality than the Baptist table had seen.

Rebecca accepted the call at Winstead "with the idea of this is what is possible." Her situated possibility meant she "cut her teeth" in ministry by preaching, leading worship, presiding at communion, visiting the sick, and offering pastoral care in the absence of a permanent full-time pastor. She recalls that the learning process felt like a "trial by fire" and at the same time she was able to overcome the intimidation factor and say, "If I can preach here, I can preach anywhere." Standing in the pulpit as a female role model (something she didn't have), Rebecca says, was an opportunity to know God's sustaining power and to embody a grace she felt was beyond her. Affirmations came in the form of young girls passing notes in worship proclaiming "girl power" and elderly women coming to her in tears, inspired by seeing a woman serve communion. In these moments Rebecca knew God's sustenance and believed she was in the right place.

Two acclaimed Baptist preachers crafted sermons from the creation stories in Genesis illustrating theological problems with gender and its entanglement with what it means to be human from biblicist and autonomist perspectives. In 1979, the year marking the start of the schism, Adrian Rogers, pastor of Bellevue Baptist Church in Memphis, Tennessee, preached at the pre-SBC Pastors' Conference. Then, in the first in a string of biblicist victories, he was elected president of the convention. Rogers's 1979 sermon, "The Great Deceiver," recounted the creation story with humor: "Cain and Abel crawled up and looked over a wall and they saw the Garden of Eden, they hotfooted it back to Adam, and they said, Daddy, we've seen the most beautiful place ... do you think we could ever live in a place like that? Adam said, we did once, boys, before your mother ate us out of house and home."[62] Rogers continued:

> It's not a sin to want to be like God. That's what all of life is all about. We want to be godly. If God had not wanted us to be like him, why did he make us in his image? ... He is right now working to conform me to the image of his son, who is God himself. And it's not a crime to want to be like God. But Satan said, "Eve, you disobey, Eve, you do your own thing, and you will be as God." That is, you'll be a little old cheap tin god of your own making. And right here and now we see Satan's fib about women's lib. It started right at this point. Satan says to Eve, "Eve, I'm going to liberate you. You see, what God had said you ought to do and ought not to do is cramping your style. You have not had the

fulfillment that you ought to have. And Eve, listen, there are great vistas out there, there are marvelous things that you can do. And after all Eve, you only go through life once, grab all the gusto you can."

Rogers said this was Satan's "cleverest lie [sounding] the most like truth." On "women's liberation" he assured listeners he was not a "chauvinist." He preached, "A woman is infinitely superior to a man at being a woman. And . . . a man is infinitely superior to a woman at being a man. And God made us different that he might make us one. Don't ever forget that it was God that made them in the beginning male and female, and God said 'That is good' and this unisex movement has been belched out of hell."[63]

The idea that men and women are infinitely and superiorly different from each other so God might "make us one" is a popular theological justification for complementarity and a biblicist understanding of gender. Rogers stamped his interpretation with God's pronouncement of "good," and he declared any alternative interpretation as Satan's "cleverest lie." By contrast, it is "no crime," he said, to be conformed by God to the image of "his son, who is God himself." However, Rogers turned the tables on Eve. Her initiative was the trouble: her desire for liberation, fulfillment, action, and agency were based on Satan's "lies" and "belched from hell." In 1979 these "claims" expressed by women sounded identical to the "freedoms" men like Rogers had enjoyed unquestioned for centuries. Rogers implied that his obedience to God justified his own ambitions for liberation, fulfillment, action, and agency. However, such ambitions for Eve (or anyone believing in "women's lib") are equivalent to listening to Satan, resulting in punishment and blame. Because of Eve's sins, everyone was thrown from the garden.

In 1988, Cindy Harp Johnson, a founder of SBWIM and a pastor in Maryland, preached from the same text, using the same rhetorical trick to tell the story of Adam and Eve.[64] When Seth asks about the "lush, verdant garden," Adam tells him a "sad story," concluding, "That's where we used to live. But then your mother ate us out of house and home." But Johnson continued: "The world has been a hard place from which to wring a blessing for a woman ever since!" From that day, Johnson said, life choices for women have been "suspect." Singleness raises "speculation that there's something fundamentally wrong . . . like a hairy back, a stone for a heart, or napalm breath in the morning—some hidden affliction that keeps us from being wanted by anybody." Marriage evokes "relief from those who believed that we couldn't have made it on our own." Remaining childless brings accusations of "idolatrous self-interest." And parenthood suggests "wasted marketplace potential." Women working outside the home are blamed as "the downfall of the family" and called names if they take men's jobs. When every possible option for women is "under suspicion," said Johnson, then we might consider "that the options themselves are the problem."[65]

Redeeming Humanity

In her sermon Johnson addressed the problem by turning to Jesus, who "redefined" the measure of "blessedness." Jesus offered blessings not to "those who fulfill arbitrary roles imposed on them for simplicity or convenience" but to "those who choose to fulfill the will of God." She interpreted *adam* in Genesis 1:26–28 as a plural noun for all people. From this rereading she argued for three ways women (and men) fulfill God's will: (1) through being a "reflection of God" in "rationality, moral choice, responsible action, and self-transcendence"; (2) through their capacity for a "relationship with God"; and (3) in their "partnership" with each other. Johnson carefully reinterpreted the second creation story in which God brings Eve to Adam as an *ezer,* which she rendered not "helper" or "helpmeet" but "divine help" in the form of partnership.[66]

In their sermons, both Rogers and Johnson addressed a theology of being human through what it means to be male and female. The questions they addressed remained ever-present in the years of Baptist struggle. Both preachers cast woman as a problem—*the problem.* However, Rogers confirmed woman as the problem when Eve listened to "Satan's lies" and tried to embody the characteristics assumed for a man, including her desire for liberation, fulfillment, and agency. Johnson shifted the logic from *woman as the problem* to *sexism as the problem.* Autonomists like Johnson preached, prayed, and argued for the full humanity of women and for partnership as the paradigmatic intent of Jesus, an ideal for human relationship between male and female. Biblicists like Rogers held out for complementarity and the asymmetrical shape of power, which continued both subtly and explicitly to cast women in subordinate roles then blame and punish them for the sins of upsetting an order established by God.

Both sermons wrestle with thorny double binds women face, whether unwittingly or knowingly. Women are understood as both cause and victim of fighting in the SBC. And women and men who work to challenge sexism are beset by entrenched sexism at every turn. The situation is nearly impossible to escape in the late modern Western world in which these pastors lived and preached. However, women themselves do not live as if they are a problem. Pastors like Rebecca demonstrate how clergywomen live and work creatively, making the most of situated possibility.

In a fundamentally new historical moment, Rebecca presided at Christ's table, and old women saw visions of themselves fully included and young women dreamed dreams of belonging and empowerment.[67] Women and girls felt sustained in faith by ministers like Rebecca, who were in the right place and time. They experienced, tasted, and witnessed a new belonging to the family of God, sustained by God's grace and divine help at work in women like Rebecca. Through God's sustaining presence, clergywomen redeemed the story of Eve and the story of Baptists. Although blamed for "eating us out of house and home," these women stood at the table offering radical hospitality, serving the bread of life and cup of a new covenant. Even as God sustained women like Rebecca, assuring her she was in the right place at the right time, her life and ministry inspired the visions of girls and boys and dreams of old women and men, who longed for a place at the table. Rebecca's life and ministry was wringing a blessing in the midst of a wider Baptist struggle over what it means to be human, a struggle that animated the years of schism and pressed toward a more vulnerable and redeemed life. Her story reinterprets the schism as more than a political war over meaning of the Bible or doctrine. Rather, it was a deeply spiritual and theological struggle over the meaning of life itself.

What sustained Rebecca in ministry and kept her going even through wilderness moments, when the flaws and foibles of the church were so blatant, was her vision for embodying "a basic congruence" between what she was doing and what she thought was important. In her preaching and practice of ministry, including her missteps, she was living toward a new way to be human, which was recognizable and identifiable to those who experienced it. What sustained Rebecca was seeing and living and preaching a redeemed way to be human. It was not that she won the theological struggle: it was not a contest with clear winners and losers. Rather, her life was a testament to the living truth of her full humanity, an incarnate word made flesh. Clergywomen entering places of ministry during the years of Southern Baptist schism were not merely symbols held up by the parties, nor were they marginalized through alienation or hostility from the Baptist context. They were also empowered in the right place and time to bring needed, graceful change to the world they served. They embodied something new, and their lives and stories offer powerful reinterpretations of Southern Baptist schism as both a psychological and theological struggle over the identity and humanity of Baptists, as well as a space for a newly emerging theology and practice of ministry.

5

Reimagining Ministry

How Clergywomen Reinterpret Schism and Remake Baptist Identity

> There's a sense of freedom, as a Baptist woman, that's important. For me, the issues of soul competency and priesthood of the believer have always been important. And as I continue on my own journey, I'm realizing how very crucial that is. A huge part of pastoring for me is making sure that I'm nurturing my own personal relationship with God and helping church members do the same. And through that relationship, encountering Scripture, worshipping and praying together . . . seeking God's presence together.
>
> —Chloe

At twenty-nine, Chloe began pastoring a small Baptist church in Virginia. She grew up attending several prominent Southern Baptist churches in the South. When she entered into an ordination process at the progressive Milesdale Baptist Church, the church invited her to write a discernment paper for herself and the congregation. The paper addressed seven topics: her personal story, education, calling, church, theology, leadership, and being Baptist. That framework guides a retelling of Chloe's story. The particularity of Chloe's story resonates deeply with the stories of other Baptist women in ministry. Read together, these stories offer new ways to understand the Baptist schism.

Chloe's story of practicing ministry reinterprets Baptist schism as a time and space not only for fighting and disagreement but also for reimagining and living into a new theology of ministry. Chloe and other clergywomen improvised the practice of ministry and reshaped Baptist identity in significant ways. From adolescence to adulthood, Chloe found ways of making and discovering meaning that departed from her parents' reliance on rational deliberation and reached instead for embodied, relational, and even mystical ways of experiencing God's purpose in and for her life. Chloe's shift resonated with widespread generational shifts in meaning making, moving away from rational belief and deliberation and giving greater attention to embodied and emotional knowing. These personal and cultural shifts contributed to the contest over what it means to be an authentic Baptist, which was at the heart of the schism. Chloe's story also shows how the era of schism was not only a psychological and cultural battleground but also a playground. In the space of Baptist freedom, Chloe plays with how to understand God's calling and with ways of remaining Baptist, despite the conflict and struggle over how that might be possible. Chloe's ordination highlights how the schism in the SBC was a contest over the reshaping of authority, making way for women to share in pastoral leadership for the first time. The novelty of Baptist women's ordination also participated in sweeping changes to church leadership in twentieth-century America as growing numbers of women entered Christian ministry.

As Baptist life splintered into multiple factions and affiliations, individual roles and identities destabilized and a contest over the future of complementarity erupted. Chloe's story of negotiating two callings—to marriage and family on one hand and to work and church on the other—shows how a neat division between callings is no longer possible (and probably never was). Family and ministry relationships offered possibilities for Baptists to confront the sins of sexism and to imagine a new kind of mutuality and authenticity in home and church. As Chloe made her way into the pastorate, she embodied the possibility of a new kind of ministry.

In the contest over gender roles for ministry, biblicists upheld the "authoritative (male) pastor" model as the only acceptable one. Autonomists argued for the "servant leader" model as the right one. Both models for ministry were (and are) troublesome for women. Chloe's story brings to light longstanding splits and fissures hidden by a predominantly male practice of ministry. Her understanding and practice of ministry provide a contrast in leadership that is embodied, relational, and spiritually integrated. Her work in ministry is a significant transforming practice, resisting the complementarity culture of Southern Baptists and renewing a culture of mutuality and shared leadership in ministry.

Chloe's Story

Chloe grew up in a family steeped in Baptist knowledge and rational piety. She taped Bible verses up around her bedroom and as a child pondered, "What is God saying to me?" Chloe says her "very Baptist" mother Lillie prioritized involvement in Baptist life, educating and informing herself about what it means to be Baptist by reading Bill Leonard's books and subscribing to *Baptists Today*.[1] Chloe recalls her mother saying about the schism, "They're trying to take away what it means to be Baptist." From South Carolina and trained as a nurse, Lillie felt "very personally affected by the struggle" among Baptists in the 1980s and 1990s. Chloe's father, Martin, an engineer, and her mother are, according to Chloe, both "very Enlightenment" and "very rational" people. She says, "Their faith is very cerebral." In her own journey, Chloe took a "much more mystical" path. Given the values of her parents' lives, she says laughingly that they may "think that I'm sometimes going off the deep end." In her family "you could think anything out. What you believed was important. Experience wasn't as firm as knowledge . . . and reading."

Chloe was baptized at age twelve. In the custom of Baptists, she walked down the aisle at Milton Heights Baptist Church at the end of a worship service in a traditional "I am accepting Christ" moment. After arriving at the front of the sanctuary, Chloe says she felt "perplexed" when a deacon sat down and asked her, "Do you understand the seriousness of this?" Chloe said, "Well, of course I do!" She says she "struggled for a year before that, sensing maybe God was calling me to this, but sensing that it was huge, and it required a lot, and not being sure I was ready." She does not recall talking with her parents about the decision, despite their roles as Sunday school teachers. Chloe says she deliberated "internally," although she considers herself an extrovert, usually talking things over with others. The persistent and intentional focus on evangelism at Milton Heights culminated one day when Chloe and her peers found themselves "shut in a classroom" and given the message *"you need to make the decision."* Chloe felt the external pressure and understood the gravity of deciding on baptism: "This connects to your soul and your eternal destination."

Pastors held significant sway in Chloe's family life. Hugh Binkley served as pastor during her childhood and early adolescence at Milton Heights. Gradually Chloe's mom began to see Binkley as "much more conservative than she realized at first." She once told Chloe about a patronizing reply he gave her: "Now, now, Lillie, you know what the apostle Paul says about such and such." The church did not ordain women as deacons or ministers. Not long after Chloe's baptism, the church called Lawrence Benson as the new pastor. Chloe recalls, "At that time, Pastor Benson was in a much different place in his view of women in the church," a position he later admitted and for which he repented. When Lillie attended a meeting to introduce Benson as a pastoral candidate, Chloe remembers her mother coming home mad. Lillie asked about women's roles as deacons and church leaders, a question to which Pastor Benson gave a "very negative" response. Thus began the search for a new church. Chloe says, "We were out of there so fast that our heads were spinning!"

Chloe's quiet father, Martin, shared her mother's feelings. Soon after leaving the church, Chloe's family went out one evening for frozen yogurt and saw another family still attending Milton Heights. When the other family asked why they had left, Chloe recalls her dad saying, "Because we don't want our girls growing up not believing that God can call them to be whatever God calls them to be." Chloe says the irony of the story is that her dad meant "lawyer or doctor, not pastor."

Chloe's family joined Brenthall Baptist Church, and Paul Sandlin became their pastor. Sandlin involved himself "in the whole Southern Baptist struggle" and offered a leading voice in the autonomist party. The church started ordaining women as deacons fifteen years before Chloe's family arrived. Women served as youth minister, children's minister, and education minister at Brenthall. Chloe and her family found "a very different theology about women" in play at their new church. Other connections played a role as well: "Paul Sandlin counseled my parents about getting married before they ever got married. But they never went to his church. My mom wanted to be a missionary nurse. My dad wanted to marry her." Paul Sandlin told Lillie she should "open her eyes to the idea that every place is a mission field." Chloe says, "That's why she decided to marry my dad. . . . I'll be eternally grateful to Dr. Sandlin for my existence. God and Dr. Sandlin."

Growing up, Chloe preferred to entertain herself and considered herself a "real homebody," avoiding church camp and youth trips. This did not, however, keep her from weekly attendance in Sunday school and worship. She recalls a wonderful Sunday school teacher who used drama and once invited Chloe "to play Jesus . . . in a very well thought out and intentional" presentation. "It was about God being present with us," says Chloe. "And I remember thinking how unusual it was that I got to play Jesus. And I also loved drama. And that was the way she made us plug in and interact." Chloe felt connected with and loved by her Sunday school teachers.

At fourteen Chloe declared she wanted to be a journalist. She wrote for her high school newspaper and attended a journalism workshop at Boston University one summer. She chose Carson-Newman College for its "sense of community" and because she might find more opportunities in its Communications Department. As a journalism major, Chloe worked with the production company and anchored the campus TV news. She graduated with the highest honors in both broadcast journalism and mass communications.

Chloe spent a year before graduation working as an intern at a local TV station. When she graduated, she accepted a job in Santa Barbara, California, a good starting position as a general assignment reporter. "Everyone there just graduated from college," she says. "We created our own family because we're all away from family and friends." Small-market television stations hire new college graduates expecting they will use first jobs as steppingstones, thus paying them modestly. Chloe recalls, "Thankfully, I could scrape by. . . . It was a good place to be, overall, because it allowed me some space to discern that, vocationally, it was *not* where I was supposed to be."

Chloe recalls the discernment unfolding: "I was at everybody's disaster in their life. . . . House fires and car wrecks. . . . And my job was to be objective." It took a while to identify the problem, but, says Chloe, "a huge issue is that I am relational in the way I minister. So I went into journalism with a crusader point of view that I'm going to change the world." The approach worked if someone's house burned down, and she could advocate for installing smoke detectors. However, says Chloe, "my job was *to not get involved* with the person in front of me." She said it "felt very soul stifling" to report the disasters and "interact with people but not truly be in a relationship."

Chloe started questioning her choices when she saw help offered by the Red Cross and the Salvation Army "right then and there, that moment!" Her work felt "not so helpful." She began to watch TV stations in larger markets, where she could expect to "move up." The situation looked the same in those markets, so Chloe began to ask, "God, is this really where you want me to be? Is this the best way?" She sensed that she possessed "a gift of being in a relationship with God" and felt that "knowing God loved me . . . was something that the world could use." Yet Chloe was less sure she was using her gifts "in the best way."

Chloe lived alone that year, attending church with the other young reporters and maintaining minimal involvement because of the intense demands of her job. She worked twelve hours shifts, carried heavy equipment, and was often on call, working longer hours if a story broke late in her shift. As a result, Chloe says, she felt the need of constant prayer to sustain her. She recalls listening to Jars of Clay's first album while driving to assignments.[2] Lillie sent Chloe an article from the Raleigh newspaper with a story about a medical doctor who embraced a mission to open a clinic in an impoverished neighborhood in the city. In the article, the doctor said, "To whom much is given much is required."[3] Chloe understood him to be "using his gift and medical education to serve the children." She says she "read that story over and over again" and felt its effects. Chloe began to wonder: "What can I do with this degree that might be more helpful?" After a year on the TV reporter's beat, Chloe received an offer from a midsize TV station in Myrtle Beach, South Carolina, but she turned it down. In her discernment process she concluded that nonprofit public relations would be more in line with her desires, and she accepted a PR job for the YMCA of Raleigh, a career change she never regretted.

Chloe moved back home with her parents for a brief time. Then she found a housemate and continued working in nonprofit public relations for the next two years. During that time she became reengaged with Brenthall Baptist Church, and there, two significant relationships developed: one with Matt, who eventually became her husband, and a second with a ministry group that became the occasion for Chloe to hear a clearer sense of calling to ministry.

Early in her reentry at Brenthall, Chloe heard about a partnership with Bethel Baptist Church, an African American church extensively involved in social justice ministries on the other side of the city. Chloe's involvement in the partnership began one Sunday when Brenthall's associate pastor, Neal Fogel, preached from James: "Faith without works is dead."[4] At the same time, recalls Chloe, the church launched a partnership with Bethel built on a $1 million anonymous donation "specifically for missions." Brenthall's pastor called the pastor at Bethel and said, "I understand you have a lot of missions in Raleigh-Durham that are reaching out to the communities. We have all this money. Is there some way we can partner?"

As she sat in worship that day, Chloe says, "I remember it sounded like really good news to me." She attended a breakfast meeting where the pastor from Bethel told stories about their residential programs for women and for men in recovery from addictions and a home for people living with HIV/AIDS. The African American congregation, says Chloe, "is in one of *the worst* parts of Raleigh-Durham." Some of Chloe's African American co-workers at the YMCA urged her not to go, saying, "Chloe, the cops don't even go to that area." They told her about a drug-dealing corner called "the bloody something." Bethel sat at the center of a "very, very bad neighborhood."[5]

The partnership with Bethel became a pivotal relationship in Chloe's life for several reasons. It began with an embodied response to the news: "I remember, when this pastor was describing all these things, feeling tingling all over my body. Just so excited about this . . . hearing it as really good news and knowing that I wanted to get involved." At the same time Chloe decided to end a struggling, long-term dating relationship. At that point, she says, "I really started to plug in. . . . And I initiated a ministry of the single women at Brenthall with the women that were in Hope House," one of the recovery programs at Bethel. Her desire and enthusiasm led her to invite her Sunday school class to join the ministry, making connections that lasted "long after the two churches dissolved their relationship." Chloe met Matt when as part of the Brenthall-Bethel partnership they attended a recovery celebration together.

Chloe immersed herself in the ministry at Hope House. "The pastor told me that the women needed fellowship with other women." Chloe's group took pizza and guitars and they ate, prayed, and sang. Chloe's interest in her PR job began to wane, but she found going to Hope House "exciting, energizing and interesting." She began to think, "I could do this all the time. This might be my vocation, might be my calling." Over the months that followed, Chloe prayed and felt a growing sense of call, and she saw her own gift of relationships with the women of Hope House. She began to ask herself, "How do I become better trained to do this kind of work?" Over the next year two callings clearly emerged. Chloe explored her call to seminary and decided to apply to just one divinity school. Her relationship with Matt matured into a call to marriage. In autumn of the following year, Matt and Chloe married, and she began seminary.

The dramatic changes left Chloe and Matt, four years later, sorting through the cost of making all those adjustments at once. The challenges of beginning a marriage and graduate school at the same time, said Chloe, created "a huge issue" for them. She recalls, "I was so focused on seminary, doing well, and being invested in it, that my marriage came second. And I neglected Matt, and I regret how much I did that." Chloe and Matt began with "very different understandings of marriage." Chloe's "goal-oriented" approach led her to see Matt as a "partner to help me accomplish my goals, and I'll help him accomplish his goals. And two will be better than one to get done all the stuff we need to get done in the world." For Matt, "marriage was an end in itself... his biggest goal... the one thing he hoped for himself." He didn't articulate this until much later. Chloe says learning about their differing expectations changed her pastoral approach to premarital counseling. "Now," she says, "I always begin with expectations: How do you understand marriage? What does it mean to you?"

Chloe says she loved her first ministry placement for seminary in a homeless shelter, where she conducted intake interviews and spent time with guests. The next summer she accepted a different job at the agency, coordinating a new lunch program for a Latina/Latino community. It sounded great, and yet the experience taught Chloe things she didn't expect to learn about herself. In the challenges of the job, she says, "I started to grasp that my gifts were not in logistics and administration and organization. I need to surround myself with those kinds of people, but I do not need to do it." She says she likes to "think of all the good ideas," but working out details taxes her energy. The work caused her to become physically ill, "literally nauseated in the mornings." She began taking medication for acid reflux. Matt provided a reality check at that point by asking her, "Why? Why are you doing this?" Late in the summer Chloe finally told the staff, "I can't do this anymore. This is not good for me." The stress spilled over into her marriage, and what could have been much-needed family time outside the school demands did not materialize. As Chloe put it, "Hello! That was a huge learning!"

The seminary required Chloe, as a second-year student, to work in a church. Chloe resisted, saying, "I'm not going to work in a church. This is a waste of my time [laughs]. Put me where I'm going to be doing what I'm going to do." Chloe recalls, "I had no sense of being called to the church. The person doing that program was new. And finally, getting tired of messing with me, she said, 'Well, go find a church that has the programs that you're looking for. Let me know and we'll see about placing you there.'" Chloe agreed, and then a friend told her about Milesdale Baptist Church.

Following up on her friend's suggestion to visit Milesdale, Chloe called the pastor. She met Morgan Smith for lunch and discovered many similarities immediately. Chloe says, "We sat down and just really hit it off. And he's very into the mentoring relationship." She says he knew Chloe grew up at Brenthall and had "no idea what she was getting involved in" at the more progressive Milesdale. That day Chloe learned that Milesdale was historically an SBC church but had recently changed its affiliations to the Alliance of Baptists and the American Baptist Churches USA. The congregation ministered to the community through a recovery program, a homeless ministry, a prison ministry, and other social justice programs, and Chloe decided it sounded like a place she could go.

Chloe planned only to get involved in social ministries as an intern. However, Morgan said, "This is going to be a buffet of ministry experiences. And I want you to taste from preaching and teaching and pastoral care." The requirements of Chloe's seminary field education class lined up with that vision, insisting she "get really involved in the life of the community and their process," engaging in "all sections of the church." She decided to give it all a try and felt surprised by her love of worship and the fun of using her creative energies to plan. As her internship came to a close, Chloe gladly accepted a call to be an interim pastor at the neighboring Springside Baptist Church. During the interim, she also began an ordination process with Milesdale.

Chloe felt surprised again, this time by the elaborate ordination process. She says she appreciated writing the discernment paper because it helped her "work through" important aspects of her preparation for ministry. She recalls that other candidates before her received a message, "to go back and do more work." Ordination for ministry at Milesdale was not a "rubber stamp process" with a council in the afternoon, and a service the same night. The church required a minimum of one year of membership before beginning the process "because Milesdale would ordain women and other people who are marginalized," says Chloe. "There was concern that people would just come there, specifically, to be ordained and not really be invested in the life or the community."

Because the church is aligned with both the ABC-USA and the Alliance of Baptists, Chloe felt the importance of representing her affiliation with both groups through the discernment process and in the ordination service. The church at Milesdale appointed a mentoring team who shepherded Chloe through a time of discernment and testing, multiple meetings, and written assignments. They walked with her through her doubts, wrestling, and discernment about what ministry ought to be and what gave Chloe "joy and energy." The process lasted through her final year of seminary and during the interim pastorate at Springside Baptist Church.

After several months and rounds of meetings with deacons and her mentoring team, Chloe presented her ordination paper for feedback. Then the church convened an ordination council, made up of Milesdale members. The church deacons questioned Chloe twice, and the ordination council examined her in a two-hour meeting. The mentoring team also asked Chloe to invite mentors from her seminary to the meeting. She invited a seminary advisor and Marcie Landon, a minister at Hutchins Memorial Baptist Church and a member of the Alliance board of directors. The Alliance does not ordain or hold requirements beyond local church ordination for ministers, but Chloe wanted them to be represented. After the ordination council voted to approve Chloe for ordination, the worship planning began. Marcie Landon also assisted with planning the service "as a representative from the Alliance." Chloe incorporated the Alliance of Baptists Covenant (see Appendix C), improvising a way to identify with them intentionally.

Before the completion of her interim assignment at Springside, Chloe began to talk with a small church in Virginia about becoming their pastor. Soon after her ordination by Milesdale, Cave Hill Baptist called her as their pastor. The Virginia church has fewer than one hundred members and Chloe works officially thirty hours a week, although like many ministers she cannot always limit her work to "part time." Matt found employment easily at an accounting firm. Chloe has been the church's pastor for three years, and she says, "Right now, for the first time in my life, I think that I've felt content where I am."

Chloe grappled throughout seminary to reconcile her call to care for the needs of people with the demands of the institutional church. She said the "social justice aspect" of Milesdale's ministry engaged her interest as the most significant "value of the church": "The local church, for me, as a Christian, is what those things need to grow out of: the body of Christ in the world. . . . I felt like social justice was the need in the world. . . . People need to be fed and people need a home and . . . change needs to happen." Chloe worried that if she spent her energy and time on preaching or pastoral care, the needs for justice would go unattended.

Social justice pulled Chloe in one direction, yet in another direction she found "joy and energy in planning worship and preaching and doing pastoral visits and the process of the local church." She wondered, "Is God calling me to one thing and what I want to do is another thing? And is God going to be disappointed or upset if I don't do this work that needs to be done?" Then one of her professors helped to shift her thinking. He said, "Chloe, your gift is to empower and inspire and mobilize the church. You are one person. You can go out and work in those places if you want. Or you can choose to bring this work that needs to be done to the church and inspire and empower the church to do this work." When she accepted that the very place giving her joy and energy might also be the place of her calling, she decided to keep moving toward the church.

Chloe also found help as she wrote about the theological tension and struggle in her field education course papers. Her supervisor, an Episcopal priest and spiritual director, repeated a "constant mantra," saying, "Your call is what brings you joy and energy. That's how you know what your call is." The priest said to her, "Chloe, if you do something that is not your true calling, you're taking it away from a person who is called to that work." Chloe countered with, "You've got a gazillion people doing this work and there's still not enough people." Thinking more about it, Chloe connected her struggle to a saying of Howard Thurman: "Don't ask yourself what the world needs, ask yourself what makes you come alive. And then go and do that. Because what the world needs are people who are alive."[6] She says, "I started to think, well, maybe that wasn't heresy and maybe . . . [laughs] all these people were right. And that perhaps this was what I was called to. And I certainly was finding lots of energy and joy, and I was really excited about it."

Chloe asked her *next* question: "Well, why would God call me to this? There's no place for me to serve. So why would God give me this desire in my heart?" In response to that question, Chloe says she learned a lot from her friend Eric

Winters, a "gay Baptist man who shared the same question." She says Eric argued with God, asking, "Why would you call me to this? Because there's going to be no place for me, and I'm just going to be hurt." His story and sermons about his call and struggle inspired Chloe to continue in the direction of pastoral ministry.

Chloe says her transition from seminary to the interim work at Springside Baptist Church and then the pastorate of Cave Hill Baptist Church in Virginia felt "really wild . . . and amazing." The pastor search committee from Cave Hill contacted her mentor, Morgan. He recommended Chloe to them, urging her to send in her resume. Chloe agreed but thought the church would not call her so it would be a "waste of time" to apply, and she didn't follow through quickly. However, the search committee called her, asking for her materials just before the spring Alliance of Baptists convocation. When she emailed her materials, they discovered that both she and they would be attending the convocation. "Meeting in person," says Chloe, dramatically changed the process.

A few weeks later the committee interviewed Chloe by phone. Then they drove to meet her and Matt and talk with them over dinner. She said the personal meetings, "changed Morgan's perspective" about her "going to a small church." He wanted Chloe to search for an associate position in a larger church, which he thought would be healthier. However, Morgan felt persuaded by the "intentionality of people" from Cave Hill. The committee also visited Springside Baptist Church, where Chloe served as the interim pastor. Next they brought her to Cave Hill to visit the church without the awareness of the congregation.

Finally, the committee brought Chloe to Cave Hill for a full interview, Sunday morning preaching, and meeting the congregation. The church met in business session and voted on that Sunday night. Chloe says, "I knew in a church that size I would not come unless it was completely and utterly unanimous." When her cell phone rang on the trip home that evening, Chloe learned the church had voted unanimously to call her. She and Matt moved in October. The committee interviewed Chloe as their only candidate, and she and the search committee saw it as a "miraculous kind of process."

Cave Hill is a small congregation with about fifty active members, begun two decades earlier as a mission from a larger church in the area. The membership includes both "blue-collar and white-collar" workers. Some are "barely getting by," and others are academic and medical professionals. When it comes to leadership and church decision making at Cave Hill, Chloe says, "the church had a good system established when I arrived. It's a church council model. There are five ministry groups and the chair of each of those ministry groups relates back to a church council." Chloe does not vote in church council, but she is a "voting member of the church."

Chloe remembers feeling glad that when a worshipper approached her with questions or concerns, she could say, "Thank you for sharing that. But, as a pastor I don't decide, totally, what happens in worship." And she could take the concerns to the worship ministry group. She says she feels "thankful for the process in place *before they hired* me." While participating in a training program for young Baptist leaders during her second year at Cave Hill, Chloe learned more about family systems and self-differentiation. She says she hopes to teach what she is learning from Edwin Friedman about "a small group of leaders who are *pulling* the rest of this church . . . trying to get everyone else to get excited, and come on board . . . seducing, cajoling, and encouraging." She talks to lay leaders about why the arrangement is not working for her. She hopes that together they can "find a better model." She thinks they are receptive to the "long-term work."[7]

In her second year at Cave Hill, Chloe mentored a younger woman working as an intern from a nearby seminary. Like Morgan, Chloe "loved the mentoring relationship." She enjoyed working with Sandy, who "added a great deal to the Cave Hill community." One insight Chloe gained from that relationship is the significance of "trusting in that sense of call. There are so many external forces that can cause us to begin to doubt the call." She says it is easy to get caught up in questions: "Is there a place for me? How can this be my call? Where could I serve?" However, she says, "if you're getting a true sense of 'This is where I'm supposed to be,' then you probably are."

In considering what it means to her to be a Baptist woman in ministry, Chloe says it is "the freedom of being Baptist" that appeals to her. She says, "I have some Methodist women friends who have been accused, in ordination processes, of having problems with authority. And these friends of mine, I don't think have problems with authority nearly as much as I do [laughs]." Chloe says, "There's a sense of freedom, as a Baptist woman, that's important. For me, the issues of soul competency and priesthood of the believer have always been important. And as I continue on my own journey, I'm realizing how very crucial that is. A huge part of pastoring for me is making sure that I'm nurturing my own personal relationship with God and helping church members do the same. And through that relationship, encountering Scripture, worshipping and praying together . . . seeking God's presence together." She notes that about half her church claims a "Baptist identity" and others come because in the "mixed community" they "feel loved when they're there." She often discusses with them "why *I'm* Baptist, and why that's important to me. Why that's important to *my* identity."

Chloe says of her spiritual practice: "Several women's voices have affirmed the same message . . . to trust my internal sense of self . . . to not be so externally dependent on who I am and where I'm going." She says she is learning to hear herself more clearly. She connects this quest with her childhood love of the Bible and "straining to hear God" and asking, "What is God saying? What is God thinking?" The women's voices help, says Chloe, "to hold my internal sources and dialogue in higher esteem: I'm created by God and that is a way God is speaking to me." Prayerful guided imagery, the use of holy imagination, and reading authors like Rabbi Tirzah Firestone are helping Chloe expand her understanding of God and to embrace the feminine divine.[8] Contemplative prayer helps her "quiet down and hear God." Three years into her ministry at Cave Hill, Chloe is integrating more of her spiritual practice into the daily work of ministry.

Chloe says, "The thing I love about the local church is that I love the diversity of my work. I love that I do get to meet with people, and I also get to preach and I also get to create worship experiences . . . and walk with people on their journeys." She finds the work exciting and a source of contentment, although she admits to looking always toward the future. And she sees greater equity between her callings to work and family: "I'm thirty-two now and actually beginning to see having a personal life may be *happily* as important as my [ministry] vocation." For now, says Chloe, "I'm more interested in living a balanced, whole life."

Remaking Baptist Identity through Reimagining Ministry

Like other clergywomen, Chloe practices ministry in a way that reinterprets the Southern Baptist schism as a space for creating and discovering a new theology of ministry. The new theology and practice of ministry embodied in her story fleshes out a new expression of Baptist identity, emerging from a struggle that ended in schism but also in clarity. A close reading of Chloe's story, in dialogue with stories of other women in ministry, offers four dimensions of the struggle and emerging identity that together make a portrait of Baptist ministry, taking shape in a crucible of conflict and change over time.

The first dimension of Chloe's stories about her ministry practice, resonating with other clergywomen, reframes the work of meaning making by situating it in an embodied and relational space of knowing rather than in deliberation or rational modes of belief and decision. The second dimension surfaces when Chloe's parents move the family to a new congregation. They chose through the transition to remain Baptist and recast their Baptist identity to embrace a fuller sense of vocation for their daughters, contributing both to Chloe's vocational discernment and to her Baptist loyalty. Chloe's ordination process demonstrates a third dimension of struggle and a new way of negotiating the meaning and practice of the "priesthood of all believers." By rejecting both the authoritarian and servant-leader roles, which prevailed in the struggle between men, she participates in reshaping authority as an embodied and relational practice grounded in gifts and calling. That shift was more than just a change for Baptists: Chloe's ordination also participates in a substantial shift in which women's ordination and pastoral ministry dramatically changed the face of Christian ministry in the United States, reconfiguring the shape and the stakes of authority in congregational leadership. The final dimension noteworthy for analysis is found in Chloe's twin calls to ministry/work and marriage/family, which elucidate the Baptist struggle between complementary and mutuality as key to authenticity in relationships at work, home, and society. Chloe's stories and transforming practice of ministry reinterpret Baptist schism as not only a battleground between politically opposed forces but also a playground for renegotiating Baptist ministry, authenticity, and identity.

Chloe's lifelong quest for answers to basic questions of meaning and faithfulness—"What is God saying to me?"—is a story of attending to her own situated knowing, which takes its form in relational, emotional, and embodied practice.[9] Chloe understands questions of meaning in a qualitatively different way than her parents. She describes her parents as rational and deliberative and sees herself as mystical, relational, and emotional. She thinks they worry that she might be "going off the deep end." The changing emphasis on meaning making from Lillie and Martin's generation to Chloe and Matt's generation captures vividly a cultural shift away from rational deliberation toward situated knowing. Baptists participated in the larger change taking place across the landscape of American religion.[10]

In each season of her life Chloe asked questions of meaning. As an adolescent she held an internal dialogue about baptism, grasping the seriousness of the situation and wrestling over her decision for a full year. As she discerned her vocational choices while working as a TV news reporter, Chloe asked, "God, is this really where you want me to be?" She felt that her relationship with God ("knowing that God loved me") was a gift "the world could use." She integrated other questions about life's meaning and God's involvement in that meaning into her work of ministry. For example, after coming to a better understanding of the differing expectations she and Matt brought to their marriage, she began asking couples in premarital counseling about their understandings and expectations of marriage.

In describing the process of making important decisions, Chloe regularly notes how her body gives her vital information. In the time of discerning a vocational call, she feels excitement, literally a "tingling all over," when she hears about the partnership between Brenthall and Bethel, and she takes the embodied knowing as a sign of the rightness of her choice to pursue the opportunity.[11] She describes feelings of helplessness when reporting the news of other people's disasters, and later she describes physical distress and illness during the summer work of setting up a lunch program for the Latina/Latino community. These embodied indicators help Chloe discern and move toward a calling that is personally fulfilling, attends to the needs of others, and responds to God's Spirit. She does not depend solely on reason to find her way toward knowing what to do, as she believes her parents' generation might. She trusts her body, relationships, and emotional responses to give her pertinent information for making good vocational decisions.[12]

The generational shift in Chloe's family story highlights how the SBC schism is an instance of larger shifting in American Christianity away from responding to religion as a matter of right belief or rational deliberations or shoring up rules and roles by the faithful.[13] Chloe's story of being corralled with other children in a room to make a "salvation decision" typifies the earlier model.[14] In the new direction, Baptists respond to religious experiences of potential new members—children or adults—with an increased interest in spiritual practice, exploring questions and doubt, making room for "not knowing," and acting as stewards of spiritual gifts for life and work.[15] The changes in practice show a shift that is generational, situational, and historical. The shift in emphasis from Lillie and Martin's rational deliberation to Chloe and Matt's situated knowing provides a contrast in modes of Baptist identity. The shift also shows the growing divide between autonomists and biblicists as a flowering of longstanding tensions in Baptist history.[16]

Other Baptist clergywomen describe experiences of calling and leading that are embodied, emotional, relational and concerned foremost with meaningfulness. For example, before Margaret Hess became an American Baptist pastor and preaching professor, she grew up in a traditional Southern Baptist home and at First Baptist Church in Danville, Virginia. As a teen she felt caught up in the "Jesus Movement" and went to "every revival service and prayer meeting" she could. More times than not, she found herself moved, even "propelled to the altar," and "saved more times than beef stew." When she attended Meredith College her religion professors opened "a whole new world" for her: "Something began to shift in my relationship with God. My faith was less anxiety driven and more characterized by trust. Faith became less about 'being saved' and more about figuring out how to align myself with God's just and compassionate activity in the world." When Hess preached her first sermon in seminary, she felt surprised by her own passion. She experienced preaching as "a mystical experience" that "connected to God in a deep and transforming way."[17] Chloe's and Margaret Hess's descriptions of mystical and embodied experiences of discernment and of ministry point to a major shift in emphasis underway among Baptists.[18]

In a contrasting example, Dorothy Patterson, one of the architects of biblicist revisions of the 2000 Baptist Faith and Message, describes how leadership and decision making ideally work in a complementarian relationship. With an example from her own marriage to Paige Patterson, she says, "We have an interchange of ideas about it, and [Paige] will share his feelings and he wants to hear my feelings and many times we finish that and we've already come to a meeting of the minds. We've already made a decision and there is not really the necessity for submission to come into play in the sense of my giving into his wishes against my own preferences because we have decided together." In Patterson's description of discernment, feelings and relationality are certainly important, yet the emphasis is on rational deliberation, meeting of minds, a decision together, and the role of submission. The decision-making pathway assumes both particular family roles for wives and husbands and a commitment to timeless roles understood as prescribed in Scripture.[19]

The schism is one in a long line of Baptist controversies that are a study in the tensions of modern identity.[20] Having arisen at the turn of the seventeenth century, early Baptists took on the indelible imprint of enlightenment dilemmas. One enlightenment struggle remains woven into the fabric of Baptist identity, expressing itself in churchly politics and alignments. In Baptist parlance, at one side stands the individual's God-given freedom, right, and responsibility to experience, to choose, and to act from internal moral conviction. This aspect of Baptist identity depends heavily on feeling, affection, and the evocative, mystical power of God. On the other side stands the appeal to God's timeless revelation in Scripture and the rules and roles prescribed therein providing guidance for all decision making.[21] This side appeals to rational, deliberative clarity for taking action and following the direction already given by God. Both sides appeal to the presence and power of God, the inspiration of the Spirit, and the Lordship of Christ. Yet as the decades unfolded and fissures between Baptists opened up, tensions increased, and contentious parties formed, each staking identity more solidly on one side or the other of a growing chasm.[22] The meaning- and decision-making narratives by Hess and Patterson are examples of the ongoing negotiation of meaning making in the SBC schism. Each narrative holds within it the shadows of the other. And Chloe's story highlights how a generational shifting of emphasis was underway, moving from rational deliberation to greater embodied, relational practice, which guides decision making and meaning making.

Chloe's story of growing up Baptist during the height of controversy showed how her family took the Baptist battles seriously and made choices that supported their daughters' ongoing growth and development. When Lillie learned the new pastor would not support women's leadership, the family departed "so fast our heads were spinning," says Chloe. Her father thought his daughters deserved a church space open and supportive of nontraditional professions for women.[23] Finding a new church helped the family remain Baptist *and* remake that longstanding identity. The changed situation supported Chloe's vocational discernment and deepened her commitment to remaining a *Baptist* pastor.

Other clergywomen often found the freedom of being Baptist, even amid the fighting between parties, a necessary aspect of discerning vocation and identity. In 1981 Royal Lane Baptist Church in Dallas, Texas, ordained Nancy Ellett. Work in collegiate ministry and clinical pastoral education at Baptist institutions helped her discern and clarify her call to pastoral ministry. Later, working as a youth minister at Royal Lane, Nancy "discovered what a wonderful—and free—place the church could be!" She stated, "I could not have been more fortunate in finding a congregation that has blessed and encouraged me and has continually allowed me to grow as a minister."[24]

In various situations of mentoring, Chloe discovered Baptist churches could be spaces for playful growth, contexts for remaking Baptist identity, and not solely concerned with enforcing roles, rules, or guidelines.[25] When Chloe began her field education at Milesdale Baptist Church, the pastor invited her to engage in a "buffet of ministry experiences." Her seminary professor also insisted she get "really involved in the life of the community and their process," immersing herself the whole church. These mentors invited Chloe into an open space where she discovered a love of preaching, pastoral care, and creating worship.

Chloe clarified her calling to ministries of justice through empowering a congregation, but she struggled with why God would call and wondered if she should pursue ordination when opportunities to serve in Baptist churches remained rare for women. Eric Winters inspired her through his life and story as a gay man, and through his preaching, assuring her that there was a place for her among Baptists. His friendship and peer mentoring allowed Chloe to play with the idea that although opportunities for women remained limited, she could belong and contribute to a Baptist church.

As a new pastor, Chloe mentored a young woman preparing for ministry. In that relationship she learned that one can "trust the sense of call." With growing experience and hindsight, she could see how internal and external "forces" stir up doubt and bring on questions that she asked herself in seminary: "Is there a place for me? How can this be my call? Where could I serve?" Yet over time her confidence grew and she could say, "If you're getting a true sense of 'this is where I'm supposed to be,' then you probably are."[26]

Despite the widespread conflict and tension that animated late-twentieth-century Baptist life, the years of schism offered a playground as well as a battleground for remaking Baptist identity and ministry. In 2000 biblicists changed the Baptist Faith and Message to confess the church as a place where believers are "governed by [Christ's] laws," replacing the 1963 confession, which declared the church "committed to [Christ's] teachings." This change suggests how biblicists adopted the meaning of "church" as a place where rules and laws of faith are enforced in subtle protest to autonomist ideas about a space where questions are asked and faith is discovered.

Both the 1963 and 2000 confessions declare that in Christ believers should engage in "exercising the gifts, rights, and privileges invested in them by His Word... seeking to extend the gospel to the ends of the earth." However, biblicists' 2000 revision remade the qualifications for exercising spiritual and pastoral gifts: "While both men and women are gifted for service in the church, the office of pastor is limited to men as qualified by Scripture." During the years of schism, biblicists reimagined the church as a place where "scriptural" roles should govern church jobs and identity for women, men, and children. During those same years, autonomists also appealed to Scripture and reimagined church as a place of service, leadership, and giftedness for both women and men. For example, the Alliance of Baptists crafted a covenant committed to the "freedom of the local church under the authority of Jesus Christ to shape its own life and mission, call its own leadership, and ordain whom it perceives as gifted for ministry, male or female."[27] Both parties refashioned Baptist identity in their own images of it, codifying and adopting their differences through confessions and covenants. The schism didn't merely split the issue of Baptist identity into opposing forms, however. New articulations of church and Baptist identity multiplied and emerged in the wake of schism. Chloe and others incorporated ideas of freedom, relationality, and giftedness, expanding the variety of Baptist identities and reinterpreting schism as a playground for exploration and renewal.[28]

Chloe's story of ordination reinterprets schism in the SBC as both a contest over reshaping ecclesial authority and an instance of major change in American religion wrought by the growing number of women entering ministry. Both reinterpretations can be situated within a longstanding Baptist tension between clergy and laity over the meaning and practice of authority. The cherished Baptist belief and practice of the "priesthood of all believers" holds together this tension and serves as a major point of contention between autonomists and biblicists.[29]

Chloe worked through her discernment for ordination by engaging in a year-long process that included written reflections, prayer and conversation with church members and ministers, and engagement with a seminary professor and a minister from another congregation. The mutually shared process treated her authorization for ministry as a matter of group consensus building to affirm the gifts and calling of God in Chloe for the church. The process held the tension creatively between clergy and laity, honoring both the congregation and the ministers in its unfolding. Chloe's story of ordination is neither typical, nor a complete anomaly. It is exemplary of the ways autonomists resisted the biblicist assertions of greater pastoral authority during the late 1980s.

More than a decade before Chloe's ordination, the SBC passed a resolution solidifying the aspirations of the biblicist party regarding pastoral authority. The 1988 Resolution On the Priesthood of the Believer claimed that the doctrine could be used neither "to justify wrongly the attitude that a Christian may believe whatever he so chooses and still be considered a loyal Southern Baptist" nor "to justify the undermining of pastoral authority in the local church." Although the resolution affirmed the doctrine of the priesthood of believer(s), it prohibited its use from undercutting "the role, responsibility, and authority of the pastor." Passing the resolution formalized a shift away from congregational authority and toward greater pastoral authority, which assumed a male pastorate and added another victory for biblicists in their program of change for the SBC.[30]

Milesdale Baptist Church chose to ordain women and others typically marginalized, adopting an extended and carefully discerned process involving the entire congregation. Their choice illuminated a divergent path through the authorizing practice of Baptist ordination. By authorizing Chloe (and others at the margins) for ministry, Milesdale reshaped the longstanding tension between clergy and laity through the practice of ordination and instantiated the priesthood of all believers in a particular new way. The contest over authority for Baptists played out in a formal set of rules (cast as convention resolutions), but the same dispute presented itself in the local practice of ordination.[31] Women seeking ordination opened up more explicitly the meaning and theological significance of the practice and provided a focal point for interpreting the meaning of authority more broadly in congregations.[32]

The shift in authority was not solely a Baptist dispute over the meaning and uses of power in church decision making. It was also part of a widespread cultural change in authorizing women to lead many denominations of Christian churches. Of all the changes to ministry in two millennia of church practice, the full authorization and growing enfranchisement of women (in some denominations) is among the most dramatic.[33] Since 1950 the number of women serving as pastors with full pastoral authority in churches and ministry settings has gone from negligible to normative in many U.S. denominations. In 2012, clergywomen made up 9.4 percent of American Baptist pastors. Women make up nearly 30 percent of the clergy serving as pastors in Disciples (Church of Christ) congregations. In 2011 United Methodists clergywomen made up 29 percent of the total number of United Methodist pastors. Presbyterians and United Churches of Christ clergywomen each constituted 27 percent of their total numbers of pastors serving congregations.[34] Among churches affiliated with Southern Baptists in 2012, the numbers with women as pastors remains virtually nonexistent. Calling a woman as pastor in a Southern Baptist congregation is a nearly certain way to find one's congregation removed from fellowship by the local association and/or state Baptist convention.[35] Among CBF churches, the numbers in 2012 reached an all-time high, with women pastoring 90 of 1,800 churches (5 percent). Alliance churches are the most friendly to female pastors, with women pastoring 43 of 139 churches (31 percent). Approximately twenty-two hundred Baptist women in the SBC, Alliance, and CBF are ordained and serve in a numerous capacities as ministers.[36]

In the early 1990s, former SBC missionary and Southern Baptist Theological Seminary graduate Kathy Manis Findley worked as a hospital chaplain. She asked her SBC church in Arkansas to ordain her, hoping the request would harm no one. However, Findley's request stirred up a controversy that included "cruel words, harsh criticism and rejection." Church members feared SBC censure. A "bitter business meeting" about her potential ordination ended with some church members leaving the congregation and Kathy's husband Fred resigning from his paid position as minister of music. A small band of alienated members took a road trip to connect with other more supportive Baptist congregations. Eventually, North View Baptist Church in El Paso, Texas, extended an invitation to ordain her. Kathy received blessings, prayers, affirmation, and encouragement from "former missionary colleagues, seminary friends, professors, fellow chaplains, Methodist and Presbyterian friends." The group of supporters started Providence Baptist Church in Little Rock, Arkansas, and called Findley as their pastor. She says the "harsh criticism and rejection forced me to expand my faith community and empowered me with courage."[37] Rather than accept the initial rejection or leave Baptist life in defeat, these Baptists, in partnership with Findley, found another path for authorizing the gifts of their pastoral leader, founding a new church and naming it for God's presence in their midst.

A contest over ecclesial authority took shape in the years of schism both in the convention scuffles and in local settings where women asked for ordination. The change from an all-male clergy to ministry shared by women and men participated in a larger democratization of ministry in the United States in the twentieth century, a change in which even progressive Baptists remain at the early adopters phase.[38] Autonomists at Milesdale and Providence churches affirmed the priesthood of all believers by extending leadership to women and reshaping authorizing practice of ordination to fit the new situation.

Chloe's story of negotiating two callings, one to her work and one to her marriage, reinterprets schism in the SBC as a theological struggle between cultures of complementarity and mutuality, each claiming to be the authentic Baptist way of relating between genders.[39] Her story also shows how theological disputes between parties leading to schism were riddled with the sins of sexism and how clergywomen found a different way through the split to experience grace and participate in redemption.

Schism became a contest over what it means to be "authentically Baptist." For instance, Lillie worried that "they're trying to take away what it means to be Baptist," naming the stakes of the struggle. Biblicists claimed in the 1988 Resolution On the Priesthood of the Believer that to be a "loyal Southern Baptist," an authentic Baptist, meant to avoid "undermining ... pastoral authority in the local church." Neither should one "misinterpret, explain away, demythologize, or extrapolate out elements of the supernatural from the Bible." Authenticity for biblicists meant literal belief in the Bible and a specific kind of pastoral authority.[40] Autonomists grounded Baptist authenticity in personal religious experience of the freedom of God and subsequently the freedom to live out of that experience in community.[41] Following the logic of their basic commitments, autonomists called for mutuality in marriage and servanthood in ministry as authentic forms of Baptist loyalty. Biblicists insisted on complementarity in all relationships as the authentic and biblical standard for marriage and ministry.

Chloe did not give up a career in ministry to marry Matt, as her mother Lillie gave up a desire to become a missionary in order to marry Martin. Chloe's spouse moved and found work in a new city to support her calling and career as a pastor. This does not suggest that Lillie did not find fulfillment in her work as a nurse or support within her chosen family. The observation highlights how Chloe's choice was not as readily available to Lillie: the situation had changed.[42] The pastor who officiated Martin and Lillie's wedding asked Lillie to "open her eyes to the idea that every place is a mission field." Implicitly he asked her to close her eyes to the calling she felt to be a missionary nurse, a request that might be perceived four decades later as a denial of one's authentic self and calling.[43] By contrast, Chloe did not face a choice of one over the other but pursued a career in ministry *and* her marriage to Matt. Authenticity in this case is not loyalty to a "true self" but how one navigates multiple demands and desires.[44]

Chloe and Matt began their marriage with differing expectations, callings, and needs. After completing seminary, Chloe realized that she had not given adequate attention to her marriage and needed to renegotiate expectations and hopes with Matt. After some relational work and three years into the pastorate, Chloe says she felt for the first time a sense of contentment and living into her desire for "a balanced whole life." She learned that "filling roles" for ministry/work or marriage/family did not match her lived experience. The two callings compete as well as support each other, and "filling roles" is not an adequate way to imagine fulfillment in either call.[45]

Interwoven and embedded in the structures of complementarity are sins of sexism.[46] Attempts to displace the complementarity model of family and work continued as a central part of the autonomist struggle for justice and redemption in the years of schism.[47] The struggle in the SBC was not only a pragmatic struggle over who could do what jobs or play which roles in a family. Clergywomen perceived the struggle as a practical and theological challenge to the structures of sin instantiated in certain arrangements of family and ministry. Baptist clergywomen exemplified the challenge to the sins of complementarity by choosing to pursue vocations that included both family and work. Chloe's life demonstrates that questions of how to structure a family or pursue a call to ministry are ongoing negotiations, sometimes struggles, and not merely an exercise in filling prearranged roles. Biblicists who defend complementarity don't in reality "merely fill roles" either, yet in defending "God's delegated order" as a corollary to "biblical authority," they disregarded the sense of spiritual and theological authenticity that permeates Baptist culture.[48] By this logic, biblicists saw clergywomen as examples of sin.[49] Women pursuing ordination *and* family life surfaced hidden sins of sexism. The Baptist struggle over authenticity woven through the schism was not simply a contest between self-fulfillment and sinfulness but also a struggle over the very human negotiations that are required for living, loving, and working, which are also occasions for grace and redemption.

When biblicist rhetoric asserted ministry as a role to be filled by a male pastor leading his congregation with authority, autonomists countered by insisting on a role for pastor as servant leader. Many women embraced the servant leader role. Ester Tye Perkins became the first female (interim) pastor of a Baptist church in South Carolina in 1983, when her husband died. Prior to that, they served together, he as pastor and she as minister of music and education, for five years. The church asked her to become the interim pastor, and a few months later they ordained her. She said, "I do not see this ordination as involving manhood or womanhood, but servanthood. . . . God called my husband into the ministry and through the years we had a shared ministry. This is my opportunity to continue it. As for women being liberated, Jesus Christ liberated me many years ago."[50]

Both assertions of authoritative male pastor and servant-pastor created a dilemma for women. Some clergywomen found another path through the tensions that did not adopt either the biblicist or autonomist strategy but took a third way. Preaching in 1984 at the Southern Baptist Women in Ministry meeting in Kansas City, Kansas, Lynda Weaver-Williams, a pastor from Kentucky, developed the meeting's theme: "Exercising Our Gifts." The theme, she says, reflected the SBWIM Steering Team's effort "to express in a positive way what we as women in ministry are trying to do. We are not demanding our rights or asserting our freedom. We are simply asking for the opportunity to exercise our gifts. In the name of One who blessed us with gifts, we only want a chance to do what we've been called to do."[51] The idea was not new but as old as the Bible itself, and it was more than a rhetorical strategy for countering the false dichotomy between (male) authority and servanthood in ministry. Weaver-Williams commends a way to live into ministry that is relational, embodied, and situated in Baptist life yet also in the larger context of God's calling and gifts. Chloe and hundreds more lived creatively in this complex situation, experiencing God's grace and redemption, reimagining ministry, and reinterpreting the SBC schism as a context for joyful, creative, and life-giving ministry for everyone, even women.

Chloe and other Baptist women entering ordained ministry across four decades reimagine pastoral practice such that it reinterprets schism in the SBC as a potential space of improvisation and renewal for ministry rather than merely a space of hostility and conflict. Chloe understands ministry as nurturing herself and others and "practicing the presence of Christ in community." In one sense Chloe's articulation of ministry is nothing new and lines up with centuries of practice. The major difference is that she is a woman, and as such the careful unfolding of her narrative shows how her story elucidates splits and fractures that already existed in Baptist identity. Her narrative also expresses a wider and deeper set of cultural changes extending beyond the Baptist world, and it displays her practices of ministry, which improvise and embody a new theology of ministry.[52] Chloe's life and ministry as an ordained pastor offer newly situated possibilities for Baptist ministry and identity that foreground relational and embodied knowing and focus on discernment and giftedness for callings that matter.

None of the clergywomen interviewed in this book considers herself Southern Baptist today. Many remain Baptist, yet by making explicit the many fissures already present in the Baptist experience, clergywomen played a significant role in the emerging schism. Previously excluded from the realm of ordained ministry, when women began pastoring and leading, they challenged the rhetoric of both biblicists and autonomists about appropriate roles and opened up new ways of living their Baptist identities. Clergywomen found personal and corporate clarity; they challenged notions of ministry, making the complexity of vocation more evident and exposing previously hidden sins of sexism. Their lives are also occasions for redemption and grace, and they are part of one of the most dramatic and significant changes to ordained ministry since the Christian church began.

Although Baptists have long struggled with how best to make decisions and find meaning in life, the years of schism further opened a divide between rational deliberation and embodied, situational knowing. Autonomists gravitated to the latter, and they still tried to appeal in a satisfying way to deliberative arguments for their stance. Biblicists embraced the deliberative approach, offering elaborate arguments that all but ignored embodied, situational knowledge of God's presence and call in women's lives. However, the result was not simply to polarize Baptist identity into oppositions. Chloe's life and ministry exemplifies new articulations and improvisations on the Baptist ideas of freedom, relationality, and giftedness to renew Baptist identities. The move shows in hindsight how schism created both a battleground and a playground for Baptist identity.

The years of schism included a protracted argument over ecclesial authority. Autonomist and biblicist parties recast their understandings in the confessions and covenants they wrote, voting them in or out at annual meetings. Meanwhile, the debate played out in the local authorizing practice of ordination itself. Women requesting ordination brought larger disputes to the foreground, and some churches conferred authority through ordination and calling such that they embodied their commitments to Christ, Scripture, and the priesthood of all believers. Women moved gradually into authorized roles in churches across the ecclesial landscape participating in a permanent change to the face of ministry in America. Behind the curve of change, Southern Baptists who embraced women in ministry either departed from or were ejected by the SBC.

Another fragmentation in the Southern Baptist split was created by the pull between cultures of complementarity and mutuality. As growing numbers of women embraced their calls to both ministry and family, they brought to the surface the often hidden sins of sexism and broke open the question of how to be an authentic Baptist. Filling roles no longer adequately captured the complexity and negotiation required for Baptists to navigate a lived experience of identity and vocation. Baptist clergywomen not only embodied the split in the denomination but also renewed Baptist identity and reimagined ministry. The new frameworks that they adopted through practice resisted the complementarity culture of Southern Baptists and reimagined a culture of mutuality and embodied, relational leadership for ministry.

Conclusion

A widespread lack of attention to both women and the category of gender in the existing analysis of Southern Baptists and their conflicts over the last forty years left open a pathway for reinterpreting the fracturing of the Southern Baptist Convention. The untraversed pathway also left open a way to consider the psychological underpinnings and implications of schism. Taken together, these two approaches, refracted through the stories of ordained Baptist women, offer a new interpretation for a living Baptist history, which remains contested. By considering the positions taken by both the autonomist and biblicist parties on issues of women's ordination and gender roles in church, home, and society, the multivalent dynamic of splitting comes more clearly into focus. Clergywomen were often perceived at a distance as the very symbols of the Baptist struggle. Women also experienced the splitting firsthand in the fracturing of important relationships in their families and their faith communities. The social fractures also divided their thinking and action at times, presenting them with dilemmas that required creativity and imagination to navigate. Social and psychological splitting came easy amid tensions of belief and practice that are inherent in the larger Baptist history.

In a Baptist subculture of complementarity, institutionalized forms of splitting gender, power, and work permeated Baptist lives through weekly programs of piety and annual cycles of observance in Baptist churches, including Sunday school, missions classes with achievement programs, printed educational materials, financial campaigns for missions, and weekly worship. Baptist women (and men) experienced the dilemmas of complementarity as they navigated the expectations of their families and considered a sense of God's calling for their lives, starting in Sunday school and summer camp and extending through college and seminary. In the struggle between following a pathway of dutiful daughters and coming to an intersection where Baptist piety and feminism encouraged a new direction toward ministry, women struggled over the very future of complementarity. On one hand they expressed a clear desire to undo it and replace it with mutuality, but in other more subtle and unwitting ways they reproduced complementarity with all its dilemmas. Nevertheless, clergywomen found ways to live creatively between mission and submission, and as they negotiated these internal and relational dynamics, they also participated in sweeping changes to Baptist identity that took shape in the years of schism. Rather than languish in the crucible of conflict, women enrolled in more education, accepted the authority of ordination, and embraced the call of churches, becoming shapers and changers of Baptist identity.

Although the birth of women's ordination in Southern Baptist life was and remains a novelty, it was also possible because of the space made by longstanding tensions in Baptist polity and history. The U.S. context fueled the creative tensions of belief and practice in Baptist life. Baptist theology was not simply amorphous in the democratically oriented U.S. Republic, with each person deciding for him- or herself, yet neither was Baptist theology set out as uniformly accepted orthodoxy. The creative tensions of Baptist life provide an improvisational space in which new influences and social conditions interact with longstanding practices of faith and articulations of belief, producing new iterations of Baptist faithfulness.[1] Within the tension between dramatic conversion and nurturing faith, clergywomen found both *salvation and calling* that transformed their lives and sent them with confidence in the direction of becoming pastors. In the tension between the authority of the biblical text and the authority of spiritual and religious experience, clergywomen experienced themselves competent to hear and respond to God's call, even while those around them continued to debate their legitimacy.[2]

By joining the ranks of the ordained, Baptist women highlighted the gender inequality that was bound up in the tension between clergy and laity in the *priesthood of all believers*. Women's entrance into ordained roles showed how that priesthood was mainly available to male clergy and existed as a male domain, leaving laity and women in a different and less powerful ecclesial space. Clergywomen and other autonomists worked to reframe relational spaces of their faith communities, and personal narratives, so that "all believers" might embody something closer to equality and welcome women more fully into the priesthood.

In the tension between autonomy of a local church and the need for churches to cooperate in shared mission, clergywomen found the opportunity for ordination and service. On the principle of *voluntary association,* each church could choose and many took the risk to break with tradition and ordain or call women, authorizing them as ministers. At the institutional level, while Baptists were splitting and unable to cooperate, clergywomen and their supporters founded one of the early cooperative organizations in a constellation of moderate to progressive Baptist groups, Southern Baptist Women in Ministry (later Baptist Women in Ministry). The group majored on support for women in ministry yet also functioned as a catalyst for fracturing the longstanding political synthesis of Southern Baptists.

In the Baptist tension between loyal citizenship and the protest over state infringements on religious freedom, clergywomen often positioned themselves as dissenters and sought recognition as those speaking within a Baptist tradition for the *separation of church and state,* with mixed results. In the case of each historic Baptist tension, the two major parties of Southern Baptist life embroiled themselves in conflict, spitting the social and spiritual space of Baptist life, but in very practical, everyday ways, clergywomen and others navigated the tensions to find a third way that moved them beyond the stated controversies and into new creative and improvisational ways to be Baptist.

Conclusion

More than one's "baptistness" was at stake in the years of schism, however. Deep symbols and powerful messages about the character of humanity itself circulated through Baptist life, capturing both the power and the vulnerability of human being in the everyday interactions of a subculture of complementarity. When women challenged the normative assumptions by stepping into places of authority and power, they made explicit a set of implicit struggles over the meaning of human existence embedded in Baptist theology and practice. Women's participation and leadership in the rituals of preaching, presiding at communion, and baptizing believers allowed a visual, embodied, and sustained critique of the injustices and the brokenness of humanity, taking form in institutionalized sexism and racism. Those same ritual functions also afforded opportunities for healing and redemption for women and for whole communities of faith. Ultimately at stake in the wider Baptist fracturing was a struggle over what it means to be human and how Baptists perceive God's presence as both a sustaining force through suffering and a healing force for redemption and renewal.

As both parties participated in a renewal of Baptist identity, they also participated in larger transformations of the religious context in America.[3] Sweeping changes to the practice of ministry carried Baptist clergywomen along as congregations and other ministry sites opened up to fuller and more sustained leadership by women. The pathway to remaking Baptist identity for many clergywomen paralleled a pathway that reimagined ministry more as a practice based on calling, gifts, and spiritual presence and less as a (male) role and identity. The context of denominational fighting was certainly experienced by many white Southern Baptists as a battlefield. However, the times also functioned as a playing field for a new way to imagine and play the game of ministry. In the past the rules of the game mostly excluded women, but as they entered the playing field, women challenged the rules and upped the stakes of the game. Through the everyday practices of pastoring and offering themselves in ministry to others, women embodied and enacted a new theology for ministry, which became one of their chief contributions to the era of the schism. As traditional forms of authority for ministry eroded, clergywomen led the way in grounding their pastoral authority in leadership that embodied more vulnerable, authentic, and mutually shared approaches to being human, being Baptist, and being ministers.

Epilogue

By 2000 the votes had been cast and the fracturing of the Southern Baptist Convention was clear, if not yet complete. The breaks were not clean, and many churches and individuals continued to split and splinter their Baptist identities and loyalties in the years that followed. The fragments, like so many shards of stained glass, fell in many directions. Some individuals and a few churches released their Baptist identity altogether in the years of schism. However, many who lived through the years of fighting continued to renew their sense of being Baptist.

When Chloe started her pastoral internship at Milesdale Baptist Church in 2000, that congregation was among the small and growing number who had long since departed the SBC in the 1980s and 1990s, affiliating with the breakaway groups. Meanwhile, biblicists continued their political march into a new century that began with narrow victories in every SBC presidential election since 1979. They paid little attention to autonomist churches that had stopped supporting the convention. Through the presidential appointment process, biblicists maintained their control of every SBC agency, board, and school. They continued to capitalize on the culture of complementarity to make their case publicly, appealing to biblical passages, urging submission to powerful forces, and fanning flames of fear over the loss of control in church, home, and denomination. Biblicists consolidated their power and captured the sentiments and practice of complementarity in their revision of the Baptist Faith and Message in 2000. The confession declared that wives should graciously submit to their husbands and the role of pastor should be limited to men. Young women like Chloe were interested in neither sentiment, and they gravitated to churches that were forging Baptist identities no longer attached to the SBC. However, the 2000 revision became a litmus test for employment, funding, chaplaincy endorsement, and missionary service throughout the convention and even into state and associational organizations.

By 2000 Rebecca was in her second call working with Habitat for Humanity, and like Chloe, she had long since given up her affiliations with the SBC. Many autonomist churches and individuals had taken their votes, mostly with their feet and their church budgets, to depart the SBC. In the new century, autonomists were consolidating their own power in organizations that pulled away in the 1980s and 1990s. Interestingly, the new groups, Baptist Women in Ministry, the Alliance of Baptists, and the Cooperative Baptist Fellowship, also occasionally capitalized on cultural notions of complementarity emphasizing a "positive" articulation that the gifts of both men and women were needed to *complete* the picture of ministry and family. Efforts to undo complementarity continued in various forms, particularly among clergywomen who were openly accepted in the breakaway groups. Yet when autonomists walked away from the SBC, they didn't leave complementarity behind altogether. The psychological and familial structures of complementarity remain even to the present, and they can be seen in both the stories of individual Baptists and in the shape of the new organizations where women continue to play mostly supportive and secondary roles with an increasing number of exceptions.[1] Notably, in 2014, women headed the Alliance of Baptists, the Cooperative Baptist Fellowship, the Baptist Peace Fellowship in North America, Baptist Women in Ministry, and two autonomist-related seminaries.[2]

In 2001, having completed her seminary degree and a residency in pastoral care, Martha was called to Monroe Corner Baptist Church as pastor. Monroe Corner was like many autonomist churches, somewhat ambivalent, not fully decided on staying or leaving the SBC, yet forming connections and giving funds to CBF. No matter how verbally supportive Southern Baptist parents were for their daughters in the 1970s, 1980s, 1990s, or even in the new century, the patterns of submission and domination remained deeply entrenched in both the social arrangements and psychological dynamics of a westernized, American culture. In white Baptist life, a subculture of complementarity remained normative across the spectrum of Baptists from the most conservative and fundamentalist to the most progressive and liberal. Complementarity was also naturalized and universalized by appeals to the Bible and to biology. Even more significantly, although largely hidden from view, complementarity remained in the unconscious psychological dynamics fostered in white southern families, where mothers raised children at the mid- and late twentieth century in near isolation and fathers continued to work outside the home. Consequently, the seeming permanence and universality of complementarity made it impervious to attempts at change it well into the twenty-first century. Before Martha's pastorate came to a close at Monroe Corner in 2005, the dynamics of her leadership and related issues of affiliation with the SBC and/or CBF came to a head. After months of disagreement and conflict, Martha was forced into a resignation she did not desire.

Despite Martha's loss of her pastoral role, she stayed in ministry, serving a community agency. Despite Joanna's departure after conflict with her congregation over events following 9/11, she also maintained her sense of American Baptist identity and connections, holding out hope that Baptist churches might continue to make more space for women's gifts for ministry. Clergywomen like Anna, Chloe, Joanna, Rebecca, and Martha remained novelties wherever they emerged in Baptist life. They constantly presented a challenge to the conventions of gender, marriage, parenting, and religious leadership simply by their presence. And they present not only a social challenge but also a deeply ingrained psychological and theological one.

As clergywomen, alongside many others, struggled against the complementarity culture and asserted their desires for love and work as Baptists, pastors, and women in the new century, they challenged the binary splitting of gender. They continued to defy the patterns of submission and domination. They confronted the limits of complementarity culture. The entire schism of Southern Baptists into parties of autonomists and biblicists was at its deepest psychological point a struggle against the paradigm of submission and domination on one side and a struggle to maintain that status quo on the other.[3] The parties lined up pretty neatly over the differing explicit causes. Autonomists championed servant leadership, women in ministry, and the recognition of everyone's call to ministry (the priesthood of all believers). Biblicists upheld the special call and authority of the male pastor, complementary relationships for women and men in workplace and home, and called for tradition in marriage and child-rearing.[4] Yet even deeper than this overt polarization around issues that typify the split socially, both parties were also reproducing a culture of complementarity by degrees. Both were up against a longstanding and powerful construal of the human condition, which demanded a hierarchical view of humanity, disempowering most of the human population and urging submission to authorities more powerful than themselves. The effect of this kind of arrangement is the dehumanization of the disempowered. And while the same can be said of those in power, their dehumanization is less obvious, because they embody the epitome of the cultural definition of what it is to be human. The powerful enjoy the benefits of that privilege. Their complicity with the cultural definitions and practices of what it means to be human contribute to keeping others in a less-than-human position while maintaining their privilege and place of power.[5]

Nevertheless, resistances to such arrangements of power and privilege are always somewhere at work in any system of human living. When the 2000 Baptist Faith and Message was published, Anna said she "struggled big time," but she found the courage to break her connections to the SBC in 2003 so the Cooperative Baptists would endorse her for working as a chaplain. In the final three decades of the twentieth century, and well into the twenty-first, Baptist clergywomen were exemplars of such resistance. Whatever else they may have been doing, they were asserting their desire to be fully human and to do work that was fulfilling and would help them achieve basic recognition and mutual well-being. Of course, they were not always able to achieve their goals, and rarely would any of them have expressed their desires in such assertive or direct ways.

The women interviewed in this book no longer consider themselves Southern Baptist, yet the Baptist sensibility has a way of lingering in the lives of those shaped by the powerful tradition and formed for ministry in a crucible of conflict over Baptist identity. By starting with these stories, a new interpretation of the schism emerged, bringing a different palpable set of concerns into focus. Through their stories, the anatomy of Baptist schism shifts in focus and brings into sharp relief how the struggle was a gendered, psychological, and theological one. The new interpretation points out just how much was at stake for both churches and individuals living through the period of Southern Baptist schism.

Epilogue

Appendix A

Resolution on Ordination and the Role of Women in Ministry

June 1984

WHEREAS, We, the messengers to the Southern Baptist Convention meeting in Kansas City, June 12–14, 1984, recognize the authority of Scripture in all matters of faith and practice including the autonomy of the local church; and

WHEREAS, The New Testament enjoins all Christians to proclaim the gospel; and

WHEREAS, The New Testament churches as a community of faith recognized God's ordination and anointing of some believers for special ministries (e.g., 1 Timothy 2:7; Titus 1:15) and in consequence of their demonstrated loyalty to the gospel, conferred public blessing and engaged in public dedicatory prayer setting them apart for service; and

WHEREAS, The New Testament does not mandate that all who are divinely called to ministry be ordained; and

WHEREAS, In the New Testament, ordination symbolizes spiritual succession to the world task of proclaiming and extending the gospel of Christ, and not a sacramental transfer of unique divine grace that perpetuates apostolic authority; and

WHEREAS, The New Testament emphasizes the equal dignity of men and women (Gal. 3:28) and that the Holy Spirit was at Pentecost divinely outpoured on men and women alike (Acts 2:17); and

WHEREAS, Women as well as men prayed and prophesied in public worship services (1 Cor. 11:2–16), and Priscilla joined her husband in teaching Apollos (Acts 18:26), and women fulfilled special church service-ministries as exemplified by Phoebe whose work Paul tributes as that of a servant of the church (Rom. 16:1); and

WHEREAS, The Scriptures attest to God's delegated order of authority (God the head of Christ, Christ the head of man, man the head of woman, man and woman dependent one upon the other to the glory of God) distinguishing the roles of men and women in public prayer and prophecy (1 Cor. 11:2–5); and

WHEREAS, The Scriptures teach that women are not in public worship to assume a role of authority over men lest confusion reign in the local church (1 Cor. 14:33–36); and

WHEREAS, While Paul commends women and men alike in other roles of ministry and service (Titus 2:1–10), he excludes women from pastoral leadership (1 Tim. 2:12) to preserve a submission God requires because the man was first in creation and the woman was first in the Edenic fall (1 Tim. 2:13ff); and

WHEREAS, These Scriptures are not intended to stifle the creative contribution of men and women as co-workers in many roles of church service, both on distant mission fields and in domestic ministries, but imply that women and men are nonetheless divinely gifted for distinctive areas of evangelical engagement; and

WHEREAS, Women are held in high honor for their unique and significant contribution to the advancement of Christ's kingdom, and the building of godly homes should be esteemed for its vital contribution to developing personal Christian character and Christlike concern for others.

Therefore, be it RESOLVED, That we not decide concerns of Christians doctrine and practice by modern cultural, sociological, and ecclesiastical trends or by emotional factors; that we remind ourselves of the dearly bought Baptist principle of the final authority of Scripture in matters of faith and conduct; and that we encourage the service of women in all aspects of church life and work other than pastoral functions and leadership roles entailing ordination.

Kansas City, Missouri

Appendix B

Hymns, Songs, and Poems

Wherever He Leads I'll Go

"Take up thy cross and follow Me," I heard my Master say;
"I gave My life to ransom thee, Surrender your all today."

Refrain:
Wherever He leads I'll go, Wherever He leads I'll go,
I'll follow my Christ who loves me so, Wherever He leads I'll go.

He drew me closer to His side, I sought His will to know,
And in that will I now abide, Wherever He leads I'll go.

It may be through the shadows dim, Or o'er the stormy sea,
I take my cross and follow Him, Wherever He leadeth me.

My heart, my life, my all I bring To Christ who loves me so;
he is my Master, Lord, and King, Wherever He leads I'll go.

B. B. McKinney, "Wherever He Leads I'll Go"
Tune: "Falls Creek"

Spirit of God

Spirit of God in the clear running water
Blowing to greatness the trees on the hill.
Spirit of God in the finger of morning:
Fill the earth, bring it to birth,
And blow where you will.
Blow, blow, blow till I be
But the breath of the Spirit blowing in me.

Down in the meadow the willows are moaning
Sheep in the pastureland cannot lie still.
Spirit of God, creation is groaning:
Fill the earth, bring it to birth,
And blow where you will.

Blow, blow, blow till I be
But the breath of the Spirit blowing in me.

I saw the scar of a year that lay dying
Heard the lament of a lone whippoorwill.
Spirit of God, see that cloud crying:
Fill the earth, bring it to birth,
And blow where you will.
Blow, blow, blow till I be
But the breath of the Spirit blowing in me.

Spirit of God every man's heart is lonely
Watching and waiting and hungry until
Spirit of God, man longs that you only
Fulfill the earth, bring it to birth,
Blow, blow, blow till I be
But the breath of the Spirit blowing in me.

Miriam Therese Winters
Audio Recording, Joy Is Like the Rain
© 1965, Medical Mission Sisters

Holy Spirit, Comforter

Holy Spirit, Comforter come and comfort be
Rest our fears dry our tears set your children free
Long are we in bondage, sin has had its say
But we rejoice for by your voice the chains all fall away

Comfort now with courage give us peace with power
Fill us up and call us out to face this urgent hour
Long are we in bondage, sin has had its say
But we rejoice for by your voice the chains all fall away

Holy Spirit, Comforter come and comfort be
Rest our fears dry our tears set your children free
Long are we in bondage, sin has had its say
But we rejoice for by your voice the chains all fall away

Paul D. Duke lyrics
© 1982, 2010 Darrell Adams

The Weaver

I celebrate a mother God,
Gently weaving, working carefully.
I celebrate the hands of skill, creating beauty within me.
I celebrate the working of the loom, reconnecting myself,
weaving a tapestry that picks up threads of pain and anger and
grief and loss, and power and courage and strength and grace.

Here are the broken threads. This should have been solid here.
This innocence should have continued on, this openness should
have come through here, this pattern of trust should have been
right here, making a design that all would see
and say, "What beauty!"
But these threads were broken, ripped from the fabric of me, and
I was afraid to show anyone the tear.
I thought it was my fault, that all would look
and say, "What horror!"
Now we pick up this broken thread, my weaving God and me.
Now we do the work of repair, and as the fabric is made strong
I look in surprise and say to myself, "What beauty I reclaim!"
Out of the torn places, I reclaim wholeness.
Out of the broken places, I reclaim strength.
Out of the shatteredness, I reclaim power.
Out of the horror and the shame and the pain, I reclaim
openness, innocence, courage.

The Weaver will not be discouraged or deterred.
We weave fabric which no one's violence will destroy,
and I discover the beauty of me.

Amen.

> Catherine J. Foote, "The Weaver," in *Survivor Prayers:
> Talking with God about Childhood Sexual Abuse*
> (Louisville, KY: Westminster John Knox, 1994), 17.

Appendix C

Alliance of Baptists Covenant

In a time when historic Baptist principles, freedoms, and traditions need a clear voice, and in our personal and corporate response to the call of God in Jesus Christ to be disciples and servants in the world, we commit ourselves to:

1) The freedom of the individual, led by God's Spirit within the family of faith, to read and interpret the Scriptures, relying on the historical understanding by the church and on the best methods of modern biblical study;

2) The freedom of the local church under the authority of Jesus Christ to shape its own life and mission, call its own leadership, and ordain whom it perceives as gifted for ministry, male or female;

3) The larger body of Jesus Christ, expressed in various Christian traditions, and to a cooperation with believers everywhere in giving full expression to the Gospel;

4) The servant role of leadership within the church, following the model of our Servant Lord, and to full partnership of all of God's people in mission and ministry;

5) Theological education in congregations, colleges, and seminaries characterized by reverence for biblical authority and respect for open inquiry and responsible scholarship;

6) The proclamation of the Good News of Jesus Christ and the calling of God to all peoples to repentance and faith, reconciliation and hope, social and economic justice;

7) The principle of a free church in a free state and the opposition to any effort either by church or state to use the other for its own purposes.

MISSION

To keep faith with our covenant we will:

1) Make the worship of God primary in all our gatherings.

2) Foster relationships within the Alliance and with other people of faith.

3) Create places of refuge and renewal for those who are wounded or ignored by the church.

4) Side with those who are poor.

5) Pursue justice with and for those who are oppressed.

6) Care for the earth.

7) Work for peace.

8) Honor wisdom and lifelong learning.

9) Hold ourselves accountable for equity, collegiality, and diversity.

Notes

Introduction

1. All names and identifying information of the five clergywomen in this study were changed to protect the identities of the study participants and their families, churches, and schools while preserving the character of the places, their political and cultural locations within Baptist life, and their role, if any, in the schism.
2. See "SBC to Cease Endorsing Ordained Female Chaplains," *Baptist Standard,* Feb. 18, 2002, http://www.baptiststandard.com/2002/2_18/print/endorsing.html, accessed May 31, 2006; B. B. McKinney, "Wherever He Leads I'll Go," *Baptist Hymnal* (Nashville: Convention Press, 1975), 361.
3. A culture of complementarity is a concept explored in depth in this study. The basic idea is that of a culture that upholds universal differences between males and females that "complement" (or complete) each other. See pages 9–11 for a more extended discussion and analysis.
4. The protocol of this study benefitted from the oversight of two institutional review boards across a number of years (2003 to 2013). The early years of the project received oversight from Vanderbilt University in Nashville, Tennessee (IRB 020124). The more recent years received oversight from Luther Seminary in St. Paul, Minnesota.
5. The bold claim that the stories in this book constitute "paradigm cases" is based on the novelty of interpretation they together create and the idea that richer data is available in contextualized cases of experience-near reports. For a description of paradigm cases, see Bent Flyvbjerg, "Five Misunderstandings about Case-Study Research," *Qualitative Inquiry* 12, no. 2 (Apr. 2006): 223. As Flyvbjerg points out, "Social science has not succeeded in producing general, context-independent theory and, thus, has in the final instance nothing else to offer than concrete, context-dependent knowledge. And the case study is especially well suited to produce this knowledge."
6. A substantial amount of writing on the schism can be qualified as partisan, written from a convictional perspective by one party or another. Materials from the biblicist party perspective include James C. Hefley, *The Truth in Crisis: The Controversy in the Southern Baptist Convention* (Dallas, TX: Criterion Publications, 1986); and James C. Hefley, *The Conservative Resurgence in the Southern Baptist Convention* (Hannibal, MO: Hannibal Books, 1991). Hefley also published four other volumes between these first and last books in his series. From the autonomist party came the following interpretations: Walter B. Shurden, ed., *The Struggle for the Soul of the SBC: Moderate Responses to the Fundamentalist Movement* (Macon, GA: Mercer Univ. Press, 1993); Rob James and Gary Leazer, eds., *The Takeover in the Southern Baptist Convention: A Brief History* (Decatur, GA: Baptists Today, 1994); and Walter B. Shurden and Randy Shepley, *Going for the Jugular: A Documentary History of the SBC Holy War* (Macon, GA: Mercer Univ. Press, 1996). Several books attempted to chronicle the events with even-handed analysis but in the end favored one perspective or the other. Joe Edward

Barnhart, *The Southern Baptist Holy War: The Self-Destructive Struggle for Power within the Largest Protestant Denomination in America* (Austin: Texas Monthly Press, 1986), sympathetic to moderates, proposed a divorce between the parties; David T. Morgan, *The New Crusades, the New Holy Land: Conflict in the Southern Baptist Convention, 1969–1991* (Tuscaloosa: Univ. of Alabama Press, 1996), was also sympathetic to moderates. Jesse C. Fletcher wrote about the events as the official SBC chronicler in *The Southern Baptist Convention: A Sesquicentennial History* (Nashville: Broadman and Holman, 1994). Jerry Sutton offered the first lengthy analysis unapologetically from a biblicist perspective: *The Baptist Reformation: The Conservative Resurgence in the Southern Baptist Convention* (Nashville: Broadman and Holman, 2000). Two volumes of partisan literature attempted to illustrate the rhetoric used by leaders (and laity) who were firsthand participants in convention during the years of schism. See Carl L. Kell and Raymond L. Camp, *In the Name of the Father: The Rhetoric of the New Southern Baptist Convention* (Carbondale: Southern Illinois Univ. Press, 1999); and Carl L. Kell, *Exiled: Voices of the Southern Baptist Convention Holy War* (Knoxville: Univ. of Tennessee Press, 2006).

7. The most comprehensive academic studies appeared in the following order: Ellen M. Rosenberg, *The Southern Baptists: A Subculture in Transition* (Knoxville: Univ. of Tennessee Press, 1989); Bill Leonard, *God's Last and Only Hope: The Fragmentation of the Southern Baptist Convention* (Grand Rapids, MI: Eerdmans, 1990); Nancy Tatom Ammerman, *Baptist Battles: Social Change and Religious Conflict in the Southern Baptist Convention* (New Brunswick, NJ: Rutgers Univ. Press, 1990); Nancy Tatom Ammerman, ed., *Southern Baptists Observed: Multiple Perspectives on a Changing Denomination* (Knoxville: Univ. of Tennessee Press, 1993); Arthur Emery Farnsley II, *Southern Baptist Politics: Authority and Power in the Restructuring of an American Denomination* (University Park: Pennsylvania State Univ. Press, 1994); David Stricklin, *A Genealogy of Dissent: Southern Baptist Protest in the Twentieth Century* (Lexington: Univ. of Kentucky Press, 1999); Barry Hankins, *Uneasy in Babylon: Southern Baptist Conservatives and American Culture* (Tuscaloosa: Univ. of Alabama Press, 2002); Gregory Wills, *Southern Baptist Theological Seminary, 1859–2009* (New York: Oxford Univ. Press, 2009).

8. Two book-length treatments and several dissertations published since 2008 are among the first books to consider seriously women's contributions to Baptist life in the late twentieth century at length. Betsy Flowers, Susan Shaw, and I were interviewing Baptist women in the early 2000s and taking their stories into account in the new interpretations of Southern Baptist identity and shifts in Baptist life. See Elizabeth Flowers, "Varieties of Evangelical Womanhood: Southern Baptists, Gender, and American Culture" (PhD diss., Duke Univ., 2007); Eileen Campbell-Reed, "Anatomy of a Schism: How Clergywomen's Narratives Interpret the Fracturing of the Southern Baptist Convention" (PhD diss., Vanderbilt Univ., 2008); and Susan Shaw, *God Speaks to Us, Too: Southern Baptist Women on Church, Home, and Society* (Lexington: Univ. of Kentucky, 2008). As I do in this book, Shaw and Flowers follow the insistence by Ann Braude that women's history is religious history in America and to understand that religious history, women's contributions need to move from margin

to center. See Ann Braude, "Women's History *Is* American Religious History," in *Religion and American Culture: A Reader*, 2nd ed., ed. David G. Hackett (New York: Routledge, 2003), 161–78.

9. Often the institutional gains and losses determine the perspective in the studies, many of which fail even to consider a split, instead seeing the convention itself (or one of its schools or agencies) as an institutional prize won or lost. Leonard, *God's Last and Only Hope*, and Ammerman, *Baptist Battles*, make the most comprehensive arguments about the causes of the schism, but these volumes appeared in 1990, before the full divisions of the split were negotiated. Less often are the organizations that split from the SBC treated in the same analysis with the convention itself. Only Shaw, *God Speaks to Us, Too*, and Flowers, *Into the Pulpit: Southern Baptist Women and Power since World War II* (Chapel Hill: Univ. of North Carolina Press, 2012), give some attention to groups that formed out of the split.

10. The following brief review summarizes academic contributions to the analysis of the schism, and the book considers the partisan materials primarily as evidence for and the embodiment of widespread divisions.

11. The best early examples are Leonard and Ammerman, but neither devotes more than a section to the "issue" of women in the controversy. Sarah Frances Anders and Marilyn Metcalf-Whittaker, "Women as Lay Leaders and Clergy: A Crucial Issue," in Ammerman, *Southern Baptists Observed*, 214, provide statistical data about women in ministry but little in the way of analysis. Women, they say, prefer not to be portrayed as symbols of the Baptist controversy, yet their essay effects the same problem by pointing out the minority status of women in each area of Baptist life.

12. As Ammerman, *Baptist Battles*, 93–94, notes, "When fundamentalists claimed that moderates did not really believe the Bible, they were likely to point to women pastors as the perfect example of defying God's Word. And when moderates wanted to contrast their tolerance and open-mindedness with fundamentalist oppressiveness, they pointed to their acceptance of women as proof." Women not only were symbols of differences between the parties but also faced, "overt opposition . . . routine exclusion . . . invisibility, along with occasional jokes and hostile remarks."

13. Leonard, *God's Last and Only Hope*, 151, says women's role in church and society was one of the doctrinal issues that crossed the "thin line" between "inerrant Scripture and inerrant dogma." He argues that both conservatives and moderates reached "logical" conclusions about the role of women, conclusions that fit their interpretations of Scripture.

14. Ibid., 153. Leonard concludes in 1990 that women's ordination "is a major source of fragmentation for the denomination with no sign of resolution in sight."

15. Rosenberg, *Southern Baptists*, 127, understands ordained women to be ostracized as a *result* of the fighting: "The steady marginalization of the handful of women pastors is an important result of fundamentalist pressure." Farnsley, *Southern Baptist Politics*, portrays women's ordination as one of a laundry list of issues, but one that did not hold the center and was eclipsed by democratic procedures that held sway in the convention. Even Ammerman in *Baptist Battles*, who includes the most comprehensive data

collection, including surveys, participant observations, interviews, statistical analysis, and careful reading of history and textual sources, still primarily treats women as an issue rather than a source for information or analysis in the controversy.

16. Both Stricklin, *Genealogy of Dissent,* 114–41, and Hankins, *Uneasy in Babylon,* 200–239, take this approach.

17. More recent monographs consider a wider variety of "overlapping situations" akin to Edward Farley's practical theological task of "interpreting situations," which entails trying to understand the "intersituational issues" or the "impingement of other situations on the local situation." See Edward Farley, "Interpreting Situations: An Inquiry into the Nature of Practical Theology," in *Practicing Gospel: Unconventional Thoughts on the Church's Ministry,* by Edward Farley (Louisville, KY: Westminster John Knox Press, 2003), 39. Examples include Hankins, *Uneasy in Babylon;* Stricklin, *Genealogy of Dissent;* and Flowers, *Into the Pulpit.*

18. Three books fall into this category: the first academic book to address the schism, Rosenberg's *Southern Baptists;* Farnsley, *Southern Baptist Politics;* and Ammerman, *Southern Baptists Observed.* In *Southern Baptists Observed,* Ammerman brings together Baptists and non-Baptists, scholars of religion and the social sciences, and even journalists. Her framing of the book helps unify the methodological diversity of their approaches. Both Flowers and Shaw used qualitative interviewing to gather stories, and they bring a gender studies lens to their work, but neither of them utilizes psychological frameworks for interpretation.

19. A few concerns are addressed, such as charismatic leadership, grief over loss, grandiosity, and so on, but no sustained psychological analysis of the schism has been offered to date.

20. By looking at the "genealogies" of intellectual influence on the two extreme parties in the SBC schism, Hankins, *Uneasy in Babylon,* and Stricklin, *Genealogy of Dissent,* reach beyond the insularity of interpretations that keep recycling previously told stories.

21. Jessica Benjamin, *The Bonds of Love: Psychoanalysis, Feminism and the Problem of Domination* (New York: Pantheon Books, 1988), 81, says that neither essentializing gender nor disregarding it will lead to a better understanding of the character of what it is to be human. Attention to "the interaction of culture and psychological process" is needed for understanding and change to be possible.

22. Charles Darwin's six basic affects, supported in studies by psychologists and cultural anthropologists, are common to all humans (anger, joy, sadness, surprise, fear, and disgust). Volney Gay argues that although a discreet set of affects can be identified and that they share a "curve of intensity that builds up slowly then rises faster and faster, is satiated, and subsides," these affects cannot be reduced to formulas but are better understood metaphorically "through analogue devices like those available in poetic metaphor or dramatic action." See Volney Gay, *Joy and the Objects of Psychoanalysis: Literature, Belief, and Neurosis* (New York: State Univ. of New York Press, 2001), 131, 142. See also Charles Darwin, *The Expression of the Emotions in Man and Animals,* 3rd ed. (London: HarperCollins, 1998).

23. The theological framework of the human condition described in Edward Farley's *Good and Evil: Interpreting a Human Condition* (Minneapolis: Fortress, 1991) conceptualizes three interpenetrating realms of human existence: the individual/subjective, the interhuman/relational and the social/collective. Farley's realms of human being are keys in this book for interpreting Baptist identity and change. Chapters 3 and 4 tell Joanna and Rebecca's stories in ways that explore the psychological and theological effects, particularly as they relate to the relational or interhuman sphere.
24. The psychologies engaged in this study often hold general psychological ideas or beliefs that circulate culturally and reference some more complex conceptual material. When possible, the notes will point the reader to related psychological thinkers and concepts.
25. Philip E. Thompson and Anthony R. Cross address the problem of "recycling history" in their introduction to *Recycling the Past or Researching History? Studies in Baptist Historiography and Myths* (Waynesboro, GA: Paternoster, 2005), xv–xviii. They note the following factors that create the problem of "recycling the past" for Baptists: ongoing debates about Baptist origins, the great variety of sources for Baptist thought and practice, the perennial concern for Baptist identity, and dilemma of balancing primary and secondary historical sources.
26. Although Flowers, *Into the Pulpit,* and Shaw, *God Speaks to Us, Too,* give priority to clergywomen in their books, neither of them are aiming for the kind of psychological or theological analysis of clergywomen's lives attempted here. Multiple interpretations are crucial for seeing the complexity of lived human experience and its interface with the sacred.
27. For example, both Stricklin and Hankins devote a chapter to discussing the role of women in the schism. Stricklin, *Genealogy of Dissent,* 113–41, 160–61, makes a case that women seeking ordination were exemplary "dissenters," calling for gender justice in the early 1980s. By launching a movement of support and action, he argues, they became catalysts, which galvanized "fundamentalists" to commit themselves to winning the denominational apparatus of control for their cause. In contrast to Stricklin, Hankins, *Uneasy in Babylon,* 41–52, 200–239, tells the story of women's submission from the perspective of "culture warriors," who say they were galvanized not by women's ordination but by the issue of abortion to win control in the denomination and to regain a stronghold in the culture. Women's submission in home and church became an occasion to express concern about the culture crisis and offer the right response from an inerrant Bible. Conservatives used every possible opportunity to challenge the cultural norm of women's equality and gain a hearing for their other concerns. In both arguments, women play supporting or symbolic roles rather than central ones.
28. The analysis addresses the issues of race and sexuality where they arise in the stories of the clergywomen.
29. Ellen M. Rosenberg, "The Southern Baptist Response to the Newest South," in Ammerman, *Southern Baptists Observed,* 144–45. Hankins, *Uneasy in Babylon,* 107–17 ff., offers a more nuanced description.

30. In his opening chapter, Sutton, *Baptist Reformation,* 6–29, details the "theological inadequacies" of SBC professors, pastors, and leaders from a biblicist perspective.
31. Jackson Carroll, *God's Potters: Pastoral Leadership and the Shaping of Congregations* (Grand Rapids, MI: Eerdmans, 2006), 7. For 2012 statistics on women in pastoral leadership, see Eileen Campbell-Reed, "Baptists in Tension: The Status of Women's Leadership and Ministry, 2012," *Review and Expositor* 110, no. 1 *(Winter 2013): 49–64.* See also Barbara Brown Zikmund, Adair T. Lumis, and Patricia Mei Yin Chang, *Clergywomen: An Uphill Calling* (Louisville, KY: Westminster John Knox Press, 1998), which was the last book to take seriously the participation of Baptist women in changes to the larger context of ministry in the United States.
32. See Eileen R. Campbell-Reed, "Baptist Clergywomen's Narratives: Reinterpreting the Southern Baptist Convention Schism," in *Pastoral Bearings: Lived Religion and Pastoral Theology,* ed. Leonard Hummel, Mary Clark Moschella, and Jane Maynard (Lanham, MD: Lexington Books, 2010), 143–45, 170. Barry Hankins reached a similar conclusion in "Southern Baptists and the F-Word: A Historiography of the Southern Baptist Convention Controversy and What It Might Mean," in *Through a Glass Darkly: Contested Notions of Baptist Identity,* ed. Keith Harper (Tuscaloosa: Univ. of Alabama Press, 2012), 296–323.
33. Baptists also ordain men and women as deacon ministers, who are not typically professional ministers, nor do they regularly carry out all pastoral functions. However, performing any pastoral task is open to any baptized believer authorized by a Baptist congregation. Baptist deacons are typically lay men and women who serve and/or lead in congregations along with pastoral ministers (clergy). The term "clergywomen" also communicates outside Baptist life to indicate the full pastoral authority of ministry granted in ecclesial communities. The use of the term follows Constant H. Jacquet Jr.'s definition in Eileen W. Lindner, ed., *Yearbook of American and Canadian Churches* (Nashville: Abingdon Press, 2010): clergywomen are those "ordained to the highest level of ministry carrying full rights and privileges within their church." See Zikmund, Lumis, and Chang, *Clergywomen,* 171–72.
34. Because the meaning of the "priesthood of all believers" is among the points of contention between Baptists, the tension between clergy and laity is central to understanding the meanings of ordained ministry and the disagreements between the parties.
35. I coined the terms autonomist and biblicist in my 2008 dissertation. See Campbell-Reed, "Anatomy of a Schism" (PhD diss., 2008).
36. The term "schism" comes up occasionally in the literature about the SBC controversies, often as "schismatic." The term "anatomy" is used in at least one article by Larry L. McSwain, "Anatomy of the SBC Institutional Crisis," *Review and Expositor* 88, no. 1 (Winter 1991): 25–35. The term is often used, however, to describe religious break-ups and institutional splits through history including the eleventh century split between the eastern and western churches.
37. Ammerman, *Baptist Battles,* 178, notes that "the primary symbols in this denominational fight were the Bible on one side, and freedom, on the other." Ammerman also identifies through surveys and interviews (72–73 ff.) five groups on a continuum:

self-identified fundamentalists, fundamentalist conservatives, conservatives, moderate conservatives, and self-identified moderates. These are important distinctions for getting at the subtleties of self-understanding among Southern Baptists of the 1980s, but in the end polarization defined the schism and most everyone was forced to identify with one group or another, thus the choices: autonomist party and biblicist party. See Ammerman, *Baptist Battles,* 78–80. In the accounts written from the left wing of the Baptist controversy, labels for two opposing parties are most often called "moderates" and "fundamentalists." The labels favored in the literature from the Right are usually "liberals" and "conservatives." Both "liberal" and "fundamentalist" are used pejoratively by opposing groups.

38. Ibid., 174–78.
39. Walter Shurden posed the question of a "cracking synthesis" in 1981. See Walter B. Shurden, "The Southern Baptist Synthesis: Is It Cracking?" *Baptist History and Heritage* 16, no 2 (Apr. 1981): 2–11. Shurden identifies multiple streams of tradition shaping the contemporary context of Baptist life and observes five stressors on the Baptist synthesis: cultural, denominational, financial, creedal, and theological.
40. The analysis in this book has an imbalance in the number of voices from each party because it prioritizes the voices of women; the effect is to allow more autonomist sympathizers into the text.
41. In her chapter on "Gender Regulations," Judith Butler, *Undoing Gender* (New York: Routledge, 2004), 43, begins to untangle the problem of gender: "the conflation of gender with masculine/feminine, man/woman, male/female, thus performs the very naturalization that the notion of gender is meant to forestall."
42. Stephanie Coontz traces this transition among others in *Marriage, a History: From Obedience to Intimacy or How Love Conquered Marriage* (New York: Penguin, 2005), 247: "It took more than 150 years to establish the love-based, male breadwinner marriage as the dominant model in North America and Western Europe. It took less than 25 years to dismantle it. . . . Marriage lost its role as the 'master event' that governed young people's sexual lives, their assumption of adult roles, their job choices and their transition into parenthood."
43. Relational theorists like Jessica Benjamin, *Like Subjects, Love Objects: Essays on Recognition and Sexual Difference* (New Haven, CT: Yale, 1995), 11–16; philosophers like Butler, *Undoing Gender,* 150–51; and pastoral theologians like Pamela Cooper-White, *Shared Wisdom: The Use of the Self in Pastoral Care and Counseling* (Minneapolis: Fortress Press, 2004), 186–93, argue for expanding understandings of identity, relationality, and gender, as complex, multiple, and fluid.
44. The language first appeared in the 1998 Resolution on the Strengthening the Marriage Covenant, http://www.sbc.net/resolutions/amResolution.asp?ID=699, accessed Jan. 21, 2014. The full Baptist Faith and Message (2000) is located at http://www.sbc.net/bfm/bfm2000.asp, accessed, Jan. 21, 2014.
45. Baptist Faith and Message, 2000.
46. Karen Seat, "Evangelicals and Women's Leadership in the Post-Palin Era," paper presented at the American Academy of Religion annual meeting, Nov. 2012, Chicago,

argues that uses and means of complementarity change over time. Her chief example is the rise to political power of Sarah Palin, Michele Bachmann, and other conservative female politicians. They represent a sea change in which "'complementarians' have sought to incorporate women's civic leadership into their existing anti-feminist narrative." She says, "While social conservatives continue to decry liberal feminism, their anti-feminist message has shifted its focus away from opposing women's full participation in modern public life to dismantling big government and modernism itself."

47. Systematic theologian Edward Farley, in *Good and Evil,* captures the philosophical and theological existentialism of this view of human being.

48. Ibid., 139–53. While the tragic structure of human being opens up the possibility for harm, corruption, and evil, it also is the space in which redemption, founding, and grace come into the human experience. Farley builds his understanding of "being founded" on Paul Tillich's classic text, *The Courage to Be* (New Haven, CT: Yale Univ. Press, 1952).

49. See Peter Fonagy, *Attachment Theory and Psychoanalysis* (New York: Other Press, 2001), 84–90, for a discussion of the concepts of splitting and projective identification as bridge issues between empirical studies of infant attachment and the formulations of theorists like Melanie Klein and Otto Kernberg, who conceptualized the necessity of sensitive and attuned care giving to function as containers for powerful feelings in infants and children.

50. Benjamin, *Bonds of Love,* 18, observes, "Once we accept the idea that infants do not begin life as part of an undifferentiated unity, the issue is not only how we separate from oneness, but also how we connect to and recognized others; the issue is not how we become free of the other, but how we actively engage and make ourselves known in relationship to the other."

51. D. W. Winnicott, *Playing and Reality* (New York: Routledge, 1971), 10: "The good-enough mother . . . starts off with an almost complete adaptation to her infant's needs, and as time proceeds she adapts less and less completely, gradually, according to the infant's growing ability to deal with her failure."

52. See Butler, *Undoing Gender,* 42: "Gender is not exactly what one 'is' nor is it precisely what one 'has.' Gender is the apparatus by which the production and normalization of masculine and feminine take place along with interstitial forms of hormonal, chromosomal, psychic, and performative that gender assumes. . . . Gender is the mechanism by which notions of masculine and feminine are produced and naturalized, but gender might very well be the apparatus by which such terms are deconstructed and denaturalized."

53. Disentangling power and gender in the women's movement of the 1960s and 1970s set off innumerable social and personal identity crises to which Southern Baptists and Baptist clergywomen were heirs. However, like previous worries over gender, Braude, "Women's History," 168, challenges the "narrative fiction" that historians of religion in America tell about the eighteenth-century declension, nineteenth-century feminization, and twentieth-century secularization of Christianity in the U.S. context.

She observes, "Because women are viewed as the less powerful half of society, their numerical dominance is interpreted as a decline in power for a religious institution."

54. Hankins, *Uneasy in Babylon,* 238–39.

55. Numerous psychological concepts could be identified and analyzed from the women's narratives for this interpretation. Two broad schools of thought inform my psychological readings of the situation. The psychoanalytic tradition, including some philosophical approaches, object relations theory, self psychology, and the relational school of thought are among the dialogue partners, and they remain at the referential level of the work. The other set of conversation partners are in pastoral theology and include a number of feminist pastoral theologians who draw on psychological concepts in their understandings of the human situation.

56. Barry Hankins shares this observation regarding historical and theological perspectives. See Hankins, "Southern Baptists and the F-Word," 302 and n. 18.

57. Corruption or corporate sin between social groups, according to Farley, *Good and Evil,* 130–35, 257–60, becomes possible when a particular good is absolutized in response to the demands and uncertainties of life. Absolutizing finite goods becomes a form of idolatry, embracing the object of need—an idea or anything temporal—for the sake of escaping vulnerability and finitude rather than remaining open to the "eternal horizon" or that which unites all other basic human passions or drives. When social groups confuse their primary aims (on the order of serving, educating, promoting justice, healing, etc.) and secondary aims (such as keeping the doors open, paying the bills, maintaining institutions, etc.), they "victimize and subjugate" other groups, losing a sense of the humanity of the "others."

58. The shift in focus to the everyday lives and practical theologies of subjects is part of a turn by academic theologians toward practice and the communal-contextual settings of lived theology. See, for example, Bonnie J. Miller-McLemore, "Pastoral Theology as Public Theology: Revolutions in the 'Fourth Area,'" in *Pastoral Care and Counseling: Redefining the Paradigms,* ed. Nancy Ramsay (Nashville: Abingdon Press), 45–85.

59. My thanks go to Richard Carp for introducing this idea in a workshop at the American Academy of Religion in 2009.

60. Randall Lolley, Eileen R. Campbell-Reed, Pope A. Duncan, Pete Hill, and Nancy A. Thurmond, eds., *Findings: A Report of the Special Study Commission to Study the Question: "Should the Cooperative Baptist Fellowship become a Separate Convention?"* (Atlanta: Cooperative Baptist Fellowship, 1996).

61. See Mark Chaves, *Ordaining Women: Culture and Conflict in Religious Organizations* (Cambridge: Harvard Univ. Press, 1997), 14–18, 104–5, passim. Baptist beginnings for women's ordination are sporadic and hard to trace. See Pamela R. Durso, "She-Preachers, Bossy Women, and Children of the Devil: Women Ministers in the Baptist Tradition 1609–2012," *Review and Expositor* 110, no. 1 (Winter 2013): 36–39. Durso identifies several isolated instances of Northern/American Baptist and Seventh Day Baptist women being ordained to ministry in the nineteenth century.

62. Ammerman, *Baptist Battles,* 64.

63. The Elliott controversy was sparked in 1961. The Baptist Faith and Message revisions began in 1962 and were delivered in 1963 at the Kansas City convention, with a stated intent "to build upon the structure of the 1925 Statement, keeping in mind the 'certain needs' of our generation." Baptist Faith and Message, 1963, http://www.sbc.net/bfm2000/bfmcomparison.asp, accessed Dec. 30, 2015. For a recounting of the events, see Ammerman, *Baptist Battles,* 63–65. Ironically, the statement about Jesus Christ was removed in the next revision in 2000.
64. Durso, "She-Preachers, Bossy Women, and Children of the Devil," 38–39.
65. In early 1965, Baptist Press noted that the membership of Southern Baptist churches grew to "10.6 million Baptists [who] are members of 33,388 churches." "Mission Gifts Pass $100 Million Mark," Baptist Press, Feb. 23, 1965, http://media.sbhla.org.s3.amazonaws.com/2014,13-Feb-1965.pdf, accessed Nov. 30, 2014. The "total SBC membership reported for 1965–66 in February was 10,952,463." "United Methodist Church Bigger than SBC, Maybe" Baptist Press, July 7, 1967, http://media.sbhla.org.s3.amazonaws.com/2423,07-Jul-1967.pdf, accessed Nov. 30, 2014.
66. Hefley, *Conservative Resurgence,* 32–33, describes Pressler's initial meeting with Patterson.
67. Leon McBeth reports: "Between 1964 and 1978 perhaps fifty or more women have been ordained in Southern Baptist Churches." He then published a list of fifty-eight women compiled by Helen Lee Turner. See Leon McBeth, *Women in Baptist Life* (Nashville: Broadman Press, 1979), 154–55. See Charles W. Deweese, *Women Deacons and Deaconesses: 400 Years of Baptist Service* (Macon, GA: Mercer Univ. Press, 2005), 121–24.
68. Ammerman, *Baptist Battles,* 204–7. The role of the Committee on Resolutions is to receive proposed resolutions, decide if they are appropriately worded, and present them to the body for a vote. As the committee shifted from autonomist to biblicist in its makeup during the 1980s, motions were more likely to reflect biblicist values. Ammerman also points out that the resolutions were often used or referenced by the various SBC agencies that wished to justify work that might otherwise be considered off center. For example, the Christian Life Commission prior to 1979 would appeal to resolutions about abortion or women or race that supported their work. After the parties began to polarize, new leaders of SBC agencies would make similar appeals to resolutions that supported biblicist causes.
69. One of the outcomes of the second Genesis controversy was the formation of the Baptist Faith and Message Fellowship. The group and its publication, the *Southern Baptist Journal,* took "an aggressive path from the first publication, attacking 'liberal' professors and through letter and print, challenging leaders to affirm their conservative positions." Fletcher, *Southern Baptist Convention,* 247.
70. *Findings of the Consultation on Women in Church-Related Vocations* (Nashville: Southern Baptist Convention, Sept. 20–22, 1978), located at the Southern Baptist Historical Library and Archives, Nashville.
71. Shurden, in *Struggle for the Soul of the SBC,* 280–86, assessed the "moderates" as being stymied by several myths about the changes to the SBC. He says they denied

the changes would last, believed in a pendulum swing that would bring power back their way, thought "fundamentalist" infighting would break the stronghold, thought fundamentalism would not survive culture changes, did not believe in fundamentalists' financial ability to support the SBC, thought new leadership would mellow over time, and didn't think the changes would impact local Baptist churches. None of these beliefs proved true, and the SBC did not return to the synthesis or balance formerly enjoyed by moderates.

72. Ammerman, *Baptist Battles,* 174–78.
73. For more about the history of Southern Baptist Women in Ministry (later Baptist Women in Ministry) and the role women played in the fracturing, see Eileen Campbell-Reed and Pamela R. Durso, "The State of Women in Baptist Life, 2007: A Twenty-Five-Year Retrospective of Baptist Women in Ministry," Baptist Women in Ministry, Atlanta, June 2008. See also Flowers, *Into the Pulpit,* 95–101, passim.
74. Ammerman, *Baptist Battles,* 223–24. See Appendix A.
75. Shurden and Shepley, *Going for the Jugular,* 248.
76. Hefley, *Conservative Resurgence,* 310–11.
77. Shurden and Shepley, *Going for the Jugular,* 261.
78. For example, the shift in focus can be seen in the name changes: SBWIM dropped "Southern" in 1996. The Southern Baptist Alliance changed to the Alliance of Baptists in 1992. See Alan Neely, "The History of the Alliance of Baptists," in Shurden, *Struggle for the Soul of the SBC,* 101–28. The Cooperative Baptist Fellowship considered several names but determined to take a name that intentionally set it apart from the SBC.
79. Flowers, *Into the Pulpit,* 76–86, demonstrates how conservative women developed the arguments for complementarity.
80. Ammerman, *Baptist Battles,* 94, observes women faced "overt opposition . . . routine exclusion and invisibility, along with occasional jokes and hostile remarks" and even being booed by crowds at SBC meetings.

Chapter 1

1. Although other embodiments are possible, this discussion addresses three, cultural, relational, and internal, to show their interrelation. "Embodiment" refers to an incorporation of a cultural world, what Pierre Bourdieu calls "habitus" and as such makes available a kind of knowing that is not merely representational, rational, or logical in the formal sense. See Pierre Bourdieu, *The Logic of Practice,* trans. Richard Nice (Stanford, CA: Stanford Univ. Press, 1990), 9–10, 52–56, passim.
2. Ordination and subordination are each contested ideas and practices and are not mutually exclusive. There is no simple move from one to the other, and the complexity of embodying both simultaneously is part of the anatomy of the schism under discussion.
3. Henri Nouwen, *Wounded Healer: Ministry in Contemporary Society* (New York: Doubleday, 1972).

4. Witnessing was a Baptist practice of giving testimony of one's faith to friends, co-workers, and strangers, inviting a conversion experience from hearers.
5. See "SBC to Cease Endorsing Ordained Female Chaplains"; McKinney, "Wherever He Leads I'll Go."
6. Susan Shaw describes finding "shared threads of identity" among women who stayed and women who left the SBC over the last four decades in *God Speaks to Us, Too,* 20.
7. Anders and Metcalf-Whittaker, "Women as Lay Leaders and Clergy," 214, invoked a similar image: "Ordained women are naturally controversial and symbolic, and they are aware of it. They sit at the heart of the fundamentalist-moderate controversy, representing each side's cause—either to be purged from the Southern Baptist Convention as the embodiment of liberalism or to be held up in triumph as the symbol of open-mindedness and independence."
8. Ammerman, *Baptist Battles,* 93–94, observes that clergywomen became "symbolic of the division facing the convention." She illustrates her point: "When fundamentalists claimed that moderates did not really believe the Bible, they were likely to point to women pastors as the perfect example of defying God's Word. And when moderates wanted to contrast their tolerance and open-mindedness with fundamentalist oppressiveness, they pointed to their acceptance of women as proof."
9. These "new" groups include the Alliance of Baptists, Cooperative Baptist Fellowship (CBF), Baptist Peace Fellowship of North America (BPFNA), Baptist Women in Ministry (BWIM), and other state and special interest organizations that are part of a moderate to progressive constellation of Baptists.
10. Bill Leonard identifies a "clergification" of Baptist polity, which extends a longstanding tension between laity and clergy, adopts a business model for administrating church affairs, and trains, hires, and ordains more specialists for ministry. Although he sees changing role of clergy as a "symptom of the fragmentation" in the SBC, he doesn't consider ways that women's ordination further complicates the change. See Leonard, *God's Last and Only Hope,* 81–84.
11. Resolutions passed at conventions hold no binding power. Each church is autonomous, and authority flows officially from churches to the convention. However, in practice, the SBC exercises tremendous accrued authority on its member churches, and it speaks as a representative body to public media and others outside the SBC. See Ammerman, *Baptist Battles,* 204–7. Specific resolutions about women are recorded in SBC annuals for 1972, 1973, 1974, 1977, 1979, 1980, 1981, 1983, and 1984. Susan M. Shaw, "Gracious Submission: Southern Baptist Fundamentalists and Women," *NWSA Journal* 20, no. 1 (Spring 2008): 51–77, argues that the rhetoric of these resolutions created "a small and tightly controlled ideological circle restricting gender roles for women." She also argues that women's lived experience in the SBC was more complex than the rhetoric reflected.
12. Flowers, *Into the Pulpit,* 57–58, argues that conservative women in the SBC built a "a grassroots movement" of Bible studies and retreats that "provided and shaped, the rhetoric of submission." Male pastors (often their husbands) helped to organize a widespread opposition to feminism and the ERA and linked those causes to "homo-

sexuality, pedophilia, abortion, and the demise of the nuclear family." Resolutions at the SBC and seventeen state Baptist conventions resulted from the "anti-feminist campaign."

13. Fletcher, *Southern Baptist Convention*, 272.
14. Ammerman, *Baptist Battles*, 223–24. See the full resolution text in Appendix A of this book.
15. Hefley, *Truth in Crisis* 104.
16. See Appendix A of this book.
17. Ibid. The writing and passing of the Kansas City Resolution contributed to shaping the emerging definition of complementarity in Baptist circles. See this book's introduction for a working definition. See also Flowers, *Into the Pulpit*, 130–35, where she details Patterson's role in the rhetorical and definitional work of "complementarity."
18. In 2000 the SBC revised its confessional statement, the Baptist Faith and Message. In a response to feedback about their initial release of the statement, the committee responded publicly to criticism. They said in the response, "First, we faced the fact that the Bible is clear in presenting the office of pastor as restricted to men. There is no biblical precedent for a woman in the pastorate, and the Bible teaches that women should not teach in authority over men. Second, the issue of women in the pastorate demands attention in our time, when other denominations are abandoning biblical teaching and calling women to serve as pastors. Third, we spoke to the issue because Southern Baptists are united in conviction. Far less than one percent of churches cooperating with the Southern Baptist Convention have ever called a woman as pastor. For the sake of generations to come, we should state our convictions boldly." Baptist Faith and Message, http://www.sbc.net/bfm2000/bfmfeedback.asp, accessed Apr. 28, 2012.
19. *Folio: A Newsletter for Southern Baptist Women in Ministry* 2, no. 2 (Autumn 1984): 1, 6–7.
20. Stricklin, *Genealogy of Dissent*, 127.
21. Ibid. Stricklin says further, "This sort of 'incarnational' theology and practice gave progressive dissenters a mandate for placing themselves among people who needed to hear a prophetic word of reminder of God's expectations of them."
22. Ibid.
23. Wilburn T. Stancil, "Divergent Views and Practices of Ordination among Southern Baptists since 1945," *Baptist History and Heritage* 23, no. 3 (July 1, 1988): 42–49.
24. Ibid., 46.
25. Scores of cases like these are documented in the last three decades. See Bob Allen, "Georgia Baptists Cut Ties with Church Led by Woman Pastor," Associated Baptist Press, Nov. 16, 2009, http://www.abpnews.com/content/view/4575/53, accessed Apr. 28, 2012; and Norman Jameson, "Assn. Ousts Church with Woman Pastor," Associated Baptist Press, Aug. 4, 2011, http://www.abpnews.com/content/view/6626/43, accessed Apr. 28, 2012.
26. Stancil, "Divergent Views and Practices of Ordination," 43, 47.

27. Jann Aldredge-Clanton, "Why I Believe Southern Baptist Churches Should Ordain Women," *Baptist History and Heritage* 23, no. 3 (July 1, 1988): 50–55; Dorothy Patterson, "Why I Believe Southern Baptist Churches Should Not Ordain Women," *Baptist History and Heritage* 23, no. 3 (July 1, 1988): 56–62. Patterson emerged at this time as a spokesperson for biblical womanhood and manhood.
28. Patterson, "Why I Believe Southern Baptist Churches Should Not Ordain Women," 56.
29. Ibid., 56–57.
30. Ibid., 57–61.
31. Aldredge-Clanton, "Why I Believe Southern Baptist Churches Should Ordain Women," 50–55.
32. Biblicists unapologetically cast the years of schism as a battle over biblical truth. James Hefley in a partisan account of the schism reports the beginning of a coalition between Paige and Dorothy Patterson and Paul and Nancy Pressler as a shared hope to "turn Southern Baptists back to belief in an inerrant Bible." See Hefley, *Truth in Crisis*, 65. Academic studies of the SBC schism also took seriously the stakes over the meaning and use of the Bible for Southern Baptists as they divided into factions. See Ammerman, *Baptist Battles*, 63–65.
33. The relationship between schism and clergywomen's stories did not appear obvious at the beginning of this project, making a methodological point: gathering data in an open-ended way, inviting participants to frame their stories, allows indirect access to rich data about their social worlds and/or cultural contexts.
34. The intensity and explicitness of the schism took different shape at different institutions and among different women. Both Shaw, *God Speaks to Us, Too,* and Flowers, *Into the Pulpit,* demonstrate a variety of responses by women and institutions to the prevailing rhetoric and rending in Southern Baptist life.
35. For Anna the implicit and null curricula at her seminary were more dramatic and powerful in her memory than the explicit curriculum. See Elliott W. Eisner, *The Educational Imagination: On the Design and Evaluation of School Programs,* 3rd ed. (Upper Saddle River, NJ: Prentice Hall, 2002).
36. Anna's relationships with neighbors and others show how relational space or "intersubjective space" is neither one subject nor the other, but a third space between them. See Benjamin, *Bonds of Love,* 15, 22. See also Benjamin, *Like Subjects, Love Objects,* 112–13.
37. The lack of clear messages about ministry *is* a commentary on gendered expectations in Anna's church.
38. Many women, upon experiencing similar and multiple confrontations, chose to walk away from Baptist life and pursue vocational ministry in other denominations or to change vocational directions altogether. Many outsiders hear stories like these and fail to comprehend why anyone would remain within the Baptist milieu. This book focuses on the situations of those who chose to remain Baptist, but other investigations about those who departed would enrich an understanding of the dynamics.

39. Austrian analyst Sigmund Freud, the "father of psychoanalysis," influenced popular views on sexuality and essentialized views of "male" and "female" with his extensive writings. See Sigmund Freud, "Some Psychical Consequences of the Anatomical Distinction between the Sexes," in *The Standard Edition of the Complete Psychological Works of Sigmund Freud* (London: Hogarth Press, 1925), 19:233–39.
40. Physician and child psychiatrist D. W. Winnicott was influenced by yet departed from Freud. He theorized a female element of "being" and a male element of "doing" that developed sequentially in infants based on the care and handling of the mothering figure. See Winnicott, *Playing and Reality*, 76–85.
41. Winnicott improves Freud's analysis by adding the concept of males' envy toward females. Ibid., 81. See also Freud, "Some Psychical Consequences of the Anatomical Distinction between the Sexes."
42. By shifting the problem of gender from "nature" to "relationships," the possibility for change over time increases.
43. "In the beginning was the deed," says Freud, and by the deed he means the killing of the father in the primal horde, the father who previously had controlled females for his sexual pleasure and punished or expelled maturing sons if they attempted to possess the females. See Sigmund Freud, *Totem and Taboo: Resemblances between the Psychic Lives of Savages and Neurotics*, trans. A. A. Brill (New York: Dover, 1998), 138. The primal deed and its aftermath were, for Freud, not only the beginning of a relationship between father and son but also a precursor to humanity's social and cultural institutions.
44. See G. Thomas Halbrooks, "The Meaning and Significance of Ordination Among Southern Baptists, 1845–1945," *Baptist History and Heritage* 23, no. 3 (July 1988): 24–32. Licensure is less universal among Baptists and is often determined by state laws and local customs of a particular church. The question of the ordaining body, an association or a church, is also significant but contested. In my database of ordained Baptist women (collected in conjunction with Baptist Women in Ministry), only 31 of 592 women (5 percent) reported that a Baptist association took part in ordaining them. Of those, 21 were from North Carolina and Virginia, and 4 others were ordained in ABC-USA contexts. The remaining six received ordination in six different states.
45. A person's "inner life" or intrapsychic domain is populated by self-perceptions, images of others, defenses, coping strategies, fantasies, beliefs, and memories. The internal world is not separate from but interpenetrates with relational spaces. Jessica Benjamin offers the insight that the intrapsychic and intersubjective views of mind are helpful to each other rather than contradictory. The intrapsychic foregrounds material existing primarily within the mind of the individual; the intersubjective describes a shared space between subjects in relationship with each other. See Benjamin, *Bonds of Love*, 20–21.
46. See "SBC to Cease Endorsing Ordained Female Chaplains."
47. Psychological defenses arise in response to early relational experiences. Defenses are seemingly "automatic" responses to situations that are dynamically similar to the

early failures felt by the individual. Defenses occur along a broad range of functions beginning "as healthy, reactive adaptations" that can serve a person well, but they can become maladaptive if one is trying to maintain unconsciously either an avoidance of overwhelming feelings (anxiety, grief, etc.) or a fragile self-esteem. See Nancy McWilliams, *Psychoanalytic Diagnosis: Understanding Personality Structure in the Clinical Process* (New York: Guilford, 1994), 96–97.

48. Historian Samuel Hill laments the loss of the denominational "mother," describes schism as a "family struggle," names himself a "son" of Southern Baptists, and sees the losses as a "shattering of this body that has served as Total Culture in the ordering of [Baptist] lives." See Samuel Hill, "Introduction," in *Exiled: Voices of the Southern Baptist Convention Holy War,* ed. Carl L. Kell (Knoxville: Univ. Press, 2006), 7–9. Susan Shaw describes the Southern Baptist Theological Seminary as the "mother seminary" in *God Speaks to Us, Too,* 21, 156–57.

49. Benjamin, *Bonds of Love,* 96.

50. Ibid., 99. See also Nancy Chodorow, *The Reproduction of Mothering: Psychoanalysis and the Sociology of Gender* (Berkeley and Los Angeles: Univ. of California Press, 1978), 38. Chodorow's thesis is that the "structure of parenting reproduces itself.... Psychoanalysis shows us how the family division of labor in which women mother gives socially and historically specific meaning to gender itself. This engendering of men and women with particular personalities, needs, defenses, and capacities creates the condition for and contributes to the reproduction of this same division of labor. The sexual division of labor both produces gender difference and is in turn reproduced by them."

51. Benjamin, *Bonds of Love,* 112–14. Benjamin envisions a way of changing the patterns that reproduce domination and submission by "rejecting assumptions" related to early gender development and seeing that "both parents can be figures of separation *and* attachment for their children; that both boys *and* girls can make use of identification with both parents without being confused about their gender identity."

52. Ibid., 92–96. Much of Freud's analysis of women's identity is based on the idea of penis envy and gives little consideration to the total relationship of daughters to their mothers or fathers. Benjamin argues against Freud's limited reading and explores the more complex ways that boys and girls negotiate identity—including gender—by reconsidering both pre-Oedipal and Oedipal struggles between children and parents.

53. Benjamin describes an internal coexistence of both a mode of representation of one's mother that recognizes her as "another subject" with independent action, feeling, desire, and agency and "a mode of fantasy" about mothers as powerful omnipotent figures. She says, "The capacity to recognize the mother as another subject and the fantasy of maternal omnipotence are aligned with this duality. Ideally these distinct psychic tendencies of our psychic organization constitute a tension rather than, as has often been supposed, a contradiction, an 'either-or.'" See Benjamin, *Like Subjects, Love Objects,* 85–86.

54. The Southern Baptist Convention holds no binding ecclesial power over churches. Historically, Baptist churches are autonomous and connected through voluntary

cooperation around shared causes such as missions and theological education. While an acceptance of the church universal is memorialized in most Baptist confessional statements, local churches of regenerated believers answer only to God and resist external interference from other churches or the state. See H. W. Pipkin, "Ecclesiology, Baptist," in *Dictionary of Baptists in America,* ed. Bill J. Leonard (Downer's Grove, IL: Intervarsity Press, 1994). Nevertheless, the unofficial power of the SBC is expansive and pervasive enough that Martin Marty referred the SBC as headed toward becoming "the Catholic church of the South." See Martin Marty, "The Protestant Experience and Perspective," in *American Religious Values and the Future of America,* ed. Rodger Van Allen (Philadelphia: Fortress Press, 1978), 46.

55. In 1936 B. B. McKinney composed the hymn "Wherever He Leads I'll Go" and its tune ("Falls Creek"). See the full text of the hymn in Appendix B (page 149).
56. Benjamin, *Bonds of Love,* 73–74, 77.
57. Anne T. Neil, "The Servant Model," in *Proceedings of the 1983 Conference for Women in Ministry, SBC: Held in Pittsburgh, Pennsylvania, June 11–12, 1983* (Nashville: Christian Life Commission of the Southern Baptist Convention, 1983), 7–9. See also Rachel Richardson Smith, "Liberating the Servant," *Christian Century,* Dec. 16, 1981, 1313–14. Smith understood the dilemma as a Baptist student at Southwestern Baptist Seminary.
58. Christie Cozad Neuger, *Counseling Women: A Narrative, Pastoral Approach* (Minneapolis: Fortress, 2001), 45, says that "double binding or paradoxical messages" consist of "at least two contradictory messages . . . inescapably linked together, and . . . terribly damaging." The dilemma is also built on intersectional systems of racism and white privilege that put white women in the middle as both oppressor and oppressed. The systems remain invisible most of the time serving to keep them unquestioned and operational. However, more attention is needed on the role of race in social spaces that seem not to be about race. For a fuller critique of this problem, see Evelyn Brooks Higginbotham, "African-American Women's History and the Metalanguage of Race," *Signs* 17, no. 2 (Winter, 1992): 251–74.
59. Patterson, "Why I Believe Southern Baptist Churches Should Not Ordain Women," 56. See Appendix A for the language about Eve in the 1984 Kansas City Resolution.

Chapter 2

1. "Traditional" indicates gender roles typical in U.S. culture during the twentieth century, especially those prized by the white middle and upper classes. Not a monolith, the enduring practice of heterosexual, white couples included mothers who cared for home and children and fathers who earned income and offered financial support. Judith Sealander traces a history of families following World War II, demonstrating how social and political powers emphasized the domesticity of wives and mothers and valorized the public and heroic status of husbands and fathers. White women did not question these values significantly. Children became the central focus of white middle-class families, and strict rules gave way to greater permissiveness. See Judith

Sealander, "Families, World War II, and the Baby Boom (1940–1955)," in *American Families: A Research Guide and Historical Handbook,* ed. Joseph M. Hawes and Elizabeth I. Nybakken (New York: Greenwood Press, 1991), 157–81. Race and class further complicate twentieth-century understandings of gender, and privilege in U.S. families and society. See Karen Anderson, "African American Families," in *American Families: A Research Guide and Historical Handbook,* ed. Joseph M. Hawes and Elizabeth I. Nybakken (New York: Greenwood Press, 1991), 259–90.

2. Two books represent extreme views to the left and right of traditional marriage in the 1970s. Nena O'Neill and George O'Neill, *Open Marriage: A New Life Style for Couples* (New York: M. Evans, 1972), advocated for "flexible and interchangeable" roles for marriage partners. Popular among Southern Baptists, Marabel Morgan, *The Total Woman* (Old Tappan, NJ: Fleming H. Revell, 1973), called for women to "accept, admire, adapt to, and appreciate" husbands at every opportunity because submission and the burden of marital success rest with the wife. Both books uphold the idea and institution of marriage yet propose entirely different strategies for maintaining them.

3. The "all-seeing Eye" of southern religion can functions as a superego or conscience (in ego psychology). See McWilliams, *Psychoanalytic Diagnosis,* 25–29. Ana-Marie Rizzuto, *The Birth of the Living God* (Chicago: Univ. of Chicago Press), 184–90, elaborates how the seeing eye of the mother is essential for development of one's perception of God. She says, "The mirroring componenets of the God representation find their first experience in eye contact, early nursing, and maternal personal participation in the act of mirroring" (188).

4. Martha's expression of ambivalent feelings toward her mother function similarly to a psychological defense called "reaction formation," which avoids anxiety by expressing only one feeling (often the positive one) and suppressing the other. See McWilliams, *Psychoanalytic Diagnosis,* 131–33.

5. Mary Field Belenky, Blythe McVicker Clinchy, Nancy Rule Goldberger, and Jill Mattuck Tarule, *Women's Ways of Knowing: The Development of Self, Voice, and Mind* (New York: Basic Books, 1986). Belenky and her associates argued women's decision making is relationally shaped and driven, an argument verging on essentialism. Read another way, one could say women were exposed to a combination of parenting, cultural climate, and relational dynamics that fostered mature, interdependent relationships for knowing and deciding. The features of relational knowing are also present in men's development. The Belenky et al. study may have revealed universally human factors, but claiming universal features for women, not men, does not follow.

6. Martha refers to a "climate," which is much like the "field" in which one's "habitus" or embodied sense and knowing of the world is formed. See Bourdieu, *Logic of Practice,* 66–67 ff.

7. Public influence by Protestant church leaders was paradigmatic in the early-twentieth-century United States but fading by the 1960s. Martha recognizes the shift in mindset, described in 1970 by Sydney E. Ahlstrom, who argued one feature of the radical turn of the 1960s was the final eclipse of the "Protestant establishment." See Sydney E. Ahlstrom, "The Radical Turn in Theology and Ethics: Why It Occurred in the

1960's," *Annals of the American Academy of Political and Social Science* 387 (Jan. 1970): 1–13. Phillip E. Hammond agreed with Ahlstrom, arguing most of the United States experienced a "third disestablishment of religion." See Phillip E. Hammond, *Religion and Personal Autonomy: The Third Disestablishment in America* (Columbia: Univ. of South Carolina Press, 1992), 139. Hammond notes a lower impact of disestablishment in the U.S. South.

8. The work arrangement typifies the pervasive unconscious influence of complementarity culture. Martha's inexperience may have justified the lower profit share, yet if she was doing "all the work" (impossible to determine at this distance), then it raises the question of equitable sharing.

9. Martha also recalled another woman later employed by UBC as minister of music and youth.

10. In the 1970s the name Girls' Auxiliary was changed to Girls in Action. Woman's Missionary Union sponsored these weekly programs of mission study and social action.

11. During the 1980s, churches in the Southeast, especially North Carolina and Virginia, started electing female deacons to chair deacon boards. See Charles W. Deweese, *Women Deacons and Deaconesses: 400 Years of Baptist Service* (Macon, GA: Mercer Univ. Press, 2005), 124–27. Deacons in many churches remained responsible for both ministry and administrative leadership in the congregation.

12. Martha's "aha" moment shares many features of the narratives of beginning ministers. Chris Scharen and I articulate similar moments as a "birth of pastoral imagination." In such stories identity, context, and one's past preparation converge. Through reflection and integration, a shift from imagining ministry to nascent pastoral imagination means the pastor faces overwhelming circumstances, takes greater risks and responsibility, and acts responsively to a situation rather than simply following rules ("showing up" because the deacon chair asked). Martha's story shows a common developmental trajectory that leads to greater embodiment of a pastoral role and practice. See Eileen R. Campbell-Reed and Christian Scharen, "'Holy Cow! This Stuff Is Real!' From Imagining Ministry to Pastoral Imagination," *Teaching Theology and Religion* 14, no. 4 (Oct. 2011): 323–42.

13. Martha's story shows how dynamic relational patterns carry forward both formations and traditions, what Raymond Williams identifies as "three aspects of any cultural process . . . traditions, institutions, formations." The process of formation goes deeper than "socialization," Williams argues, giving this example: "In a family children are cared for and taught to care for themselves, but within this necessary process fundamental and selective attitudes to self, to others, to a social order, and to the material world are both consciously and unconsciously taught." Raymond Williams, *Marxism and Literature* (New York: Oxford Univ. Press, 1977), 115–17.

14. Kay W. Shurden, "An Analysis of the Images of Women in Selected Southern Baptist Literature," in *Findings of the Consultation on Women in Church-Related Vocations*, 49–54. Shurden considered selections from 8 magazines between 1973 and 1978, evaluating 110 periodicals.

15. Martha's story portrays the "struggle for and against selective traditions" both at the level of her family and the level of Baptist subculture. See Williams, *Marxism and Literature*, 117.
16. Deweese, *Women Deacons and Deaconesses*, 97, observes a dramatic rise in the number of women ordained as deacons and deacon chairs between 1960 and 1990. Opposition came from the Baptist Faith and Message Fellowship and the *Southern Baptist Journal*, a biblicist party group and its publication.
17. Judith Butler, "Performative Acts and Gender Constitution: An Essay in Phenomenology and Feminist Theory," in *Performing Feminisms: Feminist Critical Theory and Theatre*, ed. Sue-Ellen Case (Baltimore: Johns Hopkins Univ. Press, 1990), 526–28, argues persuasively that gender is neither essential nor revealed, but that "gender reality is created through sustained social performances," which work to uphold the "binary frame" of male and female.
18. Martha's ambivalence toward her mother and idealization of her father mirror the dynamics of relating to the SBC mother and God the father, an embodiment explored in Anna's story in chapter 1.
19. See Benjamin, *Bonds of Love*, 74–80.
20. Ibid., 220. Benjamin notes that the structure of domination is one, which can only be reversed. She points to the father-son and master-slave relationships/narratives in which domination and submission are never overcome because there is no true "outside other" and one is always the doer and one is the done-to.
21. This "freedom" is a product of white privilege, which rests on institutional racism. Laurel Schneider argues that "race and sex co-constitute a corporate merging of meaning located in human and divine hierarchies that solidify the power and make resilient the supremacy of white people, exemplified in the white male from which, in this view, all others differentiate in useful degrees of degenerate separation." See Laurel C. Schneider, "What Race Is Your Sex?" in *Disrupting White Supremacy from Within*, ed. Jennifer Harvey, Karen A. Case, and Robin Hawley Gorsline (Cleveland: Pilgrim Press, 2004), 144.
22. The book was part of a discipleship series for use in SBC churches for study on Sunday evenings. Daniel G. Bagby, *Before You Marry* (Nashville: Convention Press, 1983), 67–68 ff. Bagby portrays shared responsibility and dignity for men and women, yet the asymmetry of power remains in his descriptions. The "mutual exchange" requires a complementary relationship between man and woman, and differences are essentialized in terms of sexual identity (more than biology) as necessary for marriage union.
23. See Dorothy Kelley Patterson, *A Handbook for Ministers' Wives: Sharing the Blessings of Your Marriage, Family and Home* (Nashville: Broadman & Holman, 2002), 89. "Headship and submission must also be worked out in home life—a loving and serving leadership interwoven with a willing and respectful submission (Eph. 5:21–33; 1 Pet. 3:1–7) . . . should portray vividly and clearly femininity and masculinity and their complementarity within the role assignments given by God."
24. In 1983 pastor Deborah Griffis-Woodbery addressed the first meeting of SBWIM: "The blending of marriage, family, and ministry poses unique issues for women min-

isters. Often women ask, 'Can I be married and be a minister?' Some of us are finding that combination quite workable." *Folio: A Newsletter for Southern Baptist Women in Ministry* 1, no. 3 (Winter 1984): 1.

25. Neuger, *Counseling Women,* 45, describes "double binding or paradoxical messages" as "at least two contradictory messages . . . inescapably linked together, and . . . terribly damaging."

26. Bagby, *Before You Marry,* 78 (emphasis added).

27. Braude, "Women's History," 87–107. "Women constitute the majority of participants in religion in the United States, and have wherever Christianity has become the dominant faith in North America" (88). She also observes women are "the backbone of the vast majority of well-established religious groups. . . . Women's significance in groups considered marginal must not be allowed to obscure their centrality in maintaining . . . the 'mainstream.' Women's history is American religious history" (90).

28. Bagby's *Before You Marry* was closer to autonomist party views of egalitarian marriage. Popular marriage books among Southern Baptist biblicists included Tim and Beverly LaHaye's *The Act of Marriage: The Beauty of Sexual Love* (Grand Rapids, MI: Zondervan, 1976) and Morgan's *Total Woman.*

29. A desire for autonomy is complex because it is both a desire for freedom, agency, and resistance to harm, but autonomy is also dependent on others, so it is never simply isolation or social disconnection. Autonomy is not merely about legal or moral rights but also about vulnerability and finitude. See Judith Butler's discussion of autonomy in *Undoing Gender,* 20–25.

30. As noted, converse examples further complicate the picture. Many women worked openly to maintain the complementarity culture, and many men strived against it. For example, Flowers, *Into the Pulpit,* 57–58, shows how conservative women in the SBC created, supported, and maintained the rhetoric of submission.

31. Betty Friedan, *The Feminine Mystique* (New York: Dell, 1963), 337–42, observed how deeply rooted social mores blocked middle-class white women's attempts to free themselves from the "feminine mystique" in order to "find themselves." Kathleen faced challenges identified by Friedan: being an unpaid and little valued "housewife," facing religious arguments that working women neglect or reject husbands and children, the male wish for an ever-present mother, hostility from other housewives, and grief and loss that comes with change.

32. When Martha speaks of "autonomy," she has in mind not only a social or philosophical connotation but also a Baptist ideal. The key term "autonomy" circulated among autonomists who departed the SBC. Walter B. Shurden's books, *The Doctrine of the Priesthood of Believers* (Nashville: Convention Press, 1987) and *The Baptist Identity: Four Fragile Freedoms* (Macon, GA: Smyth & Helwys, 1993), popularized the notion. Martha's use of "autonomy" conflates or stands in for autonomy, individual liberty, soul competency, and freedom as well as individuality and agency. See also Joanna's story in chapter 3 for an analysis of these tensions.

33. José Medina, "Identity Trouble: Disidentification and the Problem of Difference," *Philosophy and Social Criticism* 29, no. 6 (2003): 655–80.

34. In *The Reproduction of Mothering, 38,* Chodorow argues that "the structure of parenting reproduces itself." She notes that "the family division of labor in which women mother gives socially and historically specific meaning to gender itself. This engendering of men and women with particular personalities, needs, defenses, and capacities creates the condition for and contributes to the reproduction of this same division of labor. The sexual division of labor both produces gender differences and is in turn reproduced by them." By remaining single and childless, Martha further disrupts the cycle of reproduction.

35. WMU's "watchword" comes from 1 Corinthians 3:9. See Catherine B. Allen, *A Century to Celebrate: History of Woman's Missionary Union* (Birmingham, AL: Woman's Missionary Union, SBC, 1987), 86-87.

36. WMU employees were among the chief organizers and supporters of the "Consultation on Women in Church Related Vocations." Ibid., 440. See also Flowers, *Into the Pulpit,* 62.

37. Benjamin, *Bonds of Love,* 133–34, says, "The route to individuality that leads through identificatory love of the father is a difficult one for women to follow. The difficulty lies in the fact that the power of the liberator-father is used to defend against the engulfing mother. Thus however helpful a specific change in the father's relationship to the daughter may be in the short run, it cannot solve the deeper problem: the split between a father of liberation and a mother of dependency. For children of both sexes, this split means that identification and closeness with the mother must be traded for independence; it means that being a subject of desire requires repudiation of the maternal role, of feminine identity itself."

38. Andrew D. Lester, "The Psychological Impact of Women in Ministry," in *Findings of the Consultation on Women in Church-Related Vocations,* 16–19.

39. Lester's presentation highlights the dilemma of reaching to overcome sexist stereotypes and assumptions that are reproduced by simply observing and naming them. In capturing dynamics felt commonly, he reproduces the same complementarity structures that he is challenging.

40. Benjamin says, "The defensive masculine stance promotes a dualism, a polarization of subject and object. The assignment of subject status to male and object status to female follows from the seemingly unavoidable fact that the boy must struggle free with all the violence of a second birth from the woman who bore him. In this second birth, the fantasy of omnipotence and erotic domination begins." *Bonds of Love,* 81.

41. Benjamin observes that "ironically, the fantasy of erotic dominance and submission expresses the deep longing for wholeness. But as long as the shape of the whole is not informed by mutuality, this longing only leads to an unequal complementarity in which one person plays the master, the other slave. And even when men and women reverse their roles . . . gender continues, consciously and unconsciously, to represent only one part of a polarized whole, one aspect of the self-other relationship. . . . The groundwork for this division is laid in the mother's renunciation of her own will, in her consequent lack of subjectivity for her children, and particularly in the male child's repudiation of his commonality with her." Ibid., 82. Chodorow, *Reproduction*

of Mothering, 181, describes twentieth-century mothers isolated in nuclear families: "Masculinity becomes an issue as a direct result of . . . being parented by a woman. For children of both genders, mothers represent regression and lack of autonomy. A boy associates these issues with his gender identification as well. Dependence on his mother, attachment to her, and identification with her represent that which is not masculine; a boy must reject dependence and deny attachment and identification." Boys repress internal feminine qualities and "reject and devalue women" and anything "feminine in the social world."

42. My analysis both over- and understates the case. Neither all, nor only, Southern Baptist men were socialized in the way this narrative portrays gender formation. Readers will readily think of exceptions. However, the narrative is compelling for imagining how complementarity continues to be reproduced generation to generation for both men and women, Baptist and non-Baptist.

43. For Southern Baptists, "missions" (plural) was the term for global and domestic missionary enterprises, while the singular "mission" is as an overlapping but not synonymous term for the purpose to which one is called by God.

44. The two internalized messages of grandiose omnipotence and nagging self-doubt are psychologically two sides of the narcissism coin. According to Heinz Kohut, a healthy, positive, and adaptive narcissism is necessary for action, creativity, and relationship. In its less adaptive form, it indicates a need for greater self-structure. Martha's admiration of church adults indicates her desire for caregivers whom she could both mirror and idealize. See Kohut, *How Does Analysis Cure?* (Chicago: Univ. of Chicago, 1984), 185–86, 198–99.

45. Martha's self-descriptions show the back and forth of seeking relational mutuality and finding it foreclosed by the complementarity pattern. Benjamin, *Bonds of Love,* 73, observes that such grandiosity "gives birth to domination." She continues, "In the absence of a differentiated sense of self and other, the vital sharing between separate minds is replaced by almost exclusively complementary relationships." The complementarity between infant and parent should offer a "prelude to intersubjective sharing. . . . But increasingly the relationship should shift in emphasis from regulation to the true exchange of recognition itself." Without that shift, complementarity will "completely eclipse mutuality."

46. Bonnie Miller-McLemore writes, "No matter how women design their lives, most would admit that conflicts between self-interest and self-sacrifice plague their solutions to questions of work and love." See Bonnie Miller-McLemore and Herbert Anderson, *Faith's Wisdom for Daily Living* (Minneapolis: Augsburg Fortress, 2008), 53. She argues that theology and practice of sacrifice arise from everyday work, family relationships, and worship, and she concludes that sacrifice can both liberate and harm.

47. Bill Leonard identifies a programmed piety among Southern Baptists that is practical in its shape and creates a powerful sense of loyalty. He says, "While there is diversity to the point of contradiction in belief and practice among SBC churches and individuals, there is also a patent uniformity, a genuinely Southern Baptist way of believing and behaving." Leonard, *God's Last and Only Hope,* 102.

48. Several times women in this book pointed to a moment of calling to missionary service during their childhood exposure to missions curriculum and church camps.
49. Enormous amounts of money and institutional capital hung in the balance of the schism. Autonomists regularly leveled criticism that biblicists were after power and money and did not contribute adequately to SBC programs. In 1979 the SBC received revenue and gifts exceeding $119 million, which they distributed to SBC agencies, boards, and schools. This was only cash flow and did not include assets of property or investments. In 1989 the same figure of receipts and distributions totaled more than $257 million. After 2005 the combined annual receipts and disbursements of SBC exceeded $1 billion annually. See the SBC annuals for 1980; 1990, 114; and 2006, 155.
50. Many other complex cultural interactions and exchanges were at work in the nineteenth- and twentieth-century missionary enterprise. See Karen Seat, *Providence Has Freed Our Hands* (Syracuse, NY: Syracuse Univ. Press, 2008). See also Willie James Jennings, *The Christian Imagination: Theology and the Origins of Race* (New Haven, CT: Yale, 2011).
51. When Baptists North and South split, Southern Baptists maintained the "rights" of slave owners and further implicated the missionary enterprise in perpetuating racist ideologies and practice. See John Lee Eighmy, *Churches in Cultural Captivity* (Knoxville: Univ. of Tennessee Press, 1987), 12–17.
52. Options for women included missionary service or a WMU career. Catherine B. Allen, *Laborers Together with God: 22 Great Women in Baptist Life* (Birmingham, AL: Woman's Missionary Union, SBC, 1987), 163–74, 235–42.
53. The provocative image "missionary position" originated with Alfred Kinsey, B. W. Pomeroy, and C. E. Martin in *Sexual Behavior in the Human Male* (Philadelphia: W. B. Saunders, 1948), in which they present a misreading of Bronislaw Malinowski, *The Sexual Life of Savages in North-western Melanesia* (New York: Harcourt, Brace and World, 1929). However, Kinsey's invention of the term is virtually lost, and in the second half of the twentieth century the metaphor of male domination (literally on top) and female submission (literally on the bottom) circulated uncritically. See Robert J. Priest, "Missionary Positions: Christian, Modernist, Postmodernist," *Current Anthropology* 42, no. 1 (Feb. 2001): 29–68.
54. Ammerman, *Baptist Battles*, 223–33, traces the skirmishes at the mission boards.
55. One reference is Matthew 25:31–46, a parable of sheep and goats. The climax of the tale comes at 25:44–46: "Then they also will answer, 'Lord, when was it that we saw you hungry or thirsty or a stranger or naked or sick or in prison, and did not take care of you?' Then he will answer them, 'Truly I tell you, just as you did not do it to one of the least of these, you did not do it to me.' And these will go away into eternal punishment, but the righteous into eternal life" (NRSV). Another reference is Matthew 20:16, coming at the end of the parable about a vineyard owner paying workers the same wage for different hours of work. The conclusion of the parable says, "So the last will be first, and the first will be last." The "last and least" are understood by CBF missionaries as the ones to be served.

56. Shaw, *God Speaks to Us, Too*, 35, found that both moderate and conservative women drew on the "priesthood of all believers" to "construct identities that embrace and express their own agency and autonomy within the varying contexts of Southern Baptist life."
57. Benjamin argues that every relationship has an imbalance of power and must contend with that reality as a part of the intersubjective space between any two "like subjects." Maintaining the creative tension is a part of the remedy to the inevitable imbalance. Complementarity collapses the tension and is thus open to greater abuse of power. See *Bonds of Love*, 66–69, 73.
58. Bill J. Leonard identifies a persistent historical tension between clergy and laity as it is worked out in the "priesthood of all believers" in Baptist life. See his *Dictionary of Baptists in America* (Downer's Grove, IL: Intervarsity Press, 1994), 4–6. See also his *Baptist Ways: A History* (Valley Forge, PA: Judson Press, 2003), 7. Joanna's story in chapter 3 includes a lengthier interpretation of the clergy-laity tension.
59. McBeth, *Women in Baptist Life*, 27–47, recounts stories of women's preaching in, testifying in, and leading Baptist churches in England and America across four centuries.
60. In chapter 3, Joanna's story is an occasion to explore the shaping influence of five perennial Baptist tensions of belief and practice. In the programmed piety of Baptist life, charismatic pastoral leaders often carried the mantle of leading weekly rituals and annual traditions.
61. Lester, "Psychological Impact of Women in Ministry," 16–19. Both claiming and accepting authority resonates with Winnicott's idea of both finding and creating relationship and meaning. See *Playing and Reality*, 47–48.
62. Lester, "Psychological Impact of Women in Ministry," 17.
63. Gay, *Joy and the Objects of Psychoanalysis*, 21–22, 90–92. Gay defines pathogenic beliefs as "theories of mind that aim to predict another person's behavior." Unconscious beliefs developed early in childhood trauma give rise to neurotic behavior/symptoms and work together to form a "patient's secret, unconscious belief system," which abides by certain rules. In a social system (for example, the SBC), pathogenic beliefs can attempt to predict the mind of the social opponent in ways that are rule bound, nonrational, and lead to suffering rather than joy.
64. Chloe's story in chapter 5 explores how clergywomen reimagined the theology and practice of ministry.
65. For a similar early ministry crisis of searching for a "real pastor," see Eileen R. Campbell-Reed, "Wisdom at the Crossroads" (Text: Proverbs 8:1–11), sermon in *This Is What a Preacher Looks Like: Sermons by Baptist Women*, ed. Pamela R. Durso (Macon, GA: Smyth & Helwys, 2010), 99–106.
66. Martha and Linda's conversation captures the emerging view of relational theorists and pastoral theologians that experience is co-constructed with meaning through shared relational, emotional, and embodied contexts. See Neuger, *Counseling Women*, 142–43. See also Cooper-White in *Shared Wisdom*, 50–54.
67. Deweese traces this history in *Women Deacons and Deaconesses*, 97–122. Some women were ordained, others were only "elected."

68. Ibid., 98–101, 105–22.

69. G. Thomas Halbrooks observed the following Baptist qualifications for ordination prior to 1945: "An inward call gifts for ministry, and an outward call.... Membership in a Baptist church was assumed." On the question of gender, "most Baptists assumed that such a call could not come to women." He quotes J. R. Graves, arguing that "'no Christian, womanly woman' would ever aspire to such a position." The question of ordination for ministry other than the pastorate was also contested. See Halbrooks, "Meaning and Significance of Ordination," 24–32; Penrose St. Amant identified this sense of inward and outward calling as a "Reformed viewpoint" explicated by John Calvin and seen as "essential prerequisites to ordination" by early Baptists. See Penrose St. Amant, "Sources of Calling in Church History," *Baptist History and Heritage* 23, no. 3 (July 1988): 3–15, 41.

70. This observation does not disparage the work of women in such roles, but points out the limits and subtlety of ways a complementarity culture endures.

71. For example, Seventh and James Baptist Church in Waco, Texas, simultaneously shifted to a pastoral care model and ordained the first five women as deacons. Deweese, *Women Deacons and Deaconesses,* 124–25.

72. Kathleen Cahalan observes the growing diversity of those practicing ministry in Roman Catholic (and Protestant) contexts: the emphasis is shifting from role, identity, and station in life toward call, practice, and giftedness for ministry. Southern Baptist women felt called and gifted, and they practiced ministry long before they were recognized for it. See Kathleen Cahalan, *Introducing the Practice of Ministry* (Collegeville, MN: Order of Saint Benedict, 2010), viii.

73. Deweese, *Women Deacons and Deaconesses,* 107–18.

74. Judith Butler asks, "Who counts as the human?" She distinguishes then between those who are "oppressed" and thus recognized, if vilified, and those who are "unreal ... unintelligible" and have "not yet achieved access to the human ... speaking only and always *as if you were* human, but with the sense you are not ... because the norms by which recognition takes places are not in your favor." *Undoing Gender,* 17–18, 30. Social recognition, and a place to appear, are key for political scales large and small. Even if the experience of "non-existence" can be reframed as one of common dissociation (it's all in your head!), the political ramifications are no less violent or dangerous if you are not able to appear. See also Mary McClintock Fulkerson, *Places of Redemption: Theology for a Worldly Church* (New York: Oxford Univ. Press, 2007), 48–51, passim.

Chapter 3

1. The "relational space" that is the focus of this chapter is equivalent to "intersubjective space" as understood by Natterson and Friedman, who define intersubjectivity as the relationship that is co-created or "the reciprocal influence of the conscious and unconscious subjectivities of two people in a relationship." They say in a therapeutic situation "the inner lives of patient and therapist have reciprocal influence on one another, responding to and creating the intersubjective situation." See Joseph M.

Natterson and Raymond J. Friedman, *A Primer of Clinical Intersubjectivity* (Northvale, NJ: Jason Aronson, 1995), 1, 11. Pastoral theologian and counselor Christie Cozad Neuger says people are not only primary actors in their own stories but also "characters in the stories and plots of other people, systems, and cultures. Changes in the plotline or interpretive lenses of *any* of these . . . mean the potential for the transformation of *all*," giving new meaning to the feminist adage "The personal is political and the political is personal." See Neuger, *Counseling Women*, 44.

2. Joanna is quoting Miriam Therese Winters, "Spirit of God," on *Joy Is Like the Rain*, audio recording, Medical Mission Sisters, 1965, a feminist influence on Roman Catholic liturgy and spiritual practice. Joanna's childhood stories reflect influences of Vatican II on everyday Catholic life with regard to liturgical practices and social teaching. See Appendix B of this book for the full text of Winter's song. In her essay "Feminist Women's Spirituality: Breaking New Ground in the Church," in *The Church Women Want: Catholic Women in Dialogue,* ed. Elizabeth A. Johnson (New York: Crossroad, 2002), 28, Winter says, "Expressions of women-church are . . . like a parallel universe within American Catholic church communities." She goes on to say the shifts in understanding authority, liturgy, and spirituality were not to replace the church but to "recover through a creative, intuitive, imaginative, instinctive reinterpretation of tradition new ways of being and behaving as Catholics, in order to live the fullness of . . . our Catholic tradition." Joanna takes a similar approach in seminary to using the tradition to critique and extend the tradition of Baptists.

3. First Baptist Church in Russetville is an American Baptist church in a midwestern state. Joanna made clear that she did not at any time consider herself personally to be Southern Baptist, although three churches in which she served in the South held historic ties to the SBC. Additionally, the dynamics of Baptist life share a common history, and Joanna's relational connections and negotiations provide insight into the relational character of Baptist life in its many forms. Nearly identical support structures and perennial conflicts can be observed in each denominational setting.

4. "Behold What Manner of Love," words and music by Patricia Van Tine, 1978, Maranatha! Music.

5. Some seminarians begin as seekers, for personal fulfillment or to answer personal (often existential) questions, while others attend with explicit vocational goals. Joanna approached seminary in both ways. See Charles R. Foster, Lisa Dahill, Larry Golemon, Barbara Wang Tolentino, William M. Sullivan, and Lee S. Shulman, *Educating Clergy: Teaching Practices and Pastoral Imagination* (San Francisco: Jossey-Bass, 2005), 56, 101–2; and Barbara Wheeler, *Is There a Problem? Theological Students and Religious Leadership for the Future,* Auburn Studies 8, Auburn Theological Seminary, July 2001.

6. In ministry Joanna hoped to make use of both knowledge and "know how," seeing the stakes of the situation and leading change. See Campbell-Reed and Scharen, "Holy Cow!"

7. In the late 1980s and early 1990s, many students from both Southeastern and Southern seminaries fled to university divinity schools and other denominational seminaries.

Joanna was intentionally not Southern Baptist and felt frustrated by assumptions in the South that all Baptists are *Southern* Baptists.

8. Historically some Baptists have practiced "laying hands on" or anointing of the sick and those in need of healing. One wonders about Joanna's experience of anointing from her childhood in the Roman Catholic Church. In late-twentieth-century Baptist practice in the United States, however, the more common use of laying on of hands is in the ritual of ordination. J. R. Tyson, "Laying on of Hands," in Leonard, *Dictionary of Baptists in America*. See also chapter 1 for Anna's ordination story.

9. "Holy Spirit Comforter," music and lyrics by D. E. Adams, (1982/2010). See Appendix B of this book for the full text.

10. Catherine J. Foote, "The Weaver," in *Survivor Prayers: Talking with God about Childhood Sexual Abuse* (Louisville, KY: Westminster John Knox, 1994), 17. See Appendix B of this book for the full text of the poem.

11. The distinction here is subtle and important for survivors of domestic violence and sexual abuse. To force members of a congregation to speak a confession that makes them perpetrators—makes the abuse "their fault"—is to reproduce violence and revictimize survivors. The concern also echoes Joanna's worry as a Baptist over the character of confessions, an issue addressed below.

12. New Testament references for taking up one's cross include Matthew 10:38 and 16:24, Mark 8:34, and Luke 9:23. One biblical reference for burdens to bear is 1 Corinthians 10:13: "No testing has overtaken you that is not common to everyone. God is faithful, and he will not let you be tested beyond your strength, but with the testing he will also provide the way out so that you may be able to endure it" (NRSV). The King James version renders it "Here hath no temptation taken you but such as is common to man: but God is faithful, who will not suffer you to be tempted above that ye are able; but will with the temptation also make a way to escape, that ye may be able to bear it." References to wives submitting to husbands are in two places. Ephesians 5:22–24: "For the husband is the head of the wife just as Christ is the head of the church, the body of which he is the Savior. Just as the church is subject to Christ, so also wives ought to be, in everything, to their husbands." And Colossians 3:18: "Wives, submit to your husbands, as is fitting in the Lord" (NIV) or "Wives, be subject to your husbands, as is fitting in the Lord" (NRSV).

13. The American Bar Association Commission on Domestic Violence reports: "In a 1995–1996 study conducted in the 50 States and the District of Columbia, nearly 25% of women and 7.6% of men were raped and/or physically assaulted by a current or former spouse, cohabiting partner, or dating partner/acquaintance at some time in their lifetime (based on survey of 16,000 participants, equally male and female)." See http://new.abanet.org/domesticviolence/Pages/Statistics.aspx, accessed July 12, 2010. See also the full report by Patricia Tjaden and Nancy Thoennes, *Extent, Nature, and Consequences of Intimate Partner Violence,* Department of Justice, NCJ 181867, July 2000, http://www.ojp.usdoj.gov/nij/pubs-sum/181867.htm, accessed July 12, 2010. The Centers for Disease Control and Prevention estimate that 25 percent of girls and 16 percent of boys are sexually assaulted before the age of eighteen. Childhood physi-

cal abuse was reported at 27 percent for girls and 30 percent for boys. See Centers for Disease Control and Prevention, http://www.cdc.gov/nccdphp/ace/prevalence.htm, accessed July 12, 2010.

14. The Revised Common Lectionary is a list of Scriptures in a three-year cycle, which cover many (but not all) the texts of the Christian Bible. Many Roman Catholic and Protestant churches follow the lectionary as a weekly guide for worship and preaching.

15. Partisan accounts include Hefley, *Truth in Crisis* and *Conservative Resurgence;* Shurden, *Struggle for the Soul of the SBC;* James and Leazer, *Takeover in the Southern Baptist Convention;* Shurden and Shepley, *Going for the Jugular;* and Kell, *Exiled*. Academic treatments also used the dramatic language: Leonard, *God's Last and Only Hope;* Ammerman, *Baptist Battles;* Stricklin, *Genealogy of Dissent;* and Hankins, *Uneasy in Babylon*.

16. C. C. Goen, *Broken Churches, Broken Nation: Denominational Schisms and the Coming of the American Civil War* (Macon, GA: Mercer Univ. Press, 1985), 6–7, 31 ff., advances the hypothesis that American identity was built upon shared religious (Protestant) identity forged in the Great Awakening. Goen adds that when those bonds were severed among Baptists, Methodists, and Presbyterians over the crisis of slavery, the divisions became both "portent and catalyst" for schism in the nation and Civil War.

17. Bill J. Leonard identifies a framework of five tensions of Baptist belief and practice in his introduction to the *Dictionary of Baptists in America,* 4–6. The tensions endured through four hundred years of Baptist history: (1) individual liberty of conscience versus the authority of Scripture, (2) the autonomy of the local church versus associational cooperation, (3) clergy versus laity, (4) religious liberty versus loyalty to the state, and (5) dramatic conversion versus nurturing process. In his more recent *Baptist Ways,* Leonard identifies three additional tensions: (1) doctrinal statements: invariably confessional, selectively creedal; (2) ordinances: sacraments and symbols; and (3) diversity: theological and ecclesial.

18. The relational tensions in Joanna's story may be implicit, yet they are common for many (or most) Baptists. The relational tensions are not uniquely Baptist, however. They also give shape to other Protestant traditions and connect to deeper relational dynamics found in the existential questions of human being. Neuger, in *Counseling Women,* 88–89, 141 ff., shows how women's coming to voice and reframing stories, is both a personal and a political act. As agents, when women change their own stories, they change one another's stories.

19. Pastoral theologian Larry Graham, in *Care of Persons, Care of Worlds: A Psychosystems Approach to Pastoral Care and Counseling* (Nashville: Abingdon Press, 1992), makes a case for the interconnections between individual psyches and the social and natural systems in which they are embedded, as well as the complex interactions of reception, synthesis, and transformation between persons and their worlds.

20. Although the question of *how* social and historical structures are internalized is significant, this chapter focuses on relational dynamics in Joanna's story to show how they reinterpret the Baptist crisis.

21. "Dramatic conversion" is Paul's Damascus Road (Acts 9:1–19) and the altar calls to walk the church aisle and declare one's self changed and saved by the power of Jesus, God, or the Holy Spirit alone. Jean Heriot outlines Max Heirich's sociological views of conversion as "1) a 'fantasy' solution to situations of psychological and social stress; 2) socialization theories which claim that the convert is influenced by prior conditioning; and 3) the analysis of interpersonal influences as significant factors in bringing converts into the group." However, Heriot notes how problematic it is for researchers to approach the topic with skepticism, which can lead to asking the wrong questions about conversion. See Jean Heriot, *Blessed Assurance: Beliefs, Actions, and the Experience of Salvation in a Carolina Baptist Church* (Knoxville: Univ. of Tennessee Press, 1994), 159–60 ff.

22. Bill Leonard says of Baptist views on conversion or regeneration, "Some suggest that such an episode involves a dramatic conversion when the sinner confronts a powerful spiritual and moral struggle, 'accepts Christ,' and receives salvation." Alternately, "most Baptist communions insist on nurturing young people to faith." The two views, Leonard notes, "may also create differences concerning the nature of conversion, its proper process, and its authentic recipients." *Baptist Ways,* 7.

23. Although the rhetoric about dramatic conversion portrays a kind of autonomous action, each of the Baptist tensions identified by Leonard, and explored through the lens of Joanna's story, are set within the framework of a faith community.

24. Baptists grew numerically in Britain, Europe, and then the Americas after the first Baptist church was founded in 1609, with steady increases in adherents and churches. Southern Baptists began with a split from Northern Baptists in 1845, and they expanded rapidly, overtaking United Methodists in the 1920s as the largest U.S. group with seven and a half million members. They doubled that number by the end of the twentieth century. See Edwin S. Gaustad, Philip L. Barlow, and Richard W. Dishno, *New Historical Atlas of Religion in America* (New York: Oxford Univ. Press, 2001), Figures C.15 and C.16, 374–75. Gaustad et al. are counting all Baptists in their figures for the early twentieth century rather than Southern Baptists alone.

25. Advocates in the 1980s and 1990s shifted the language of "victim" to "survivor," reframing possibilities for healing. For example: "Yet healing isn't just about pain. It's about learning to love yourself. As you move from feeling like a victim to being a proud survivor, you will have glimmers of hope, pride, satisfaction. Those are natural byproducts of healing." Ellen Bass and Laura Davis, *The Courage to Heal: A Guide for Women Survivors of Child Sexual Abuse,* 3rd ed. (New York: Collins Living, 1994), 189.

26. Active and passive as psychological descriptions of masculine/dominant and feminine/submissive are not adequate or accurate for describing phenomenologically the experiences of masculinity or femininity, which are culturally constructed and can be easily reversed in ways that don't reduce experience into simple polarities. Jessica Benjamin describes signs in a hospital nursery that read "I'm a boy" and "It's a girl." She notes, "The sexual difference was already interpreted in terms of complementary and unequal roles, subject and object. The aspect of will, desire, and activity—all

that we might conjure up with a subject who is an 'I'—was assigned to the male gender alone." See Benjamin, *Bonds of Love*, 85–86. Neuger, *Counseling Women*, 234, argues that women need connection in order "to develop strategies of resistance and transformation."

27. These social connections and organizations are part of the "interlocking social structures," with each one "hooking on" to the others and together constituting a recognizable Baptist way of life. See Christian Smith, *What Is a Person: Rethinking Humanity, Social Life, and the Moral Good from the Person Up* (Chicago: Univ. of Chicago Press, 2010), 257–58 ff.

28. Winnicott provides the insight from clinical analysis that creativity and conformity are contrasting ways of relating to one's world. Joanna and her friends engage in a kind of creativity, which breaks from conformity and plays with scriptural text and worship design, leading to a sense of trust for others and emerging self-identities. A process like theirs is akin to the process of relaxed ease while playing, which allows growth and self-understanding in a therapeutic setting. See *Playing and Reality*, 54–55, 65, passim.

29. Mary McClintock Fulkerson in *Changing the Subject: Women's Discourses and Feminist Theology* (Minneapolis: Augsburg, 1994), 355–72, argues that "inclusion" of women (especially without any agreed upon universal notion of "woman") is an inadequate way forward to coping with oppressions and injustices regarding gender. She critiques liberation-feminist theology for giving inadequate attention to the situated character of the social location, relations of power, and situated practices of women and the ways they make use of texts, practices, and meanings to experience "emancipatory or liberating possibilities." In other words, to interpret meaning requires a more complex social understanding of lives. Neither the "subject position" nor some unmediated "experience" are adequate categories for understanding Joanna or the changing lives of Baptist clergywomen.

30. See Leonard, *Dictionary of Baptists in America*, 4–6. The term is also called "soul liberty." Each new situation offers an experience of the sacred and a new opportunity to engage the texts and traditions for their wisdom in the situation. Molly T. Marshall, "Exercising Liberty of Conscience: Freedom in Private Interpretation," in *Baptists in the Balance: The Tension between Freedom and Responsibility*, ed. Everett C. Goodwin (Valley Forge, PA: Judson, 1997), 141, says understanding Scripture must take account of "a history of interpretation, the social location and personal experience of the interpreter, the context of the community, [and] new insights prompted by the midwifery of the Holy Spirit."

31. Marshall, "Exercising Liberty," 143–44, carefully couches individual authority for interpretation in one's participation in an ecclesial community, the life of God, and discipleship of Jesus Christ. She also points out the extreme problems in the doctrine and practice: hyperindividualism and authoritarianism.

32. Rosemary Radford Reuther traces the complexity of human relations as they are implicated in the cultural and ritual images of God through history and how women and nature are dominated in parallel fashion through Babylonian, Hebrew, Greek,

and Christian understandings of male, female, and a patriarchal image of God. See Reuther, *Sexism and God Talk: Toward a Feminist Theology* (Boston: Beacon, 1983), 72–82, 93–98.

33. Commitments to "mutuality" are no guarantee against violence or harm in relationships, according to Benjamin, but they are necessary for navigating the difficulties of recognizing otherness and surviving the inevitable negation and destruction required on the road to genuine individuation, which includes differentiation and simultaneously avoids splits into complementarity. See Benjamin, *Bonds of Love*, 82–83.

34. Each congregation where Joanna was a member, intern, or staff minister during her time in the South had historic ties to the SBC. This particular congregation was no longer affiliated with the SBC when she arrived.

35. See Sally B. Purvis, *The Stained Glass Ceiling: Churches and Their Women Pastors* (Louisville, KY: Westminster John Knox, 1995).

36. Neuger traces a process parallel to Joanna's description, shifting the framework of someone's story such that "more authentic and life-giving truths emerge from the story than they did through its original framework of meaning." See Neuger, *Counseling Women*, 135–37. Alice Miller, *The Drama of the Gifted Child: The Search for the True Self*, trans. Ruth Ward (New York: Basic Books, 2008), 101, observes, "Often a child's very gifts (his [sic] great intensity of feeling, depth of experience, curiosity, intelligence, quickness—and his ability to be critical) will confront his parents with conflicts that they have long sought to keep at bay by means of rules and regulations." It is possible to imagine that the suffering of Joanna's caregivers unwittingly inflicted or allowed pain and abuse, enforcing rules with a profound cost to Joanna's childhood development.

37. The ideal of congregational polity is also in tension with the idea of associational cooperation between and among churches. This tension in "voluntary association" is addressed below. Power exercised by the Southern Baptist Convention, however, undermines powers of the local church through its power to shape Baptist culture, despite its lack of official ecclesiastical power. See Nancy Ammerman's chapter, "Organization, Growth and Change," in which she traces the growth of influence and power in the SBC, in Ammerman, *Baptist Battles*, 44–71.

38. McBeth's *Women in Baptist Life* first traced this history. More recently, Pamela R. Durso traced it with greater global sensitivity and a broader cross section of Baptist groups in "She Preachers, Bossy Women, and Children of the Devil."

39. In her own personal therapy and through the empathic response of the pastoral counselor, Joanna reengaged her emotional life and childhood suffering, which took her along a path of internal dialogue toward greater acceptance and healing. See Miller, *Drama of the Gifted Child*, 112–13.

40. Recognition from the counselor, and the ensuing sense of freedom, opened up a potential space for Joanna's discovery and creation of a new creative vocational direction. See Winnicott, *Playing and Reality*, 54–56.

41. Although the large study of pastors conducted by Jackson Carroll concluded that a majority of pastors are satisfied, healthy, and emotionally well (if somewhat over-

weight like others in the United States), the study also identified the leading factors that "weaken commitment, foster dissatisfaction and affect health negatively" (186), including inadequate pay and benefits, unresolved congregational conflict and criticism, personal stress from conflicts, inadequate time with family, disputes over pastoral roles, loneliness, and isolation. Joanna experienced each of these factors increasingly in her time at Gentry Memorial. See Carroll, *God's Potters,* 169–87.

42. See Leonard, *God's Last and Only Hope,* 73–74, 101–3.
43. In her social analysis of the SBC parties, Ammerman found "moderates" were likely to be members of SBC churches that gave a larger percentage of money to the denomination, fostering a loyalty to the denomination. A careful examination, however, revealed that the more significant difference came at the point of education and resources. She found clergy who attended SBC seminaries and laity who attended Baptist colleges, and thus were socialized in a Baptist milieu, were more likely to participate in meetings and causes regarding the future of the SBC. As Baptists newer to the denominational scene, "fundamentalists" felt less invested in saving the denomination and more invested in doctrinal purity, cultural critique, and prophetic response. See Ammerman, *Baptist Battles,* 156–67. See also Hankins, *Uneasy in Babylon,* 39–73.
44. Having been outsiders to SBC leadership, over decades biblicists cultivated their own alternative network of connections through evangelistic revival circuits, Bible conferences, schools, and publications. See Ammerman, *Baptist Battles,* 171–73.
45. An early and highly publicized example unfolded when Prescott Memorial Baptist Church in Memphis, Tennessee, called Nancy Hastings Sehested as pastor in 1987. The Shelby County Baptist Association moved swiftly to "disfellowship" the church, setting a pattern repeated many times right up to the present. See Leonard, *God's Last and Only Hope,* 154.
46. Penny Marler reports in "A Study of the Effects of Participation in Pastoral Leader Peer Groups" on the findings of two 2008 surveys that illustrate (negatively) the lack of support felt by pastors like Joanna. Both personal support and an increased vitality of the congregation were correlated to peer group participation: "Belonging to a peer group legitimizes activities that many of pastoral leaders intuitively knew were necessary for a long and vital ministry but found difficult to squeeze into their schedules. Time of Sabbath, fellowship with friends, creative endeavors, prayer, and laughter became parts of their pastoral rhythms and therefore parts of the rhythms of their calls" (10). The studies found isolation a motivating factor for joining peer groups, especially among women: "Most female pastoral leaders [in peer groups] are a minority presence in their denominations; and many are concentrated in smaller parishes in rural areas, small towns, and inner-urban areas" (21–22). See http://www.chalicepress.com/assets/pdfs/SPEFinalSurveyReport.pdf, accessed Apr. 23, 2013.
47. Although they continue to grow in numbers, the percentage of women pastoring American Baptist Churches USA (9.4%) and Cooperative Baptist Fellowship churches (5%) is still far below other mainline congregations. Alliance of Baptists churches are more in line with other Protestant mainline congregations at 31 percent. See Campbell-Reed, "Baptists in Tension." See also Chloe's story in chapter 5.

48. The length of time in a congregation has been declining in Mainline churches like Joanna's. The Barna Research Group reports, "One of the enduring idiosyncrasies of mainline churches is the brief tenure of pastors in a church. On average, these pastors last four years before moving to another congregation." See http://www.barna.org/barna-update/article/17-leadership/323-report-examines-the-state-of-mainline-protestant-churches, accessed Apr. 26, 2013.

49. With Roger Williams as their "apostle of responsible freedom," Baptists in America have been conscientiously objecting to the union of church and state since the colonial period. See Edwin Gaustad, "Responsible Freedom: Baptists in Early America," in *Baptists in the Balance: The Tension between Freedom and Responsibility,* ed. Everett C. Goodwin (Valley Forge, PA: Judson Press, 1997), 275–85. From the colonial period through the early years of the republic white Baptists, with some exceptions, also participated in foreclosing the political space of "freedom" by structuring it to benefit themselves.

50. Radical religious liberty exceeds mere toleration and champions each individual and group who pursue religious conviction wherever it takes them (short of fraud, force, or murder, disallowed by the state). However, these assumptions applied mainly to white male landowners and/or citizens of European dissent in both the Americas and Europe during the three centuries of political battles over religious liberty.

51. Many skirmishes on the convention floor and in the Baptist papers between biblicists and autonomists erupted over conceptions of religious liberty embedded in fights over prayer in public schools, school vouchers, and public displays of the Ten Commandments. See Hankins, *Uneasy in Babylon,* 144–56.

52. Benjamin argues in *Like Subjects, Love Objects,* 22–23, that "mutual recognition should include the notion of breakdown, of failure to sustain that tension, as well as account for the possibility of repair after failure."

53. The name-calling was rampant. References for these examples include Shurden and Shepley, *Going for the Jugular:* "W. A. Criswell could savagely and publicly malign [moderates] as 'skunks' in his 1988 Pastors' Conference address" (230, 235); "Document 47: Randall Lolley's Bramble Bush Sermon at the 1990 Forum" (250 ff.); "Document 46: New Story: Vestal's Presidential Bid" (244–45). See also Hefley, *Conservative Resurgence,* 162–64.

54. Daniel Vestal, "The History of the Cooperative Baptist Fellowship," in Shurden, *Struggle for the Soul of the SBC,* 253–74. Hefley *Conservative Resurgence,* 309, captures a plethora of terms in this sweeping statement in his final chapter: "The turnaround in the [SBC] represents primarily a 'resurgence' in conservative theology as applied to the doctrine of Biblical inspiration. The SBC reversal of a liberal drift is unique in American Christianity. Never before have conservatives in a major denomination overcome the opposition of the ecclesiastical establishment, including most of the denominational editors, and turned the body back to its theological roots to such a decided extent."

Chapter 4

1. Rebecca's story highlights the continuity between discipleship and vocation. See Cahalan, *Introducing the Practice of Ministry,* 49–50: "Ministry is the vocation of leading disciples in the life of discipleship for the sake of God's mission in the world."
2. The theological framework explicated in Farley's *Good and Evil* shapes the arguments of this chapter. Thus a tragic structure of the human experience and it's irreconcilable passions (for survival, connection, and reality) are occasions for both evil and redemption and give shape to interpretations of both Rebecca's experience and conditions of the SBC.
3. Preaching as theological work (talk of God and humanity), incarnational practice (word becoming flesh), and articulation of struggle (lament over human tragedy) will be the primary understandings of sermons as sources for understanding and interpreting schism in this chapter. Rebecca shared her written sermons with me, and she speaks of her own preaching at many points in her narrative. The chapter's analysis engages published sermons by ten leading Baptist voices preached in settings from local weekly worship to the annual SBC and SBWIM meetings.
4. Architectural spaces of Southern Baptist churches often reflect the commitment to preaching, with a chancel dominated by a pulpit that towers over the communion table and virtually blocks the view of the baptistery from the perspective of worshipers gathered in a typical SBC sanctuary.
5. Rebecca's stories yield a "surplus of meaning" that cannot be fully included or accessed. See Paul Riceour, "Rhetoric-Poetics-Hermeneutics," in *From Metaphysics to Rhetoric,* ed. Michel Meyer (Boston: Kluwer Academic, 1989), 137–49. This surplus makes narrative forms of theology compelling, offering a depth and range of possibilities that cannot be reduced to formal doctrines or logical arguments, which are secondary and derivative. Both psychology and theology are secondary, interpretive modes of discourse working with complex, shifting, and contested meanings.
6. Rebecca is using the chemical term "osmosis" in a common metaphorical sense. The online *Oxford English Dictionary* gives two definitions: (1) "A process by which molecules of a solvent tend to pass through a semipermeable membrane from a less concentrated solution into a more concentrated one, thus equalizing the concentrations on each side of the membrane," and (2) "The process of gradual or unconscious assimilation of ideas, knowledge, etc." Oxford Dictionaries, http://oxforddictionaries.com/definition/osmosis?region=us, accessed Aug. 12, 2011.
7. In Baptist churches it is common practice for individuals coming to a decision about faith or baptism to "walk the aisle" or "come forward" in a worship service to express their desire for—or experience of—change to pastor, congregation, and God. The "outward" expression of "inward" conversion for Baptists is usually expressed by full-immersion baptism or dipping under the water rather than pouring (affusion) or sprinkling (aspersion). See William R. Estep, "Baptism, Baptist Views," in Leonard, *Dictionary of Baptists in America,* 40–41.

8. "Surrendering to full-time Christian service" is Baptist language for embracing a vocational call to live one's life of faith publically. See Leonard, *God's Last and Only Hope,* 2.
9. For more about living amid parental expectations, see Martha's story in chapter 2.
10. A large number of faculty departed Southern Baptist Theological Seminary and Southeastern Baptist Theological Seminary during the late 1980s and early 1990s. Between 1989 and 1993, nearly twenty, over a quarter of the full-time faculty, resigned from Southern to take other posts. By the late 1990s only a small handful of moderate faculty remained. The transformation of seminary leadership from boardroom to classroom was essentially complete by the mid 1990s. See Hankins, *Uneasy in Babylon,* 82–88.
11. In the late 1980s and early 1990s, "Baptist houses of study" opened at several university-related divinity schools across the South, and new Baptist seminaries sprang up as alternatives to the SBC schools.
12. This problem is not unique to research universities, although they may present particular problems related to ministry curricula, which are slightly different than freestanding seminaries. Rather, seminary education in the United States and North America as a whole is in a constant struggle to prepare students adequately for the life-world of church ministry when they are also accountable to the rigors of a university model of education. University models insisting on a scientific understanding of knowledge production are less concerned with love, wisdom, grace, forgiveness or justice, which are primary for an adequate theological education. Some schools navigate the space of tension between church and academy better than others. See David H. Kelsey, *To Understand God Truly: What's Theological About a Theological School* (Louisville, KY: Westminster John Knox, 1992), 227–51.
13. The master of divinity (MDiv) is the basic professional ministry degree, usually requiring a preaching course. The two quotes in this paragraph are from Rebecca's sermon, "Fearfully and Wonderfully Made."
14. A 2008 study of clergy sexual misconduct revealed the following: "In the average American congregation of 400 persons, with women representing, on average, 60% of the congregation, there are, on average of 7 women who have experienced clergy sexual misconduct." More than 90 percent of the "sexual advances" by clergy happened in secret. From the executive summary available online, http://www.baylor.edu/clergysexualmisconduct/index.php?id=67406, accessed Dec. 3, 2013. See Mark Chaves and Diana S. Richmond Garland, "The Prevalence of Clergy Sexual Advances toward Adults in Their Congregations," *Journal for the Scientific Study of Religion* 48, no. 4 (Dec. 1, 2009): 817–24.
15. The "systems issue" that Rebecca points to may seem to be a local problem at Winstead, but it is precisely the isolation that keeps the system working for churches in a sexist culture. As Karen Lebacqz and Ronald G. Barton in *Sex in the Parish* (Louisville, KY: Westminster John Knox, 1991), 236, observe, "Until such time as women are genuinely equal with men in our culture, there will be power differentials between men and women that raise ethical questions. These power differentials exist because of sexism, and they are not overcome by the efforts of any one person or pas-

tor. Until such time as patterns of child rearing in our culture are changed, it is likely that men will tend to genitalize their deep feelings. These patterns are cultural patterns not weaknesses of character of a few misfit pastors. In order to develop healthy patterns of sexual relating in the church, the cultural patterns have to be changed."

16. Lebacqz and Barton summarize the paradox in Rebecca's story: "At one and the same time, we must understand conduct on the part of clergy and the very human elements that engender that very inappropriate conduct. When sexual misconduct [by male clergy] happens, it is difficult to talk about having empathy for the women who are abused without appearing to condemn and blame men. It is difficult to talk about having sympathy for the male pastor without appearing to belittle and deny the pain of the women. Yet this is precisely the paradox with which we must work, for we are convinced that only by trying to understand all the dynamics at work can we arrive at an adequate ethical framework." Ibid., 237.

17. The observation of pieties of power and pieties of vulnerability comes from looking carefully at the rhetoric and actions of the parties in the schism. In a similar vein, Eighmy, *Churches in Cultural Captivity,* 19–20, argues that churches "forfeited their prophetic role" in society regarding slavery by cooperating with other churches only for "missions," by focusing too intently on individual morality, and by submitting to social pressures beyond the church to sanction slavery. Following slavery, the establishment of Jim Crow laws, growth of the black prison population and share cropping, as well as a rising number of lynchings in America, continued the implication of Southern Baptists (and all white Americans) in perpetuating the doctrines of white supremacy and black inferiority. The residue of those beliefs outlived slavery and Jim Crow, and they remain enshrined in institutions like Southern Baptist churches and denominational structures. Thus the pieties of power and vulnerability are relative to the more durable structures of race that endure to the present. See Michelle Alexander, *The New Jim Crow: Mass Incarceration in the Age of Colorblindness* (New York: The New Press, 2012).

18. For more about Patterson's role in the schism, see Hankins, *Uneasy in Babylon,* 38, 51–52, passim.

19. Patterson published the article, "Stalemate," in a special issue of the journal of New Orleans Baptist Theological Seminary, reprinted as "Document 31: Paige Patterson's Article in *The Theological Educator,* Special Issue, 1985," in Shurden and Shepley, *Going for the Jugular,* 141–56. Patterson gives biblical and historical examples, including the Jerusalem Conference, the Reformation, and the Landmark controversy, without elaboration.

20. Ibid. The predictions did not come to pass quite as Patterson had hoped. Growth in the number of churches and adherents in the SBC slowed considerably in the late 1990s and 2000s. Doubts regarding the accuracy of denominational statistics and losses from the schism finally led to admissions that the SBC was declining. See Cary McMullen, "Any Way You Count It, Fewer Southern Baptists," *Paltka Daily News* online, http://www.adherents.com/largecom/baptist_fewerSBC.html, accessed Dec. 3, 2013. Additionally, belief continues to be very significant for Southern

Baptists, although not as absolute in defining membership or adherence as in the past. See Chloe's story in chapter 5 for more about shifts from belief to practice.

21. Ibid, 142–43.
22. For more on Marshall's influence on the movement among Baptists to ordain women, see Eileen R. Campbell-Reed, "Molly Truman Marshall: Living Icon for Beholding the Spirit's Renewal of the Church," *Perspectives in Religious Studies* 41, no. 2 (2014): 121–36.
23. Molly Marshall, "Singing the Lord's Song: Psalm 137:1–4, Colossians 3:12–17," in *Costly Obedience: Sermons by Women of Steadfast Spirit,* ed. Elizabeth Smith Bellinger (Valley Forge, PA: Judson Press, 1994), 12–15. *Folio* 3, no. 2 (Autumn 1985): 2 reported 350 registrations and more than 500 in attendance at the 1985 SBWIM meeting in Dallas.
24. Marshall, "Singing the Lord's Song," 12–13.
25. Ibid., 14.
26. Ibid. Minimally autonomist leaders felt the risk to their careers in ministry when they took political stands in the SBC. Some, like Marshall, understood the call of Christ as choosing vulnerability. This was not true for *all* autonomists, and women took greater risks given their social vulnerability.
27. Marshall, "Singing the Lord's Song," 15.
28. Ten years after preaching this sermon, Marshall lost her job as a tenured professor at Southern Seminary. See *Battle for the Minds,* produced and directed by Steven Lipscomb (Los Angeles, 1997). See also Robison B. James, "Molly Marshall," in *The Dictionary of Heresy Trials in American Christianity,* ed. George H. Shriver (Westport, CT: Greenwood Press, 1997), 242–51. Anna's story in chapter 1 explores the double bind of theological vulnerability in the "servanthood dilemma."
29. Farley, *Good and Evil,* 106–9, describes the necessity of understanding meanings for biological survival and as well as interdependence on one another and the social environment.
30. Molly T. Marshall, *What It Means to Be Human* (Macon, GA: Smyth & Helwys, 1995), 119, poses vulnerability as an essential aspect of human existence as a "created, limited, interdependent reality."
31. Rebecca's story, as well as the messages of Marshall and Patterson, touch on the "tragic character" of the most basic human passions for survival, agency, relationality, and reality. The passions strive across the "unclosable gulf between desiring and desired" and cannot finally be reconciled, yet fulfillment comes in a limited sense to make life livable. See Farley, *Good and Evil,* 109–10.
32. Most Baptist historians and theologians maintain this point. See Bill Leonard, *Baptists in America* (New York: Columbia Univ., 2005), 142–48. Brian Haymes, "Baptism: A Question of Belief and Age?" *Perspectives in Religious Studies* 27, no. 1 (Mar. 1, 2000): 125–30, traces the theological questions surrounding the age of accountability and meaning of baptism, comparing British and American Baptists.
33. Leonard, *Baptists in America,* 144–47, traces historical disputes and divisions over baptism, focusing particularly on the Landmark controversy, in which founder,

J. M. Pendleton declared a succession of all true New Testament faithful to be immersed (baptized) and all others to be outside the true faith.

34. Ordained white Baptist women resolved the dilemma of being Baptist and female in a range of ways. Conservative Southern Baptist women resolved the dilemma in a different range of ways. Elizabeth Flowers traces the conservative pathways, often bundled together as "biblical womanhood," in *Into the Pulpit,* 68–86. African American women in black Baptist churches faced yet another pathway in the dilemma of being Baptist and female, complicated further by racist ideologies built on slavery and Jim Crow.

35. Nancy Hastings Sehested, "We Have This Treasure," in *Costly Obedience: Sermons by Women of Steadfast Spirit,* ed. Elizabeth Smith Bellinger (Valley Forge, PA: Judson Press, 1994), 1–5.

36. Fletcher, *Southern Baptist Convention,* Appendix 2, 399.

37. James T. Draper Jr., "Southern Baptists: People of Deep Beliefs," president's address, June 14, 1983, Southern Baptist Convention Press Kit Collection, Southern Baptist Historical Library and Archives, Nashville.

38. Meaning and identity are both created and discovered, as attested to in the work of psychiatrists such as Winnicott, *Playing and Reality,* 54–55, 67–71, and theologians such as Wendy Farley, who follows on from her father Ed Farley's work to explore how *desire*—to know, to be known, and to find meaning—is a symbol of humanity's great existential work in this age. See Wendy Farley, *The Wounding and Healing of Desire: Weaving Heaven and Earth* (Louisville, KY: Westminster John Knox, 2005), 19–20. The "discovery" angle of meaning is not the finding of some pre-existing self (or "true self" as Winnicott posited) but rather an acknowledgement of the social sources of the "self" and the networks of meaning available in a given time and context. See Charles Taylor, *Sources of the Self: The Making of the Modern Identity* (Cambridge: Harvard Univ. Press, 1989), 511.

39. Eighmy, *Churches in Cultural Captivity,* 8–9, 89.

40. Debates about vocation heat up when "calling" is reduced to vocation of ordained ministry, as happened in the 1970s and 1980s, when more women claimed vocations of ordained ministry. See Stancil, "Divergent Views and Practices of Ordination," 42–49.

41. Vestal, "History of the Cooperative Baptist Fellowship," 252.

42. Ibid.

43. James C. Hefley self-published a series of books from the biblicist camp taking this perspective. See *Conservative Resurgence.*

44. Ibid., 78–79.

45. Ibid., 78.

46. The man commenting was Kerry Peacock. The rally was held at First Baptist Church in Euless, Texas. The quote appeared in "Political Activities Escalate as SBC Approaches," *Word & Way,* June 8, 1989, 9, as quoted in Hefley, *Conservative Resurgence,* 79.

47. Hefley, *Conservative Resurgence,* 81. The source of this quote, Hefley says, is "from my notes and tape recording of interviews with Vestal in the press room" (90 n. 22).
48. Vestal, "History of the Cooperative Baptist Fellowship," 253–74.
49. Vestal's story recounts beginnings of the Cooperative Baptist Fellowship, part of the longer fracturing as groups left the SBC by degrees over time. The CBF departure was the largest in terms of numbers.
50. It is a misunderstanding to think that grief and lament over loss are an end to the story. Baptists on both sides did appear in seasons to be stuck on the losses and the rancor that accompanied them. To notice clarification and renewal is not a gloss on the pain but an acknowledgment that the story did not end in loss or division, although the divisions remain and the losses are still felt and lamented in many quarters.
51. Ann Taves, "Sexuality in American Religious History," in *Retelling U.S. Religious History,* ed. Thomas A. Tweed (Berkeley and Los Angeles: Univ. of California, 1997), 27–56, traces a number of instances in the formation of the state where women bear an extraordinary weight of both vulnerability and blame for sexual expression inside and outside of marriage, abortion and contraception, and homosexuality. Taves argues that earlier European and canon law, which embodied patriarchal oppression on the basis of gender, race, and class, shaped the relationship between sexuality and the formation of the American state(s).
52. Martha's story in chapter 2 and Joanna's story in chapter 3 explore the production, reproduction, and undoing of complementarity.
53. Fred H. Wolfe, "Here's Hope, Southern Baptists (Zechariah 4:1–10)," June 19, 1990, Southern Baptist Convention Press Kit Collection, Southern Baptist Historical Library and Archives, Nashville. Galatians 5:15 "If, however, you bite and devour one another, take care that you are not consumed by one another" (NRSV).
54. Ibid.
55. Both churches identified with the autonomist party. See Betty Winstead McGary, "Becoming Community," in *A Costly Obedience: Sermons by Women of Steadfast Spirit,* ed. Elizabeth Smith Bellinger (Valley Forge, PA: Judson Press, 1994), 37–42.
56. Ibid. McGary references Henri Nouwen, *Lifesigns* (New York: Doubleday, 1986), and Dietrich Bonhoeffer, *Life Together,* trans. John Doberstein (New York: Harper & Row, 1954). Bonheoffer's chapters on "Ministry" and "Confession and Communion" get at this quality of listening and speaking, which break through isolation to community.
57. McGary, "Becoming Community," 39–40.
58. Butler, *Undoing Gender,* 19, captures the connection between grief and desire eloquently: "Let's face it. We're undone by each other. And if we're not, we're missing something. If this seems so clearly the case with grief, it is only because it was already the case with desire. One does not always stay intact. It may be that one wants to, or does, but it may also be that despite one's best efforts, one is undone, in the face of the other."

59. These are the elemental passions explored by Farley in *Good and Evil*, 97–117.
60. Ibid., 112. Farley's elemental passions "do not point to three separate referents"—something like self-fulfillment, being founded by the other, or finding meaning. Rather the passions are united in "an eros for the eternal." Nothing concrete or finite finally "fulfills the passions." The passions and their referents are more simply "how agents exist in the world."
61. Ibid., 122–23. Farley observes both the "benign alienation" of "incompatibility and competition" and the "ontological alienation" that is a structural interruption and a perpetual state.
62. Adrian Rogers, "The Great Deceiver," in Shurden and Shepley, *Going for the Jugular*, 14–23.
63. Ibid., 18–19.
64. Cindy Harp Johnson, "Blessed Is She," in *Costly Obedience: Sermons by Women of Steadfast Spirit*, ed. Elizabeth Smith Bellinger (Valley Forge, PA: Judson Press, 1994), 47–53. She originally preached her sermon on Mother's Day in May 1988, at Fourth Baptist Church, Upperco, Maryland.
65. Johnson is naming double binds experienced by women. Neuger, *Counseling Women*, 44–46, also discusses the problem of double binds, urging her readers to resist the idea that women (people) *are* problems. Instead pastors and counselors should see women as people *with* problems to be addressed.
66. Johnson "Blessed Is She," 50, cites Psalm 121:1–2, Psalm 146:3, 5, and Psalm 33:20 as examples in which the help comes to a human person from God. Other examples of the use of *ezer*, she argues, indicate times when partnership between humans resulted in something greater than any one person could accomplish alone.
67. Acts 2:17–18, 21 (NRSV): "In the last days it will be, God declares, that I will pour out my Spirit upon all flesh, and your sons and your daughters shall prophesy, and your young men shall see visions, and your old men shall dream dreams. Even upon my slaves, both men and women, in those days I will pour out my Spirit; and they shall prophesy. . . . Then everyone who calls on the name of the Lord shall be saved."

Chapter 5

1. *Baptists Today*, a newspaper sponsored by the autonomist party, communicated concerns and perspectives of the party's causes.
2. Jars of Clay released *Jars of Clay* in 1995.
3. Luke 12:48b: "From everyone to whom much has been given, much will be required; and from one to whom much has been entrusted, even more will be demanded" (NRSV).
4. James 2:15–17: "If a brother or sister is naked and lacks daily food, and one of you says to them, 'Go in peace; keep warm and eat your fill,' and yet you do not supply their bodily needs, what is the good of that? So faith by itself, if it has no works, is dead" (NRSV).

5. This story highlights in multiple ways the intersections of race, class, and gender in church cultures. Through systems of institutionalized racism and pervasive white privilege at work socially, Chloe is able to experience a sense of calling and purpose and see the "good news" of the situation that leads to some healing for the harms of a broken community. And while partnership between the churches sounds admirable, it also raises questions of paternalism and how the one-directional flow of resources may serve to keep locked in place the long-standing systems that benefit Brenthall members and harm Bethel members. The concept of intersectionality was coined by Kimberle Crenshaw, "Demarginalizing the Intersection of Race and Sex: A Black Feminist Critique of Antidiscrimination Doctrine, Feminist Theory, and Antiracist Politics" *University of Chicago Legal Forum* (1989): 139–67.
6. Gil Bailie, *Violence Unveiled* (New York: Crossroad, 1996), xv, attributes the quote to Howard Thurman.
7. Chloe refers to Edwin H. Friedman's insights about small groups, triangulation, and the work of individuation. See Friedman's *Generation to Generation: Family Process in Church and Synagogue* (New York: Guilford, 1985), 213–15, passim.
8. See Rabbi Tirzah Firestone, *With Roots in Heaven: One Woman's Passionate Journey in the Heart of her Faith* (New York: Dutton, 1998).
9. For an articulation of ministry as embodied, relational practice, see Campbell-Reed and Scharen, "Holy Cow!" 323–42. See also Patricia Benner, "Using the Dreyfus Model of Skill Acquisition to Describe and Interpret Skill Acquisition and Clinical Judgment in Nursing Practice and Education," *Bulletin of Science, Technology and Society Special Issue: Human Expertise in the Age of the Computer* 24, no. 3 (2005): 188–99. Benner articulates the embodied and relational aspects of learning judgment and salience for professional practice.
10. Chloe's experience is captured in philosopher Charles Taylor's observation about tensions since the Enlightenment between "disengaged reason" and "creative imagination." He sees basic agreement about the goods of society (i.e., freedom, human rights, justice, benevolence, self-fulfillment, free expression, etc.), yet he shows at length how contentious disagreements hover just below the surface of civility about the sources of these goods, which have roots in oldest theistic sources from the Judeo-Christian traditions, the Enlightenment tradition of rational reasoning, and the romantic tradition. He shows the variety of problems that result from pursuing only one set of goods to the exclusion of the others, and he cautions against "the error of declaring those goods invalid whose exclusive pursuit leads to contemptible or disastrous consequences." Taylor, *Sources of the Self*, 511.
11. Chloe's description of the "partnership" is more accurately a one-directional flow of resources from the predominantly white Brenthall Baptist Church to a community served by the black Bethel Baptist Church. Michael Emerson and Christian Smith point out that the SBC has a long history of promoting church growth through the "homogenous units principle," which promotes racially separated congregations, allowing white congregations such as Brenthall to remain oblivious to the power dynamics of white privilege and to reproduce structural racism. See Michael O.

Emerson and Christian Smith, *Divided by Faith: Evangelical Religion and the Problem of Race in America* (New York: Oxford Univ. Press, 2000), 150–51.

12. Chloe believes her parents primarily used deliberation to make decisions, which does not mean they never trusted intuition or emotion. The shift under discussion is a subtle matter of emphasis. Both forms of decision making are present even when one is emphasized over the other. Taylor, *Sources of the Self,* 513, argues for "personal resonance" as crucial for the work of discovering meaning. He says there are "important issues of life" that can only be resolved through personal engagement, giving the example of "why it matters and what it means to have a more deeply resonant human environment and . . . affiliations with some depth in time and commitment. These are questions we can only clarify by exploring the human predicament, the way we are set in nature and among others, as a locus of moral sources. As our public traditions of family, ecology, even polis are undermined or swept away, we need new languages of personal resonance to make crucial human goods alive for us again." Feminist theologians and philosophers advocate for attending to embodied, emotional, and relational experience as primary sources for faithful discernment and theological reflection. For example, Elaine Graham says, "What is normative and authentic for the Christian community is enacted and embodied in *praxis*. It is these diverse pastoral practices that reveal, and construct, the dominant frameworks of meaning and truth. The activities of fostering moral ways of life, story telling, promoting human development, and perusing gender equality are undertaken because the community has inherited, and inhabits a particular set of truth claims." See Elaine Graham, *Transforming Practice: Pastoral Theology in an Age of Uncertainty* (London: Mowbray, 1996), 112–14, 138–39.

13. Baptist history includes a long and complex relationship between an emotional versus a reasoned faith. Some periods and groups favor one over the other. Thus the inherited traditions carry the differing commitments and values with them and are reproduced with new tensions in each new context and generation. For example, the earliest Baptist writing calls for both worship that is "spirituall proceeding originally from the hart" and also a defense of sacred Scriptures as the "fountayne of all truth; the ground and foundacion of our fayth." John Smyth, "Differences of the Churches of the Separation, 1608," in *A Sourcebook for Baptist Heritage,* ed. H. Leon McBeth (Nashville: Broadman Press, 1990), 14–18.

14. In the 1920s the Baptist Sunday School Board advocated laying foundations for conversion to Christian faith during ages four through eight, promoting active "evangelization" of children from age nine upward. By the 1960s the age of children professing faith and being baptized ranged between six and eight years old. Corralling children to make "decisions" imposed a rationalized model of belief and choice on children that approached emotional manipulation. It also ignored the historic Baptist principle of regenerate church membership based on mature accountability for following Christ. See G. Thomas Halbrooks, "Children and the Church: A Baptist Historical Perspective," *Review and Expositor* 80, no. 2 (Spring 1983): 179–88.

15. Ibid., 183–85. Halbrooks observes four Southern Baptist approaches to understanding the relationship of children to the church: "1) non-members, 2) prospects, 3) potential disciples, or 4) maturing participants." The tensions between the differing views

capture the ongoing tensions among Baptists. Biblicists hold fast to the children as prospects and continue to "convert" children to faith at younger and younger ages. Autonomists gravitated toward understandings of potential growth and maturing faith, although they still maintain a need for conversion and baptism to mark accountable faith and church membership.

16. Chloe's story illustrates a change related to the generational changes in religion demonstrated by David Campbell and Robert Putnam in their meta-study of American religiosity, *American Grace: How Religion Divides and Unites Us* (New York: Simon & Schuster, 2010), 72–76, 93–96. Change over time in religion can be generational, developmental, or by period of time. The shift in seeing ministry from "role and identity" to "calling and giftedness" is a generational shift, reflecting aftershocks of 1960s questions to authority. See also Cahalan, *Introducing the Practice of Ministry*, 49–52.

17. Margaret (Meg) B. Hess, "When I Am Preaching, I know in My Bones that I Am Doing What I Was Born to Do," in *Courage and Hope: The Stories of Ten Baptist Women Ministers,* ed. Pamela R. Durso and Keith E. Durso (Macon, GA: Mercer Univ. Press, 2005), 94–104.

18. Chloe and Margaret Hess are part of a long tradition of mystical and embodied experience in the history of the church. Yet in the twentieth century, Baptists made a mass appeal to rational deliberation as the way of faith. In Gary Furr and Curtis W. Freeman, eds., *The Ties that Bind: Life Together in the Baptist Vision* (Macon, GA: Smyth & Helwys, 1994), multiple authors describe conversionist, contemplative, and corporate spiritualities. Bill J. Leonard, "Southern Baptists and Conversion: An Evangelical Sacramentalism," 9–22, argues the intensity and popular appeal of conversion gave it the status of sacrament for Baptists. E. Glenn Hinson, 69–82, "The Contemplative Roots of Baptist Spirituality," traces the roots of contemplative prayer and spirituality among Baptists. Chloe learned both types of spiritualities but felt more at home in the contemplative.

19. Patterson's story is in Shaw, *God Speaks to Us, Too,* 186–89.

20. Many historians portray Baptist controversies as fights over explicitly religious and *Baptist* issues. For example, Walter Shurden's book *Not a Silent People: Controversies that Have Shaped Southern Baptists* (Nashville: Broadman, 1972) sketches Baptist controversies of the nineteenth and twentieth centuries over slave ownership and segregation, history, church, theology, and the Bible. He sees the fights as "identity crises." However, *Baptist* struggles in all their particularity are also embedded in a context of struggle over (post)modern religious identity, which is explored more carefully by philosophers such as Charles Taylor in *Sources of the Self.* See footnotes 10 and 12 above.

21. Bill Leonard discusses the tensions that perennially animate Baptist life in *Baptists in America*, 88. See Joanna's story in chapter 3 for more on "soul competency."

22. Southern Baptists were not an isolated case of fracturing over questions of modern identity and gender roles. For example, Lutheran Church-Missouri Synod, the Christian Reformed Church, and the Episcopal Church in America all experienced fractures in the 1970s and 1980s in which women's ordination functioned as a fault-

line issue. Chaves traces these historical trends in *Ordaining Women,* 101–12. See also Zikmund, et al., *Clergywomen,* for a discussion of denominational variances regarding views of women's ministry.

23. Openness and support capture the character of "potential space," a term used naturally by Chloe's dad and conceptualized by Winnicott in *Playing and Reality,* 110. He says, "It is useful, then, to think of a third area of human living, one neither inside the individual nor outside in the world of shared reality. This intermediate living can be thought of as occupying a potential space." In this space a baby learns to play and an adult experiences art, culture, religion, and a way to discover and make a meaningful life.

24. "Profile: Nancy Ellett," in *Folio: A Newsletter for Southern Baptist Women in Ministry* 2, no. 3 (Winter 1985): 4. Following her ordination, Nancy Ellet Allison later served as a missionary and chaplain. More recently, she pastored a United Church of Christ church.

25. Philosophers Stewart and Hubert Dreyfus argue that professional skill is "never produced by interiorizing the rules that make up the theory of a domain" and show how "rule-based performance will never be more than competent." In fact, they argue that even in situations that are governed by bureaucratic rule following, wise experts must be able to override the rules when their intuitions call on them to do so. Hubert L. Dreyfus and Stuart E. Dreyfus, "Peripheral Vision: Expertise in Real World Contexts," *Organization Studies* 26, no. 5 (2005): 779–92.

26. Chloe's accumulation of experiences over three or four years of ministry helps her perceive the possibilities in a situation with greater confidence and maturity. For more about how ministry is learned as a practice over time, see Cahalan, *Introducing the Practice of Ministry,* 130–41; and Christian Scharen, "Learning Ministry over Time: Embodying Practical Wisdom," in *For Life Abundant: Practical Theology, Theological Education and Christian Ministry,* ed. Dorothy C. Bass and Craig Dykstra (Grand Rapids, MI: Eerdmans, 2008), 265–88.

27. Comparison of 1925, 1963 and 2000 Baptist Faith and Message, http://www.sbc.net/bfm/bfmcomparison.asp, accessed Aug. 30, 2012. See Appendix C of this book for the Alliance of Baptists Covenant.

28. Chloe's story offers a window into one "expanded sense of identity" and a growing attention to multiplicity of internal self-perceptions, relational selves, and sacred multiplicity, even within bounded systems. See, for example, Pamela Cooper-White, *Braded Selves: Collected Essays on Multiplicity, God, and Persons* (Eugene, OR: Cascade, 2011). Baptist scholars continue a longstanding argument over the "irreconcilable thesis." Barry Hankins traces the ways multiple parties used arguments against each other over time, concluding that all sides in the recent schism are in fact Baptist. Hankins, "Southern Baptists and the F-Word, 296–323. I reached a similar conclusion in 2008. See Campbell-Reed, "Anatomy of a Schism," 284–87, 298–303. Theologically, the playful expansiveness in tension resounds with Edward Farley's elaboration of "being founded" within a tragically structured existence. He says in *Good and Evil,* 157, "The powers of freedom are not just the absence of the dynamics of idolatry

but powers of existing in the mode of faith. Creativity, vitality, wonder, and love are not just other names for organic satisfactions or the passions for reality and subjectivity." Rather, freedom is "the power to exist in the face of the tragic element of a specific dimension."

29. Arthur Emery Farnsley II explores of the actions and arguments of Southern Baptists at their annual conventions, concluding that a struggle for political power brought the schism. Even the language of "priesthood of all believers" (autonomist) versus "the priesthood of the believer" (biblicist) reflected the contested status of the idea and practice between parties. See Farnsley, *Southern Baptist Politics,* 75–89.

30. Ibid., 82–86 Farnsley interprets the vote as (1) a contest about the "nature of authority," (2) a loss for moderates, and (3) a concession to conservatives over their "preference for strong, charismatic pastors."

31. According Wilburn T. Stancil, historically, Baptist ordination existed in a "fundamental tension between function and office." Ordination has been a local, autonomous church choice and practice. In some regions, associational bodies performed ordinations. The meaning and function of ordination remain widely pragmatic; a "need for functional leadership" has justified ordained ministry for Baptists. See Stancil, "Divergent Views and Practices of Ordination," 42–49.

32. As a functional and pragmatic practice, the meaning of Baptist ordination remains open to multiple interpretations, inviting it to become a site of contest and dispute. See also Anna's ordination story in chapter 1.

33. Carroll observes in *God's Potters,* 14: "The opening of ordination to women in many Protestant denominations in the mid-1970s is, arguably, one of the most important changes ever to affect ordained ministry."

34. ABC-USA Professional Female Summary, Aug. 7, 2012. The Christian Church (Disciples of Christ) reports 3,334 clergy-serving congregations, with 29.7 percent of the clergy being women. Suzanne McKay to author, e-mail, Oct. 11, 2012; "Ministers Council Task Force on Women in Ministry Report to Ministers Council Senate," 2, Aug. 2011, http://www.ministerscouncil.com/WIM%20Resources/documents/MCW IMTFreport2011.pdf, accessed July 22, 2012; Kristin Knudson, "Women, Clergypersons of Color Earn Less: Less Seniority, Lower-paying Pulpits Lend to Pay Gaps," *The Flyer: General Commission on the Status and Role of Women in the United Methodist Church,* Nov. 2011, http://www.gcsrw.org/WomenClergypersonsofColorEarnLess.aspx?tr=y&auid=9865498, accessed July 20, 2012; "Religious and Demographic Profile of Presbyterians, 2008: Findings from the Initial Survey of the 2009–2011 Presbyterian Panel," http://www.pcusa.org/media/uploads/research/pdfs/fa1108panel.pdf, accessed July 20, 2012. Specialized clergy for Presbyterians include all ministers serving beyond local congregations (i.e., chaplains, denominational staff, etc.).

35. See, for example, the story of Mount Airy Baptist Association's ousting of Flat Rock Baptist Church when they called Bailey Edwards Nelson as pastor in the summer of 2011. Bob Allen, "Assn. Ousts Church with Woman Pastor," Associated Baptist Press, Aug. 4, 2011, http://www.abpnews.com/archives/item/6626-assn-ousts-church-with-woman-pastor, accessed July 15, 2012.

36. Durso says, "In 2012 the total number of women ordained since 1964 in churches affiliated with Baptist bodies located mostly in the South is upwards of 2,200." "She-Preachers, Bossy Women, and Children of the Devil," 42.
37. Kathy Manis Findley, "This Is My Story . . . ," *Folio: A Newsletter for Southern Baptist Women in Ministry* 11, no. 4 (Spring 1994): 7.
38. Everett M. Rogers, *Diffusion of Innovations* (New York: Free Press, 1983), identifies five stages in the diffusion of new social ideas or practices: innovators (first 2.5 percent), early adopters (13.5 percent), early majority (34.5 percent), late majority (34.5 percent), and laggards (last 16 percent).
39. In the wider evangelical world, and heavily influenced by Southern Baptists, the Danvers Statement on Biblical Manhood and Womanhood (1988) captured the "complementarian position." In rebuttal, the Christians for Biblical Equality group produced a different but also evangelically influenced statement, Men, Women & Biblical Equality (1990). These statements crystallize in position papers the polarizing debates over the wider meanings and practices of gender in the SBC during the years of schism.
40. The 1988 Resolution on the Priesthood of the Believer, http://www.sbc.net/resolutions/amResolution.asp?ID=872, accessed Oct. 5, 2012. See also Hankins, "Southern Baptists and the F-Word," 311–12.
41. In the firsthand accounts of the founding of CBF and the Alliance, the image of freedom and the emphasis on personal spiritual renewal are common themes. See, for example, Neely, "History of the Alliance of Baptists," 101–28; and Vestal, "History of the Cooperative Baptist Fellowship," 253–74.
42. The world for women in the 1960s—especially in the South where Chloe's parents married—prioritized a (middle class white) woman's place in home and family over personal fulfillment through work or career. For a thick description of the 1960s world, see Friedan, *Feminine Mystique*.
43. In retrospect, Chloe says from a family systems perspective Martin's stability and dependability also appealed to Lillie, who experienced a father who was "playful and free-spirited" but not always a steady presence or provider. Thus Sandlin's pastoral advice also gave Lillie permission to choose a stable, dependable partner while simultaneously reproducing the gendered expectations of the day. In each generation discernment about vocations of marriage and work are complex in many less-than-obvious ways. In the twentieth century, a pursuit of "authentic self" has preoccupied much of the therapeutic culture, popular psychology, and blossoming self-help literature. Philosopher Charles Taylor argues that the language of "self-fulfillment" is not always a form of selfishness but rather an effort at authenticity as best as one understands for the age in which she or he lives. See Charles Taylor, *The Ethics of Authenticity* (Cambridge: Harvard Univ. Press, 1991), 120. See also the chapter "The Age of Authenticity," in *A Secular Age*, by Charles Taylor (Cambridge, MA: Belknap, 2007), 473–535.
44. Graham, *Transforming Practice*, 128–30, argues that the work of understanding "human nature" cannot be reduced to any one "true self." Older theological anthropologies made this precise mistake, considering maleness to be normative (or true). Choice, agency, and practice are central for "the process by which human nature

is realized and transformed." Cahalan, *Introducing the Practice of Ministry*, 37–39, argues that vocation encompasses more than work: "Part of discovering our vocation in adulthood is discerning God's call in how to live through committed relationships" in marriage, celibacy, or the single life.

45. In "A Feminist Looks (askance) at Headship," in *Does Christianity Teach Male Headship? The Equal-Regard Marriage and Its Critics,* ed. David Blankenhorn, Don Browning, and Mary Steward Van Leeuwen (Grand Rapids, MI: Eerdmans, 2004), 49–62, Bonnie Miller-McLemore argues that mutuality is "easier said than done" because definitions of mutuality are contested ("sloppy") and because "concrete demands of domestic life often drop out of the equation." In Chloe and Matt's case, both factors were at work.

46. Mutuality as a model for marriage is not free of the possibility of sin, but as a structure holds open relatively greater possibility for resisting the sins and harms of sexism by making space for each person's self expression and needs.

47. In *Genealogy of Dissent,* 120–21 ff., David Stricklin argues that three sources fed Southern Baptist women's call to ministry: the influence of twentieth-century Baptist social reformers, activists in the wider women's movement, and training for evangelism, missions, and organizing in Woman's Missionary Union. The resulting "unintentional undercurrent of radicalism" led to women seeking to embody these movements of God's justice through answering a call to ministry and defying existing structures of women's subordination, even while working within ecclesial structures.

48. In *God Speaks to Us, Too,* 6, Shaw shows through stories of more than a hundred Baptist women (lay and ordained) how a sense of authenticity and Baptist piety are embodied in complex and tension-filled identities. Baptist women, argues Shaw, "believe in their own competence in matters of religion . . . exhibit a strong sense of agency and autonomy—they are able to act and govern themselves . . . within a social context that defines the parameters of the choices available." Women in her study don't "merely fill roles" but practice their lives of faith in complex and contested ways. See also Rebecca's story in chapter 4.

49. See also Anna's story and biblicist views of women's sinfulness in chapter 1.

50. "Profile: Ester Tye Perkins," *Folio: A Newsletter for Southern Baptist Women in Ministry* 1, no. 2 (Fall 1983): n.p.

51. Lynda Weaver-Williams, "Exercising Our Gifts," *Folio: A Newsletter for Southern Baptist Women in Ministry* 2, no. 3 (Winter 1985): 1–2.

52. In *Transforming Practice* (138–39), Graham argues against Scripture and doctrine *alone* as adequate to formulate pastoral practice. Within communities of shared praxis, the values embedded in women's lived experience not only critique the received tradition but also embody the transforming impulses of a liberatory gospel. Graham opts for "understandings of human identity as forged in and through practice; glimpsed in the process-orientated perspectives of feminist theological anthropology." Chloe's lived experience and the interpretations of the other stories show the significance of struggling to redefine the practice of ministry and renew faithful life in the era of schism.

Conclusion

1. This improvisational character is in some ways what biblicists were concerned about regarding changes to Baptist belief and practice. On the other hand, they were just as likely as autonomists (and other religious groups) to improvise and recreate new beliefs and practices, although they repeatedly framed their orthodoxy as unchanging.
2. For a description of five major tensions of belief and practice among Baptists, see Leonard, *Dictionary of Baptists in America,* 4–6.
3. Early studies of the Baptist schism emphasize the significance of the relationship between conservative Baptists and to the national religious and political Right. For example, see Rosenberg, *Southern Baptists;* and Ammerman, *Baptist Battles.* These early studies appeared as the religious Right was rising on national political stage in the United States.

Epilogue

1. In 1984, 14 women pastored Southern Baptist churches. In 2006, 117 women served as pastors and co-pastors in churches affiliated with the Alliance of Baptists, CBF, Baptist General Convention of Texas, and Baptist General Association of Virginia. Campbell-Reed and Durso, "State of Women in Baptist Life," 284–85. In 2012, 150 women pastored churches in the same groups. See Campbell-Reed, "Baptists in Tension," 54.
2. The CBF elected Suzii Paynter coordinator in 2013. The Alliance staff is team led, and the 2014 team included Paula Clayton Dempsey, Carole Collins, and several women in part-time roles. Of course women have always headed BWIM, and Pamela R. Durso was elected executive director in 2009. In 2004 Central Baptist Theological Seminary elected Molly T. Marshall president, making her the first woman to serve in such a role in Baptist theological education in the United States. In 2009 Gail R. O'Day was elected as dean of the Wake Forest Divinity School, a school rooted in Baptist history and currently embracing an ecumenical identity.
3. Flowers, *Into the Pulpit,* 54–58, works to articulate the story of women in the biblicist party who were indeed trying to uphold the status quo, and they were also working to articulate the necessity of separate roles and domains for women and men in order to "shape a rhetoric of submission."
4. These ideals are institutionalized in the 2000 Baptist Faith and Message, and with SBC ties to the Council on Biblical Manhood and Womanhood formed in 1987. See Hankins, *Uneasy in Babylon,* 225, 228.
5. This form of power is tied unavoidably to violence: "On the level of discourse, certain lives are not considered lives at all, they cannot be humanized; they fit no dominant frame for the human, and their dehumanization occurs first, at this level. This level then gives rise to a physical violence that in some sense delivers the message of dehumanization which is already at work in the culture." Butler, *Undoing Gender,* 25.

Index

Adams, Darrell, 76, 150
agency, 11, 21, 25–26, 37–38, 40–43, 83, 105, 107, 114–15, 170n53, 175n29, 175n32, 179n56, 183n18, 192n31, 201n44, 202n48
Ahlstrom, Sidney, 172n7
Aldredge-Clanton, Jann, 9, 35–36
Alliance of Baptists, 65, 89, 123–24, 126, 132, 134, 143–44, 153–54, 165n78, 166n9, 187n47, 201n41, 203nn1–2; Alliance of Baptists Covenant, 124, 153–54, 199n27. *See also* Southern Baptist Alliance
ambivalence, 8, 30, 38, 49, 55, 57, 59–61, 63–65, 69–70, 76, 80, 144, 172n4, 174n18
American Baptist Churches USA (ABC-USA), 6, 20, 71, 73, 75, 78–79, 82, 84, 104, 123–24, 130, 134, 144, 169n44, 181n3, 187n47, 200n34
Ammerman, Nancy Tatom, 156n7, 157n9, 157n11, 157n12, 157n15, 158n18, 160n37, 161n37, 164n68, 165n80, 166n8, 187n43
Anders, Sarah Francis, 157n11, 166n7
Anna, 1, 3, 6, 8, 11–13, 15–18, 21–22, 25–32, 34, 36–45, 144–45, 168nn35–37, 174n18, 192n28, 200n32, 202n49
Armstrong, Annie, 65
authenticity, 40, 105, 118, 129, 135–36, 138, 141, 201n43, 202n48
authority, 1–2, 11, 16, 35, 66–67, 75, 84–87, 110, 134, 140–41, 179n61, 200n30; biblical, 9, 16–17, 35, 84–85, 90, 136, 140, 147–48, 153, 167n18, 183n17; congregational, 133, 138; decision-making, 86; ecclesial, 58, 133, 135, 138, 166n11; of experience, 143, 185n31; external, 84; God's delegated order of, 9–10, 12, 20, 32–33, 45, 103, 136, 147; internal, 84; of Jesus Christ, 132, 153; lack of, 55; locus of, 85; male, 42, 44, 63, 67, 90, 100, 110, 118, 136–37, 145; pastoral, 11, 22, 66–67, 110, 112, 133–36, 138–39, 141, 145, 160n33; problems with, 2, 127, 198n16; reshaping of, 118, 128, 133–34, 141, 181n2, 198n2; in the SBC, 55; sources of, 9, 61, 138, 166n11
autonomists, 8, 14, 18, 61, 64, 66, 72, 90, 97, 120, 130, 132–33, 135–40, 143–45, 161n40, 164n68, 175n32, 178n49, 192n26, 194n55, 198n15, 200n29, 203n1; and complementarity, 3–4, 63, 68–70; on cooperation, 87; defined, 7–9, 161n37; developing alternative agencies, 15, 19–20; leadership, 8–9; on marriage, 56–57, 59–60, 135; on models of leadership, 22, 118, 135–36; and mutuality, 85, 135; preaching examples, 22, 94, 102–16; projecting fears, 12–13; publications, 155n6, 175n28, 195n1; on separation of church and state, 89, 188n51; treatment of women, 25, 31–36, 45, 58
autonomy, 33, 38, 42, 52, 57–59, 62–63, 88, 175n32, 179n56, 202n48; and desire, 41, 45, 49–50, 61, 175n29; individual/personal, 9, 58–59, 84, 88, 175n32; lack of, 177n41; local church, 9, 87–88, 90, 140, 147, 183n17; shared, 61. *See also* agency; soul competency

Bagby, Daniel, 9, 59–60, 174n22, 175n28; *Before You Marry*, 59, 174n22, 175n28
baptism, 49, 58, 94–95, 102, 106–7, 119, 129, 141, 189n7, 192nn32–33, 198n15
Baptist Faith and Message: 1963 revision, 15–16, 36, 132, 164n63, 199n27; 1998 addendum, 20; 2000 revision, 10, 15, 20, 30–31, 41, 130, 132, 143, 145, 161n44, 167n18, 199n27, 204n4
Baptist Faith and Message Fellowship, 164n69, 174n16
Baptist: early history, 184n24, 188n49, 197n13; ecclesiology, 166n11, 170n54; identity, 2–4, 7, 14, 20–22, 47–48, 56, 63, 67, 90, 94, 106, 117, 127–33, 137–39, 141, 143, 145, 156n8, 159n23, 159n25; paradigms of marriage, 60, 128–29, 135, 145; piety, 4, 48, 65–66, 72–73, 82, 108, 139 202n48; polity, 21, 66, 72, 80–81, 86–87, 90, 106, 140, 166n10
Baptist History and Heritage Society, 34–35
Baptist Joint Committee on Public Affairs (BJC), 89
Baptist Peace Fellowship of North America (BPFNA), 79, 144, 166n9
Baptist Student Union, 96
Baptist Women in Ministry (BWIM), 143–44, 165n73, 166n9, 169n44, 203n2. *See also* Southern Baptist Women in Ministry (SBWIM)
Baptists Today, 118, 195n1

Barton, Ronald G., 190n15, 191n16
Benjamin, Jessica, 158n21, 162n50, 169n45, 170nn51–53, 174n20, 176n37, 176nn40–41, 177n45, 179n57, 184n26, 186n33, 188n52
Benner, Patricia, 196n9
Benson, Lawrence, 119
Bethel Baptist Church, 121–22, 129, 196n5, 196n11
Bible, 1, 9, 33, 35, 60, 90, 94–95, 109, 118, 127, 137, 157n12, 166n8, 183n14; authority of, 9, 16, 35; battle for, 3–4, 36, 104, 111, 160n37, 168n32, 198n20; and gender, 8–9, 12, 144, 167n18, 193n34, 201n39, 203n4; harmful texts, 85; imagery, 81, 106, 113–15; inerrancy/literal truth, 16, 36, 104, 135, 159n27, 168n32; interpretation, 15–16, 116, 135; and ordination, 34, 36, 104, 111, 160n37, 168n32, 198n20; studying, 63, 73, 77, 166n12, 187n44. *See also* scripture
biblicists, 3, 56, 72, 90, 138–39, 145, 155n6, 160n30, 161n37, 168n32, 178n49, 198n15, 200n29, 203n1; advocating for "Christian nation," 89, 188n51; defined, 7–9; on church, 132; interpretations of schism, 14; and megachurches, 87; leadership, 8; on marriage, 56–57; on models of leadership and pastoral authority, 22, 66, 118, 130, 133, 137–38; organizing, 187n44; preaching examples, 22, 94, 102–16; projecting fears, 12–13, 32–33; publications, 175n28, 193n43; and complementarity, 13, 58, 60–61, 63–64, 68–70, 85, 135–36, 203n3; gaining leadership in SBC, 10, 15–20, 97, 143, 164n68, 174n16; views of women, 25, 31–36, 39–40, 44–45, 174n16, 202n49
Binkley, Hugh, 119
biological determinism, 38, 48, 144
Belenky, Mary Field, 172n5
Bourdieu, Pierre, 165n1; Habitus, 172n6
Braude, Ann, 156n8, 162n53, 175n27
Brenthall Baptist Church, 119–23, 129, 196n5, 196n11
Butler, Judith, 161n41, 162n52, 174n17, 175n29, 180n74, 194n58, 203n5

Cahalan, Kathleen, 180n72, 189n1, 202n44
calling, 21, 26, 30, 36, 38–39, 42–44, 63–69, 74, 79–83, 86, 94, 96, 98, 102, 106–9, 117–19, 125, 128–30, 133, 137, 139, 141, 147, 153, 193n40, 109n16; to authenticity, 105; congregations calling women pastors, 34–35, 54–55, 113, 125–26, 134, 167n18; inward/outward, 40, 180n69; to ministry, 8, 15, 17–18, 20, 25–27, 29–30, 32, 36–37, 47, 62, 64, 68–69, 71, 83, 93, 96, 98, 106–7, 121–22, 131–32, 136, 138, 145, 202n47; and mission/purpose, 47, 51–52, 56; to missionary work, 62, 95, 136, 178n48; negotiating multiple callings, 58–59, 118, 122, 129, 135–36; piety of, 108; prophetic, 82, 88; and salvation, 21, 72, 81–83, 90, 140; to seminary, 19, 22, 96; sense of, 42, 47, 51, 53, 78, 93, 95, 123, 127, 196n5. *See also* giftedness for calling
Calvary Baptist Church, 29, 39
Campbell, David, 198n16
Candler School of Theology, 52
Carroll, Jackson, 186n41, 200n33
Carson-Newman College, 120
Cave Hill Baptist Church, 2, 125–28
Central Baptist Theological Seminary, 104, 203n2
Chapman, Morris, 19
Chloe, 2–3, 6, 8, 11–13, 15, 17–18, 22, 117–33, 135–38, 143–44, 179n64, 187n47, 192n20, 196n5, 196n7, 196nn10–11, 197n12, 198n16, 196n18, 199n23, 199n26, 199n28, 201nn42–43, 202n45, 202n52
Chodorow, Nancy, 170n50, 176n34, 176n41
Christianity Today, 32
Clinical Pastoral Education, 54–55, 77, 131
Collins, Carole, 203n2
communion, 60, 94, 101, 112–13, 115–16, 141, 189n4
complementarity, 7, 32, 38, 47, 68, 85, 110, 130, 179n57, 201n39; challenges to, 10, 21, 23, 58, 60, 66, 72, 81, 84, 112, 118, 136, 138, 143–45, 184n26, 194n52; culture of, 3–4, 9–12, 21, 28, 51, 57–61, 63, 68–69, 72, 135–36, 138–39, 141, 143–45; defining, 9–10, 47, 155n3, 162n46, 167n17; failures of, 85, 136; future of, 4, 21, 45, 48, 61, 63, 70, 118, 139; justification for, 114, 144, 165n79, 174n23; and marriage, 10, 41, 60, 65, 90, 135, 144; and mutuality, 70, 129, 135, 138, 176n41, 177n45, 186n33; reproduction of, 13, 23, 60, 63, 66, 68, 110, 115, 139, 143–45, 175n30, 176n39, 177n42, 180n70; in work and ministry, 60, 68, 80, 135, 144, 173n8
Consultation on Women in Church-Related Vocations (1978), 17, 57, 62, 67, 176n36
controversies: Elliott controversy, 15–16, 164n63; Landmark controversy, 192n33, 191n19. *See also* Southern Baptist Schism

conversion, 64, 82, 84, 140, 166n4, 189n7, 197n14, 198n15, 198n18; dramatic, 82–84, 90, 140, 184nn21–23, 198n15; as nurturing process, 82–84, 90, 140 184nn22–23, 198n15
Coontz, Stephanie, 161n42
Cooperative Baptist Fellowship (CBF), 1, 9, 15, 19–20, 30–31, 41–43, 65, 89, 104, 134, 143–45, 165n78, 166n9, 178n55, 187n47, 194n49, 201n41, 203nn1–2
Criswell College, 103
Criswell, W. A., 8
Cross, Anthony R., 159n25
Crowder Seminary, 74–75, 97–98

Darwin, Charles, 158n22
Davis, Addie, 16, 22
Dempsey, Paula Clayton, 203n2
desire, 4, 11, 13, 25, 27, 43, 51–52, 60, 63, 66, 73, 94, 108–11, 114–15, 121–22, 125, 136, 139, 192n31; authoring/owning, 10–11, 13, 26, 37–39, 44, 61; and autonomy, 41, 45, 49–50, 59, 61, 175n29; deepest human 112, 192n31, 193n38; and grief, 194n58; to be human 145, 170n53; to work in ministry/be ordained, 10, 26, 29, 34–35, 37–40, 43–45, 51, 135, 144; submitting to the desired, 43, 61; women as desiring subjects, 25, 39, 43, 176n37, 184n26
Deweese, Charles W., 173n11, 174n16, 179n67
disestablishment of religion, 172n7
domination, 36, 63, 74, 83, 111, 174n20, 176n40, 177n45; and abuse, 74, 83; and submission, 3–4, 22, 40, 48, 58–59, 61, 65, 170n51, 174n20, 178n53; and subordination, 10, 13, 26, 31, 38–39, 41–42, 44–45, 59, 60, 144–45. See also submission; subordination
double binding, 10, 12, 43, 60–63, 67, 70, 103, 110, 115, 171n58, 175n25, 192n28, 195n65
Draper, James T., Jr., 8, 107
Dreyfus, Hubert and Stewart, 199n25
Durso, Pamela, 163n61, 186n38, 201n36, 203n2

Eleanor Witek Center (EWC), 75–77
Ellett, Nancy, 131, 199n24
Elliott, Ralph, 15–16; *The Message of Genesis*, 16
embodied, 33, 38, 44, 60, 83–84, 105–6, 130, 138, 141, 179n66; practice of ministry, 22, 85, 118, 128–30, 131, 137–38, 141,

196n9, 197n12; salvation, 83–84; schism, 21, 25–26, 30–31, 34, 36, 39–40, 45, 110, 116, 138, 202n48; sexism/racism, 93, 194n51; theology, 33, 101, 105–6, 110, 113, 115–16, 128, 137, 141, 167n21, 189n3, 202n47, 202n52; ways of knowing, 4, 117–18, 122, 128–30, 137–38, 172n6, 196n9, 197n12, 198n18. See also embodiment; women as symbols
embodiment, 106, 165n1, 174n18; of Baptist identity, 4, 33; of liberalism, 166n7; of pastoral role, 173n12; of principle, 33, 45; of SBC schism, 26, 36, 45, 157n10. See also embodied; women as symbols
Emerson, Michael, 196n11
Emory University, 52
enduring tensions of Baptist belief and practice, 21, 71–72, 81, 90, 140, 179n60, 183n17, 184n23, 197n13, 197n15, 198n21, 203n2. See also salvation and calling; soul competency; priesthood of all believers; voluntary association; separation of church and state
Eve, 18, 32, 44, 113–15, 171n59

Farley, Edward, 158n17, 159n23, 162nn47–48, 163n57, 189n2, 192n29, 195nn59–61, 199n28
Farley, Wendy, 193n38
Farnsley, Arthur Emery, II, 157n15, 200nn29–30
feminism, 3–4, 61–62, 65–66, 72, 75, 82, 84, 100, 103, 139, 162n46, 166n12, 175n31, 181n2, 185n29, 197n12
field education, 52–53, 74, 83, 123–25, 132
Findley, Kathy Mannis, 9, 134–35
Firestone, Rabbi Tirzah, 128
First Baptist Church of Benson, 53–54, 68–69
First Baptist Church of Florence, 54, 67
Flowers, Elizabeth "Betsy," 156n8, 157n9, 158n18, 159n26, 165n79, 166n12, 167n17, 175n30, 193n34, 203n3
Flyvbjerg, Bent, 155n5
Fogel, Neal, 121
Folio: A Newsletter for Southern Baptist Women in Ministry, 33
Fonagy, Peter, 162n49
football imagery, 31, 33, 39
Foote, Catherine J.: "The Weaver," 76, 151
founded, being, 11, 94, 112, 162n48, 195n60, 199n28
Francis Marion College, 54
Freud, Sigmund, 169nn39–41, 169n43, 170n52; Primal deed 169n43

Index

Friedan, Betty, 175n31, 201n42
Friedman, Edwin, 127, 196n7
Friedman, Raymond J., 180n1
Fulkerson, Mary McClintock, 180n74, 185n29

Gatlinburg Gang, 9
Gay, Volney, 158n22, 179n63
gender, 3–5, 7, 14, 21–22, 25, 41, 43–44, 47, 56, 63, 71, 80, 86, 89–90, 93–94, 102–3, 106–7, 110, 112–13, 144; binary, 10, 58, 144, 161n41, 174n17; as a category, 58, 81, 139, 169n42; defining, 9–10, 158n21, 161n41, 161n43, 162n52; equality/justice, 20, 159n27, 197n12; expectations of 103, 168n37, 175n31, 201n43; expressions of, 58, 70, 176n41, 201n39; ideals, 56, 63, 135; and identity, 48, 56, 170nn51–52; inequity, 39, 65, 81, 106, 110, 140, 180n69, 184n26, 185n29, 185n32, 194n51, 201n39; intersectionality, 196n5; and leadership, 66, 68; and power, 37, 45, 63, 162n53; production of, 21, 40, 95, 170nn50–51, 174n17, 176n34, 177nn41–42; roles, 31, 48–50, 72, 85, 95, 110, 113–14, 118, 130, 139, 147–48, 166n11, 171n1, 198n22; split, 12–13, 41, 56–59, 63, 65–66, 68, 72, 85, 139, 144; understandings of, 12, 38–39, 85, 105, 114, 172n1. *See also* complementarity; double binds; Southern Baptist Schism
Gentry Memorial Baptist Church, 78–80, 86–90, 186n41
Gilmore, Martha, 33–34
Girls' Auxiliary/Girls in Action (GA), 51, 61, 173n10
Graham, Elaine, 197n12, 201n44, 202n52
Graham, Larry, 183n19
Griffis-Woodbery, Deborah, 174n24
Grove Baptist Church, 29, 39

Habitat for Humanity, 93, 101, 108, 143
Halbrooks, G. Thomas, 169n44, 180n69, 197n15
Hammond, Phillip E., 173n7
Hankins, Barry, 159n27, 199n28
healing, 4, 13, 71, 76–77, 81, 83–85, 89, 109–12, 141, 163n57, 182n8, 184n25, 186n39, 196n5
Hefley, James, 168n32, 188n54, 193n43, 194n47
Heirich, Max, 184n21
Henry, Carl F. H., 32
Heriot, Jean, 184n21
Hess, Margaret, 130–31, 198n18

Higginbotham, Evelyn Brooks, 171n58
Hill, Samuel, 170n48
hymnody: "Behold What Manner of Love," 73; "Holy Spirit, Comforter," 76, 150; "Spirit God in the Clear Running Water," 72, 149–50; "Wherever He Leads I'll Go," 1, 30, 41–44, 149, 155n2

identity, 10–13, 22, 45, 56–59, 61, 63, 66, 96, 109, 116, 127–28, 131–32, 161n43, 166n6, 173n12, 198n22, 199n28, 202n52; American, 183n16; crisis of, 12, 21, 48, 55, 68–70, 162n53, 198n20; formation of, 13, 66–67, 193n38; men's, 63; pastoral, 4, 53, 141, 180n72, 198n16; reimagined, 4; sexual/gender, 12, 59–60, 170n51–52, 174n22; women's, 170n52, 176n37. *See also* Baptist: identity
infants, 11–12, 162nn49–51, 169n40, 177n45
"interpreting situations," 158n17
intersubjective space, 54, 159n23, 168n36, 169n45, 177n45, 179n57, 180n1, 183n19; as "potential" space, 199n23
intrapsychic domain, 169n45

Jacquet, Constant H., Jr., 160n33
Jars of Clay, 121
The Jesus Movement, 130
Joanna, 1–3, 6, 11–13, 15–16, 20–22, 71–91, 144, 159n23, 175n32, 179n58, 179n60, 181nn2–3, 181nn5–7, 182n8, 182n11, 183n18, 183n20, 184n23, 185nn28–29, 186n34, 186n36, 186nn39–41, 187n46, 188n48, 194n52, 198n21
Johnson, Cindy Harp, 9, 114–15

Kernberg, Otto, 162n49
Kinsey, Alfred, 178n53
Klein, Melanie, 162n49
Kohut, Heinz, 177n44

Landon, Marcie, 124
leadership, 2, 34, 41, 50, 66, 68, 83, 86, 91, 103, 117–18, 126, 128, 132, 144, 153, 158n19, 200n31; authoritative model, 12, 22, 118, 128, 135–37, 145; men's, 60, 62, 66–67; pastoral, 6–7, 18, 22, 32, 66–68, 88, 107, 118, 148; servant-leader model, 12, 22, 43, 118, 128, 136–37, 145, 153; of SBC 10, 17, 130, 165n71, 173n11, 187n44, 190n10; women's, 5–7, 16, 18, 22, 32–34, 36, 39, 57–59, 62, 68, 77, 82, 88, 101, 107, 113, 118, 131, 135, 141, 144, 148, 160n31, 162n46, 174n23

Lebacqz, Karen, 190n15, 191n16
Leonard, Bill, 118, 157nn9–10, 157nn13–14, 166n10, 177n47, 179n58, 183n17, 184nn22–23, 192n32–33, 198n18, 198n21
Lester, Andrew, 9, 62, 67–68, 176n39, 179n61
Lindsay, Homer, Jr., 108
lived theology, 14, 105, 163n58
Lolley, Randall, 9, 33

Malinowski, Bronislaw, 178n53
Marler, Penny, 187n46
Marshall, Molly Truman, 9, 103–5, 185nn30–31, 192n22, 192n26, 192m28, 192nn30–31, 203n2
Martha, 2–3, 6, 8, 11–13, 15, 17, 20–22, 47–70, 144, 172n4, 172nn6–7, 173nn8–9, 173nn12–13, 174n15, 174n18, 175n32, 176n34, 177nn44–45, 179n66, 190n9, 194n52
Marty, Martin, 171n54
McBeth, Leon, 164n67, 179n59
McGary, Betty Winstead, 9, 111–12, 194n56
McKinney, B. B., 149, 171n55
meaning: co-constructed, 179n66; to be human, 4, 22–23, 45, 70, 93, 102–3, 105, 107, 110, 116, 141, 145; making, 14, 22, 93–94, 105, 112, 117, 128–29, 131, 179n61, 186n36, 193n38, 195n60, 197n12, 199n23; surplus of, 189n5
Mercer University, 96–97, 108
Meredith College, 130
Metcalf-Whitaker, Marilyn, 157n11, 166n7
Midwestern Baptist Theological Seminary, 34
Milesdale Baptist Church, 117, 123–25, 132–35, 143
Miller, Alice, 186n36
Miller-McLemore, Bonnie, 177n46, 202n45
ministry: changing models of, 4, 7, 26, 34, 118, 128–30, 132, 134–35, 137–38, 141, 160n31, 198n16; definitions of, 189n1, 196n9; gifts for 26–27, 42, 72, 107, 133, 180n69, 180n72; learning in, 68, 93, 102, 113, 132, 199n26; as practice, 141, 196n9, 199n26; practice of, 2, 4, 20, 22, 39, 53, 66, 68, 76–77, 79, 93, 99, 101–2, 113, 116–18, 128–29, 132, 137, 141, 179n64, 180n72, 189n1, 197n12, 199n26, 202n52; theology of, 4, 20, 117, 128, 137, 141. *See also* calling; vocation
missionary, 17, 19, 61–65, 87, 95–96, 120, 134–36, 143, 177n43, 178n48, 178nn50–52, 199n24; missionary position, 65, 178n53
Mohler, Albert, 104
Montrose Hill Baptist Church, 98

Monroe Corner Baptist Church, 2, 47, 54–56, 68–69, 144
Moon, Lottie, 65
Morgan, Marabel, 172n2
mutuality, 9, 26, 37, 48, 58, 61, 66, 70, 84–85, 87, 90, 129, 139, 141, 145, 176n41, 177n45; culture of, 118, 135, 138; in marriage, 60, 135, 202nn45–46; relational mutuality, 40, 43, 81, 174n22, 176n41, 177n45, 186n33

Natterson, Joseph M., 180n1
Nelson, Bailey Edwards, 35, 200n35
Neuger, Christie Cozad, 171n58, 175n25, 181n1, 183n18, 185n26, 186n36, 195n65
Nouwen, Henri, 27

O'Day Gail R., 203n2
O'Neill, George and Neena, 172n2
ordination, 1, 7, 21, 26, 39–40, 42, 56, 69, 70, 127, 165n2; authority of, 11, 66–67, 138–39; for Baptists, 7–8, 34, 36, 41, 147–48, 180n69; as embodiment of theology, 33; meaning of, 34–36, 54, 65–67, 147–48, 169n44, 180n69, 200nn31–32; practice of, 8, 68, 133–34, 138; process of, 8, 39–41, 117, 124–25, 128, 169n44, 180n69, 182n8, 200n31; seeking, 4, 8, 33, 107, 134–36, 138, 159n27; stories of, 16, 26–27, 29, 33–34, 39–40, 54, 65–67, 74, 98, 117–18, 124–25, 128, 132–34, 137, 199n24; women's, 5–8, 15–16, 18–20, 25–26, 30–36, 45, 63, 66, 68–69, 88, 94, 104, 106–7, 113, 118, 128, 139–40, 147–48, 157nn14–15, 159n27, 163n61, 166n10, 198n22, 200n33

paradigm cases, 3, 155n5
paradox, 26, 31, 37, 44–45, 94–95, 103, 105, 171n58. *See also* double binding
pastoral identity, 4, 53
pastoral health, 186n41
pastoral imagination, 173n12
pathogenic beliefs, 68, 179n63
Patterson, Dorothy, 8, 35–36, 130–31, 167n17, 168n27, 168n32, 174n23, 198n19
Patterson, Paige, 8, 16–19, 35, 103–5, 130–31, 164n66, 191nn18–20, 192n31
Paynter, Suzii, 203n2
Pendleton, J. M., 192n33
Pennington-Russell, Julie, 34
Perkins, Ester Tye, 136–37
piety, 3, 82; Baptist, 4, 31, 48, 65–66, 72–73, 82, 108, 139, 202n48; of power, 103–4,

Index

piety (*cont.*)
  191n17; practical, 63; programmed, 21, 82, 139, 177n47, 179n60; rational, 118, 129–31, 138, 196n11, 197nn12–13; Southern, 49, 52, 171n3; of vulnerability, 103, 105, 191n17
place to appear, 180n74
preaching, 22, 29, 39–40, 60, 77, 79–80, 82, 84, 88, 93–95, 98–99, 101, 124–26, 130, 132, 137, 141, 168n32, 179n59, 183n14, 189nn3–4, 190n13, 192n28; examples of, 102–16
Pressler, Nancy, 168n32
Pressler, Paul, 8, 17–19, 103, 164n66, 168n32
priesthood of all believers, 21, 36, 54, 66, 72, 81, 85–86, 90, 128, 133–35, 138, 140, 145, 160n34, 166n10, 179n56, 179n58, 183n17, 200n29; priesthood of the believer, 2, 117, 127, 200n29
psychological defenses, 6, 11–12, 68, 169n47, 172n4

race, 7, 103, 110, 112, 121–22, 159n28, 164n68, 171n1, 171n58, 174n21, 191n17, 194n51, 196n5, 196n11; intersectionality, 196n5
racism, 93, 100, 102–3, 110, 112, 141, 171n58, 174nn20–21, 178n51, 191n17, 193n34, 196n5, 196n11
Rebecca, 1, 3, 6, 11–13, 15, 17, 19, 22, 93–103, 105–10, 112–13, 115–16, 143–44, 159n23, 189nn1–3, 189nn5–6, 190n13, 190n15, 191n16, 192n31, 202n48
recognition, 26, 35, 45, 61–63, 67–68, 82, 86, 145, 177n45, 186n40; failure of, 37–41, 43–44, 82, 89, 90, 180n74; mutual, 37, 40, 42–44, 58, 61, 68, 89–90, 188n52; seeking, 43, 140; social, 180n74
redemption, 4, 7, 13–14, 22, 93–94, 102, 115–16, 135–38, 141, 162n48, 189n2
relational dynamics, 3, 9, 38, 42, 56, 81, 139, 172n5, 183n18, 183n20
relational knowing, 172n5
relational networks, 2, 81, 83, 88, 90–91, 120, 181n3, 185n27
religious liberty, 88–90, 183n17, 188nn50–51. *See also* separation of church and state
Reuther, Rosemary Radford, 185n32
Rizzuto, Ana-Marie, 171n3
Rogers, Adrian, 8, 18, 113–15
Rogers, Everett M., 201n38
Rosenberg, Ellen M., 157n15, 203n3
rugged individualism, 72, 82, 87–88

sacrifice, 21, 47, 50, 63–65, 70, 177n46
St. Amant, Penrose, 180n69
salience, 196n9
salvation, 64, 106, 130, 184nn21–22; and calling, 21, 72, 81–83, 90, 140, 183n17
Sandlin, Paul, 119–20, 201n43
Scharen, Christian, 173n12, 199n26
Schneider, Laurel, 174n21
scripture, 1–2, 86, 90, 104, 109, 117, 127, 138, 183n14, 197n13, 202n52; appeals to, 8, 35, 130–32, 147–48; authority of, 84–85, 90, 147–48, 183n17; harms of, 81, 84; inerrancy of, 157n13; interpretation of, 16, 19, 36, 84, 90, 103–4, 153, 157n13, 185n30; study of, 16, 53, 84. *See also* Bible
scripture references:
  —Genesis 1:26–28, 1–12, 113–14, 115
  —Psalm 33:20, 195n66
  —Psalm 121:1–2, 195n66
  —Psalm 137:1–4, 192n23
  —Psalm 146:3, 5, 195n66
  —Proverbs 8:1–11, 179n65
  —Matthew 10:38, 182n12
  —Matthew 16:24, 182n12
  —Matthew 20:16, 178n55
  —Matthew 25:31–46, 178n55
  —Mark 8:34, 182n12
  —Luke 9:23, 182n12
  —Luke 12:48, 195n3
  —Acts 2:17–18, 21, 147, 195n67
  —Acts 9:1–19, 184n21
  —Acts 18:26, 147
  —Romans 16:1, 147
  —1 Corinthians 3:9, 176n35
  —1 Corinthians 10:13, 182n12
  —1 Corinthians 11:2–16, 147–48
  —1 Corinthians 14:33–36, 35, 148
  —Galatians 3:28, 147
  —Galatians 5:15, 194n53
  —Ephesians 5:22–24, 182n12
  —Ephesians 5:21–33, 174n23
  —Colossians 3:12–17, 192n23
  —Colossians 3:18, 182n12
  —1 Timothy 2:7, 147
  —1 Timothy 2:13, 148
  —1 Timothy 2:8–15, 35, 148
  —Titus 1:15, 147
  —Titus 2:1–10, 148
  —James 2:15–17, 195n4
  —1 Peter 3:1–7, 174n23. *See also* Bible
Sealander, Judith, 171n1
Seat, Karen, 161n46

second Genesis controversy, 164n69
Sehested, Nancy Hastings, 9, 34, 106–7, 187n45
seminary, 7, 12, 15, 17–18, 20, 26–29, 32–33, 39–40, 82–83, 127, 130, 132, 139, 144, 181n2, 181n5; changes in SBC seminaries, 33, 97, 190n10, 192n28; experiences of, 28, 30, 37, 47, 49, 52–54, 68, 71, 74–77, 83–84, 93, 96–98, 110, 122–26, 136; models of education, 190n12; women in, 17, 69
separation of church and state, 21, 72, 82, 88–90, 140, 153, 183n17, 188n49
September 11, 2001, 72, 79, 88–89, 144
servanthood dilemma, 12, 26, 31, 40, 43, 44, 192n28
sexism, 4, 22, 28, 93, 100, 102–3, 110, 112, 115, 118, 135–36, 138, 141, 176n39, 190n15, 202n46
sexual abuse/misconduct, 73, 82–83, 100, 110, 151, 182n11, 190n14, 191n16
Shaw, Susan, 156n8, 158n18, 159n26, 166n6, 166n11, 168n34, 170n48, 179n56, 202n48
Sherman, Cecil, 9
Shurden, Kay, 57–58, 173n14
Shurden, Walter "Buddy," 161n39, 164n71, 175n32, 198n20
situated knowing, 129–30, 133, 138
situated possibility, 22, 38, 58, 113, 115, 137, 185n29
Smalley, Gerald, 51
Smalley, June, 51–52, 61
Smith, Christian, 196n11
Smith, Morgan, 123–27
soul competency, 2, 21, 72, 81, 84–85, 90, 117, 127, 140, 175n32, 183n17, 185nn30–31, 198n21, 202n48
Southeastern Baptist Theological Seminary, 33, 181n7, 190n10
Southern Baptist Alliance 18, 165n78. *See also* Alliance of Baptists
Southern Baptist Convention (SBC): agencies/structures, 5, 16, 18–19, 30–31, 109, 139, 164n68, 167n18; analysis of, 187n43; annual meeting sermons, 102–16; Bold Mission Thrust campaign, 64; Broadman Press, 16; Christian Life Commission, 164n68; Committee on Resolutions, 32, 164n68; culture of, 40–43, 166n11, 170n54, 177n47, 186n37, 187n43; early history, 65; Ethics and Religious Liberty Commission, 89; influence on wider evangelical world, 201n39; leadership, 10, 17, 33, 134, 187n44; as mother denomination, 41–44, 174n18; North American Mission Board, 1, 41, 155n2; Peace Committee, 108; programs/materials, 48–51, 56–58, 99, 103, 167n18, 174n22; relationship to local churches, 35, 138, 166n11, 170n54; resources, 61, 178n49; sanctuaries, 189n4; Sunday School Board, 197n14
Southern Baptist Convention (SBC) annual meetings: 1963 Kansas City, 164n63; 1979 Houston, 18; 1983 Pittsburgh, 106–7; 1984 Kansas City, 18, 32, 137, 147; 1985 Dallas, 104; 1987 St. Louis, 108; 1989 Las Vegas, 108–9; 1990 New Orleans, 15, 19, 108–9, 111
Southern Baptist Convention (SBC) Resolutions, 17, 21, 166n11, 167n12; Resolution on Ordination and the Role of Women in Ministry (1984), 18, 32–34, 147–48, 167n17, 171n59; Resolution On the Priesthood of the Believer (1988), 133, 135, 201n40; Resolution on the Strengthening the Marriage Covenant (1998), 161n44
Southern Baptist Journal, 164n69
Southern Baptist schism: as "battle for the Bible," 3–4, 36, 104; as "conservative resurgence," 8, 13, 19, 81, 90, 109, 111; common/previous interpretations of, 3–7, 21, 36, 71, 90, 105, 155n6, 157n9, 158n18, 158n20, 159n27, 160nn36–37, 168n32, 198n20, 200n29, 203n1; as cultural struggle, 61; era of, 10, 15–21, 113, 202n52; financial stakes of, 178n49; gendered character of, 3, 5, 7, 14, 21, 25, 31, 47–48, 56, 59, 63, 66, 68, 71–72, 80–81, 93, 102, 112, 145, 198n22; as "hostile takeover," 9, 13, 81; as living history, 5; as playground/improvisational space, 4, 22, 118, 128–29, 131–33, 137–38, 140–41; as projection of fears, 12–13; psychological character of, 3, 5–6, 14–15, 21, 25–26, 31, 47, 59, 69, 72, 84, 116, 118, 139, 145, 158nn18–19, 159n23; as reflection of larger trends in American Christianity, 129–31, 133; as reformer of Baptist identity, 3–4, 7, 14, 20–21, 48, 56, 68–70, 72, 88, 109, 117–18, 128, 130–33, 135, 141, 143–44, 198n20; reinterpretation of, 3–7, 10, 14–15, 21, 25, 45, 47–48, 59, 68, 71–72, 80–81, 93–94, 102, 105, 111, 116–17, 128–29, 133, 139, 145, 183n20,

Southern Baptist schism (*cont.*)
198n20; relational character of, 71–72, 80–83, 86–91, 106, 110–12, 170n48; as space for renewal, 86, 90, 94, 104, 109, 133, 141, 154, 194n50; spiritual character of, 93, 102, 110, 116; theological character of, 3, 5, 14–15, 21, 93–94, 102, 104–7, 110, 112, 116, 135–37, 141, 145, 159n23; unfolding in the lives of Baptist clergywomen, 13, 25, 30, 36–39, 40, 61, 84, 119, 168nn33–34
Southern Baptist Theological Seminary, 62, 97, 103–4, 134, 170n48, 181n7, 190n10, 192n28
Southern Baptist Women in Ministry (SBWIM), 18, 33, 103–4, 106–7, 111, 114, 137, 140, 165n73, 174n24, 189n3, 192n23. *See also* Baptist Women in Ministry (BWIM)
Southwestern Baptist Theological Seminary, 28, 32, 104, 171n57
splitting: of gender, 12, 84–85, 144; psychic, 6–7, 11–13, 139, 162n49; of the SBC, 13, 20, 56, 90, 139, 140
Springside Baptist Church, 124–26
stakes of the schism in the SBC, 4, 7–8, 14–15, 43, 61, 81, 83, 88, 128, 131, 135, 141, 145, 168n32, 181n6
stained glass ceiling, 1, 12, 78, 85–86, 143
Stancil, Wilburn T., 34–35, 200n31
Stricklin, David, 159n27, 167n21, 202n47
submission, 32, 44, 59, 61, 63–64, 70, 83, 130, 143, 145, 148, 166n12, 172n2, 174n23, 175n30, 203n3; and domination, 3–4, 48, 59, 65, 144–45; female, 3, 12, 35, 48, 59, 60, 62, 65, 67, 159n27, 178n53; and mission, 21, 47, 63–64, 69, 139. *See also* domination; subordination
subordination, 10, 21, 25–26, 31, 44–45, 165n2, 202n47; and domination, 13, 38–39, 41–42, 44, 59–60. *See also* domination; submission
Sunday school, 16, 21, 27, 30, 40, 48, 54, 56–58, 95, 120, 122, 139, 197n14
Sunshine Baptist Camp, 17, 95–96
Sutton, Jerry, 160n30

Taylor, Charles, 196n10, 197n12, 198n20, 201n43
theology of being human, 115, 141
Thompson, Philip E., 159n25

Thurman, Howard, 125
Tillich, Paul, 162n48
tragic structure of existence, 11, 162n48, 189n2, 192n31, 199n28

University Baptist Church (UBC), 17, 48–52, 56–58, 64, 69, 173n9

Vestal, Daniel, 9, 19, 108–9, 194n47, 194n49
Vines, Jerry, 8, 108–9
voluntary association, 21, 72, 82, 87–88, 90, 140, 170n54, 183n17, 186n37
vocation, 13, 17, 31–32, 49, 50, 57–60, 83, 136, 138, 181n5, 186n40, 190n8, 193n40, 202n44; discernment of, 68, 96, 120, 122, 128–29, 131, 201n43; and discipleship, 93, 189n1; and gender, 59–62, 64–65, 71, 82; of ministry, 15, 20, 42–43, 47, 68, 73, 76, 108, 128, 168n38, 189n1, 193n40; nurturing of, 82; as relational, 71, 83; sense of, 4, 51, 58, 128
vulnerability, 7, 10–12, 14, 22, 62, 81, 84–85, 94, 102–5, 110, 116, 141, 163n57, 175n29, 192n26, 192n28, 192n30, 194n51

Weaver-Williams, Lynda, 9, 137
Williams, Raymond, 173n13
Williams, Roger, 188n49
Willow Baptist Church, 27–28
Winnicott, D. W., 162n51, 169nn40–41, 179n61, 185n28, 193n38, 199n23
Winstead Baptist Church, 93, 98–101, 102, 110, 113, 190n15
Winters, Eric, 125–26, 132
Winters, Miriam Therese, 150, 181n2
Wolfe, Fred, 8, 111–12
Woman's Missionary Union (WMU), 21, 61–62, 173n10, 176nn35–36, 178n52, 202n47
women as symbols, 7, 12, 22, 26, 31, 34, 116, 141, 159n27; cultural, 21, 25–26, 30, 32–33, 36, 40, 45; of schism, 26, 30, 35, 45, 139, 157nn11–12, 166nn7–8; of sin, 32. *See also* embodiment
women's liberation movement, 17, 48, 51, 61–62, 113–14, 161n46, 162n53, 202n47
woundedness, 27, 71–72, 78–79, 82–86, 91, 94, 110, 154

YMCA, 121–22
Youth Builders, 95–96

www.ingramcontent.com/pod-product-compliance
Lightning Source LLC
Chambersburg PA
CBHW020407080526
44584CB00014B/1215